D0070571

LIFE on the ICE

LIFE on the ICE

No One Goes to Antarctica Alone

Roff Smith

NATIONAL GEOGRAPHIC
Washington, D.C.

Published by the National Geographic Society

Printed in the U.S.A.
Design by Ted Tucker

Library of Congress Cataloging-in-Publication Data Available Upon Request
ISBN 0-7922-9345-2

One of the world's largest nonprofit scientific and educational organizations, the National Geographic Society was founded in 1888 "for the increase and diffusion of geographic knowledge." Fulfilling this mission, the Society educates and inspires millions every day through its magazines, books, television programs, videos, maps and atlases, research grants, the National Geographic Bee, teacher workshops, and innovative classroom materials.

The Society is supported through membership dues, charitable gifts, and income from the sale of its educational products. This support is vital to National Geographic's mission to increase global understanding and promote conservation of our planet through exploration, research, and education.

For more information, please call 1-800-NGS LINE (647-5463) or write to the following address:
National Geographic Society
1145 17th Street N.W.
Washington, D.C. 20036-4688 U.S.A.

Visit the Society's Web site at www.nationalgeographic.com.

To Laura, Ethan, Lucy, and Ella
who remind me continually of the
wonders and joys of exploration.

CONTENTS

Now when I was a little chap I had a passion for maps.
I would look for hours at South America, or Africa
or Australia and lose myself in the glories of exploration.
At the time there were many blank spaces on the earth,
and when I saw one that looked particularly inviting
(but they all look that) I would put my finger on it
and say, When I grow up I will go there.

—Marlow in *Heart of Darkness*,
by Joseph Conrad

CHAPTER ONE

Antarctic Dreamings

FOR AS FAR BACK AS I CAN REMEMBER I DREAMED OF TRAVELING TO Antarctica. I think I conceived the idea before I was even aware there was such a place, or that it had a name, perhaps the first time I tromped across a blanket of fresh unbroken snow as a child and, delighted with its crystalline magic, pictured for myself a much, much bigger one spreading out before me—an infinity of snow. Later, when I discovered that such a land really existed, and that it sat in romantic isolation at the very bottom of the world, I could hardly sit still for wanting to go there. Like Marlow, the seafaring storyteller in Conrad's novel, I'd always been fascinated by maps and atlases, my eyes intuitively seeking out the farthest reaches—the loneliest archipelagos, the outermost capes, the emptiest deserts—romancing the distances, imagining myself going there one day and wondering how the world must seem from those places. In Antarctica I found intriguing possibilities: the world's last frontier, on a wilderness continent surrounded by the world's darkest and stormiest seas, and wrapped in a deep eternal winter to boot.

I read everything about Antarctica that I could get my hands on, from the illustrated editions of the old explorers' tales I found in the library at school, to my grandfather's stack of NATIONAL GEOGRAPHIC magazines, to the *Encyclopedia Britannica*. The Guinness Book of World Records, a paperback copy of which I received for Christmas when I was ten, informed me that Antarctica was the world's highest, driest, windiest, and coldest continent and that a Russian station down there, called Vostok, had once recorded an inconceivable temperature of –126.7°F, the coldest temperature ever seen on Earth (although even that frosty extreme has since been eclipsed, by a reading of –129.3°F, in 1983, also at Vostok).

And yet the more I read, the harder it was to pin down in my imagination. I was a dreamy kid and drew all of my worldly notions from books, and Antarctica seemed to occupy two very different shelves at once. On the one hand it was an alien world that seemed to belong to science fiction, with those pictures of great orange crawling vehicles creeping across a frozen wasteland and Sputnik-era, zinc-alum huts with the American flag above them in a dazzlingly empty blue sky and bulky figures suited up and goggled against the unearthly conditions. On the other hand, Antarctica was the scene of good old-fashioned rip-roaring *Boy's Own* adventure straight from the pages of Jack London or H. Rider Haggard; a stage for all those dashing Edwardian explorers—Scott, Shackleton, Amundsen, and the like—and their deed of gallant derring-do back in the early days of flying machines and motor cars as they raced each other to conquer the South Pole. Black-and-white photographs of hard, grizzled, pipe-smoking men warming themselves in front of oil-drum fires, three-masted schooners made small by icebergs, midwinter dinners in wooden huts festooned with flags and bunting, and anorak-clad expeditioners with great bulky mittens dangling by straps draped across their shoulders.

That was the trouble with Antarctica: It either seemed too far off in the future to be real, or else it came to me as echoes from a once-upon-a-time storybook past. Either way, it never belonged in the here and now, to anything like reality as I knew it, and so there seemed to be no more of a chance to get there than there would have been to go to Narnia.

But at least I had a few visual cues around me to play with. I grew up in the White Mountains in northern New Hampshire, where the temperatures could plunge to 40 below zero, nor'easters could whip up snowdrifts higher than our porch roof, and the dogsled races ran past our house. I learned to ski on a pair of cumbersome wooden skis, with bear-trap bindings, that weren't too dissimilar to the ones I saw the explorers using in those old sledging photos, and tromped around on a pair of ancient snowshoes that were also of about the right vintage. I loved winter, the colder, and snowier, the better.

I particularly liked those intensely cold nights January nights when the temperatures plunged far below zero. On those nights I liked to get up very early, in the hours of the bitterest predawn cold, and sneak downstairs for a peek at the thermometer outside the kitchen window, before anything could have a chance to warm it up, and marvel at how low the mercury had dropped in the night. Forty-three below zero was my record. Sometimes I'd slip out the door and stand on the front step, pajamas and bare feet, just to see and marvel at what such temperatures felt like, breathing in the tingling air and expelling great clouds of vapor into the night, feeling the rubbery numbness spreading over my ears and cheekbones, listening to the trees down in the woods cracking in the intense cold and looking up at the stars, as brilliant as diamonds and as sharp as needles. When I was a little older I'd get dressed quietly and venture out on my snowshoes, to tromp around the meadow by starlight, feeling bold and adventurous, enjoying the crisp Styrofoam squeak snow has in extreme cold and imagining myself an explorer.

There were human touchstones around me too, tantalizing bridges between storybook fiction and reality. My great-uncle Chester, for example, built the dogsleds for one of Admiral Byrd's expeditions back in the 1930s, and a neighbor of ours, an irascible old woman named Eva Seeley, better known as Short, was the dog breeder who'd provided the admiral's huskies. Antarctica even formed a backdrop for one of our family's enduring myths. Legend held that when the Navy approached Uncle Chester about the sleds they wanted built, and presented him with the specifications, he'd turned them down flat, despite his badly needing the work (the Depression was on), replying with classic Yankee mulishness that he built his sleds only in such and such a manner and out of a particular kind of wood: in other words, the right way. They could have it that way, or not at all. He was an enviable craftsman—or he could be when the mood struck him—and in the end it was apparently the U.S. Navy that blinked, eventually modifying their specifications to suit Uncle Chester and, as my mother, aunts, and grandparents were fond of concluding (in rather smug tones, too) when they told the story to us kids: "We never heard of any of those sleds breaking down, either."

It's a grand story, although how much of it could withstand the cold light of independent scrutiny, I do not know, but it carried a useful moral about self-reliance, faith in your abilities, and not compromising what you believe to be true.

It is a curious characteristic of childhood that it is always far easier to imagine yourself as a swashbuckling hero from a storybook, no matter how gaudy and improbable the plot, than it is to see yourself as an actual flesh-and-blood grown-up. Over the years, as I did grow up, Antarctica was put away in the attic of dreams along with a lot of other boyhood ambitions—finding lost Inca cities in the South American jungle, prospecting for gold along the Klondike, and hopping on my bicycle one day and pedaling adventurously off to ancient rose-red cities where setting suns silhouetted the minarets.

Like everybody else, I settled for other things. I did travel to the far side of the world, though, migrating to Australia when I was 23, and slotted myself into a sunny, comfortable life in the suburbs working for newspapers in Sydney and, later, in Melbourne. Over time cold weather, snowshoes, yapping sled dogs, fresh fields of snow, and a desire to travel one day to Antarctica all receded to a sort of dim vague childhood pleasantness. By the time I was 35 I hadn't seen a snowflake in years.

Somehow a little kernel of Antarctica must have remained, lying dormant, only to be awakened one afternoon many years later when I was cycling home from work along the esplanade near Elsternwick, an old bayside suburb in Melbourne's inner south, where I was living then. It came on me suddenly, this sharp recollection of always having wanted to go to Antarctica, coupled with a sense of wonderment that I could ever have forgotten such a keen desire, or allowed it to fade, for at that instant I wanted to go down to The Ice as sharply as I ever had when I was a child.

I don't know why it emerged at that moment. I've often wondered. There were no obvious visual cues that I am aware of that might have sent the synapses flashing, no penguins on an ice-cream truck, for instance; it was just another hot, sun-drenched summer afternoon, late in December, with the ornamental palms along the esplanade casting their elongated shadows on the lawns, and the cycle track ahead busy with suntanned Rollerbladers. Perhaps (it was the penultimate day of December) it was a touch of end-of-year retrospection—another year over, what have you done? A vague dissatisfaction with the present coupled with a baited line cast into the waters of faded ambitions. It might have been prompted, too, by the strangeness of an Australian Christmas, for even after many years down under I have never really come to grips with Christmas as a summer holiday; Christmas to me will always be a season of snow and frost and icicles, not coconut oil on a beach. Whatever it was, this awakening brought with it a sense of reproach: I had never even tried to go to Antarctica. I had simply assumed, and then accepted, that it would be impossible.

I rode in to work early the next morning and put in a call to the Australian Antarctic Division headquarters, down in Kingston, Tasmania, and told the woman who answered the phone that I wanted to go to Antarctica. Hearing my voice expressing this desire conversationally, as though I were inquiring about bus fares to Sydney, seemed faintly absurd. But she didn't hang up; she patched me through to another office. A man answered this time. I explained to him that I wanted to go down to Antarctica. This somehow seemed easier to say the second time around.

"Hmmm. Are you a scientist? Tradesman? A doctor, perhaps?" he asked, a heavy note of scepticism in his voice making it obvious that he'd already guessed what my answer would be. These were clearly rhetorical questions.

"Ah...well...no, but I can be!" I chirped, and then greeted him with the news that I was the next best thing, maybe even better—a journalist. He sighed. Then he began a monotonous and obviously much practiced spiel about the hard-nosed scientific aims and goals of the Antarctic program, the great expense involved in maintaining the bases and sending people and supplies down there, that it was therefore possible to send only essential personnel, and as few of them as possible.

As he spoke I could feel my crystalline hologram of Antarctica fading before my eyes, retreating back into the attic of buried dreams, and I was mulling over this, my attention drifting away down glum corridors, when a couple of words snapped me back into the present tense: His boring spiel had taken an unexpected turn and, although his tone remained as deadpan as ever, I heard him explain that from time to time writers and artists were permitted to travel down to the bases, but that of course these few scarce places were extremely hard to get, competition was fierce, and I would need to apply a year in advance.

Did I still want the forms?

Absolutely. I gave him my address at the paper and we hung up.

I sat back in my chair, grinning, knowing somehow that this was all going to work: He hadn't said no!

A week or so later the packet of forms arrived in a bulky manila envelope with the Australian Antarctic Division logo on it. I slit it open and poured the contents onto my desk. There were lots of questions, caveats, blanks to fill in, and a large white space on the back of one form where I was supposed to describe and discuss my proposal. Use extra sheets if necessary, it said.

And so I spent my lunch hour with pencil and eraser, lost in thought (being a stranger there) and rationalizing my need to go to Antarctica, crafting a proposal that I hoped might sound wise and worldly and worthily important to bureaucratic ears and trying to make myself sound a bit more like Woodward and Bernstein and a bit less like Fletch. I finished, read it over a couple of times, made a couple of minor word changes, and then set it aside in my desk drawer to "age" for a couple of days, when I'd come back and read it again with fresh eyes. I had a whole year up my sleeve, and this was too important to rush; if this didn't work I couldn't imagine what would, or where I'd go to try next, for in the week or so since my epiphany on the esplanade, that buried ember of desire to go to Antarctica had fanned itself into a driving imperative. This seemed to be the one shot in my locker. And so I tinkered with my application, off and on, polishing the prose, aiming it as finely as I could, adding things that came to me later, and cutting out those bits that sounded too flimsy or desperate.

I liked better the part of the application where you could request the base you wished to visit. They had a map of Antarctica, with four dots representing Australia's four year-round bases: Casey, Davis, Mawson, and one on Macquarie Island, a storm-tossed sub-Antarctic island about three days south of Tasmania by ship. But my eyes were drawn straight to Mawson, the farthest-flung of the bases and one of the most remote on the continent, sitting alone on a vast and empty coast nearer Madagascar than Australia, ten to twelve days by ship across some of the loneliest and wildest stretches of the southern Indian Ocean. That was the one for me. I ticked that box, gave the little stack of forms one final look over, and a quiet blessing, slipped them into a manila envelope of my own and trundled down to the post office.

Impatient weeks passed, many of them. I heard nothing. I was dying to call up and ask, but didn't want to somehow, not without some solid logical pretext. One came along about four months later, when I was preparing to go abroad on vacation for six weeks, back to the United States, and I decided it would seem natural enough for me to give the Antarctic folks a ring to tell them that I was just stepping out for a while, and might be some time—in case they needed to contact me.

"Oh, Mr. Smith, what a coincidence. I'm so glad you called," the woman on the other end of the line said in a brisk, cheerful, matter-of-fact tone. "I was just about to call you. Your application's been approved..."

I barely heard the rest; I couldn't have been more delighted if she had been the Lottery Commission on the line. The only things I remember of our conversation, after those first few thrilling words, were her telling me that I'd been granted my wish to go to Mawson, although I'd still be required to pass a physical exam, but that unless I suffered from asthma, there shouldn't be any problem. I knew I was fine on that front. I hung up ecstatic. I was going. I was really going—to *Antarctica*. I leaned back in my squeaky chair, supreme, glancing around the newsroom, half expecting the rest of the world to have taken on the rapturous glow I was feeling just then, but things were still shuffling along as usual. Phones chirped, banter was tossed around, papers rustled, and keyboards were peck-peck-pecked—all the bustle of a newsroom on a typical busy day. It seemed odd to me at that moment how a bolt of such extravagant good fortune could strike somebody in the room and yet go unnoticed.

When I returned from vacation a few weeks later, my pigeonhole at the paper was stuffed with manila envelopes and letters from the Australian Antarctic

Division. There was a note confirming that my application had been approved and that a berth had been reserved for me on the *Aurora Australis*, the icebreaker that would be resupplying Mawson. There were more triplicate forms to fill out, a sheaf of documents pertaining to my upcoming Antarctic physical, and, on a distinctly more pleasant note, a checklist for my chest, boot, glove and waist sizes for the cold-weather gear I'd be issued for my trip south. As I ticked off the boxes, this grand adventure was starting to seem very real.

Back in 1917, Sir Ernest Shackleton sent a letter to one of his many lady friends in which he wrote: "In spite of this dusty workaday life I have ideals and far away in my own White South I open my arms to the romance of it all and it abides with me now."

I hadn't even been down there yet, but my arms were open wide and already my own White South—so long in the making—had begun to exercise my imagination and take shape in my mind; a place of adventurous possibility. If I could go to Antarctica, so the new logic ran, I could do other things too. I took a hard look around and decided maybe it was high time to put a broom through the dusty workaday life I had been leading here in Melbourne. My job as a feature writer was comfortable, reasonably well-paying drudgery, but little more than that; I wanted more, and now my own White South was suggesting to me that I could have it.

I took the bold step of firing my editor, taking him aside and breaking the news that he would no longer have the privilege of editing my copy. He took his demotion rather well, I might add. I left him in his office, burdened with all the responsibilities usually associated with a six-figure salary and company car, while I spilled onto the sidewalk in front of the building, free and unencumbered and gloriously unemployed in the warm spring sunshine, and captained body and soul around the corner to where *Time* magazine had its office.

I emerged half an hour later with a commission to write a couple of articles about my forthcoming trip to The Ice, and a breezy relationship with the local editor that resulted in the offer of a staff job after I returned.

I spent the rest of the afternoon poking my nose into various other media outlets, lining up several weeks' worth of freelance work, easily enough to keep me occupied and eating regular meals until it was time to take ship, marveling that all this—like Antarctica—must have been out there, waiting, all along.

What had I been doing all my life?

CHAPTER TWO

First Icebergs

A FEW WEEKS LATER I WAS DOWN IN HOBART, WALKING ALONG THE waterfront in a soft, cool rain, marveling at the orange icebreaker tied up alongside, the *Aurora Australis*. My ship. We were leaving today, on the afternoon tide.

I'd spent the past couple of days here in town, sleeping on a couch at a friend's house, while I attended the various mandatory lectures about safety and conduct in Antarctica and receiving my issue of clothing—Sorell boots and plaid woollen shirt, heavy wool trousers, bib-'n'-brace all-weather overalls, a sturdy parka, hats, gloves, mittens, socks, sunglasses—a whole duffel bag full of clothes the like of which you'd seldom need to wear anywhere in Australia, particularly in summer. Those days had been fun and full of anticipation, but today was the big one. In a few more hours, they'd be casting off the lines and that big beautiful orange ship would put to sea, bound for Antarctica, and I'd be on board.

The plan was for us to head first for Davis, eight days or so by sea, dropping off supplies and a change of personnel at the old base there, and then continuing east along the remote Ingrid Christensen Coast to Prydz Bay and the Larsemann Hills, to deploy a team of geologists at a field camp there and some Chinese expeditioners at China's Zhong Shan base, then farther along the coast to an obscure mote of an island at the southernmost tip of Prydz Bay where we were to cache fuel drums for a midwinter tractor traverse between Mawson and Davis, and then finally to Mawson base itself.

I was carrying my Australian National Antarctic Research Expeditions-issue duffle bag, had my rucksack slung over one shoulder, and was dangling a new waterproof camera bag I'd bought here in Hobart for the trip. Trying on all that bulky cold weather clothing the previous afternoon back at the Antarctic Division headquarters had been a happy amble down memory lane. It had been a long time since I wore mittens, and putting them on and wiggling my fingers in their scratchy woollen warmth triggered a wave of nostalgia for Flexible Flyer sleds, ice skates, and snowball fights, building forts, shoveling the porch roof—wintry things I hadn't thought of in years—as well as honing memories of tromping across fresh fields of snow and imagining myself one day setting off for the farthest ends of the Earth. Here was the ultimate vindication of long-shot childhood dreams: me, walking along this Hobart waterfront on a cool, rainy November afternoon, about to take ship for Antarctica. I wanted to laugh out loud. I hustled up the gangplank, feeling like I ought to be whistling something bold and adventurous, maybe that jaunty seafaring air from the Old Spice commercials I remembered from my childhood. It was such a glorious moment, this supreme act of boarding the ship, of departure, that as soon as I'd slung my gear in my cabin, I slipped back out on deck and sauntered down the gangplank—for the simple silly childish delight of doing it all over again, climbing aboard the ship to Antarctica.

It was great fun, but I needn't have gone to the trouble; they shooed us all off the ship anyway, an hour or so before we were to cast off, and then after the crew had gone over all the nooks and crannies on the vessel, had us all board again, one at a time, with our passes in hand. They did this to thwart stowaways. It had been done, I was told, people hitching rides down to The Ice. A couple of years earlier a young guy, desperate to go down to Antarctica, didn't go ashore after coming down to see the ship depart, and managed to find himself a nice place to hide on board, only to reveal himself when they were a few days out at sea. The captain and the expedition leader were sympathetic, and I heard the guy had a grand time down there—and when they came back to Hobart, they turned him over to the Tasmanian police. Not too much came of it. I gather he wasn't prosecuted very vigorously, but now they go over the ship a bit more carefully before they put to sea. No stowaways were found this time, though, and as they let us back on board we all crowded along the railing, waving at the crowds assembled on the wharf to see off the ship.

We left in cold drizzle and a shower of confetti, with a crowd of friends and relatives huddled there to see us off. Wives and parents and fiancées smiled bravely, babies' hands were made to wave bye-bye, and mates on the wharf shouted larrikin encouragements.

Most of the people leaning against the rails beside me would be wintering at Davis or Mawson, and this would be the last time they would see those familiar faces for a year or more. Things were not so complicated for me: I was going south for seven weeks, a mere whistle-stop by the time-consuming standards of Antarctic travel. My joy at departure was unalloyed.

A blast from the ship's horn reverberated across the harbor.

A gap of water opened up between the wharf and the ship: 300 feet, then 600. The sounds of cheering faded; the crowd on the wharf shrank to specks, looking a little forlorn on the wet quayside with the soggy confetti around them. At some point, unique to each of us, the last intangible mooring between us and them slipped away and icebreaker *Aurora Australis* became a self-contained world on its own. We glided past Battery Point, leaving the hilly cityscape behind us under low broken cloud, and steamed down the Derwent, bound for the open sea. That night we were rolling in the heaving, dark waters off Tasmania's wild southwest cape, making nine knots on a bearing of south–southwest.

Weather charts showed a stormy low-pressure system sweeping toward Tasmania, and we were sailing right into it. Before we left, when we were being shown around the lifeboats and exercising our imaginations on how ghastly it would be to have to ride in them, one of the expedition doctors had gone around passing out seasickness tablets, along with a playful little warning that they hadn't nicknamed this ship "The Orange Roughy" for nothing—a bit of wordplay: the fish market name of a species of deep-dwelling Antarctic fish, and the riding qualities in heavy seas of this rescue-orange rounded-hulled icebreaker. The pills—industrial strength, she said—came in individual foil packets with instructions to take one every 12 hours.

"Take two of these," she said, passing me a couple of packets.

"Er…it says here you should take only one…"

She smiled at such naiveté. "Take two."

So I took two, slept like a dead man that night, and woke the next morning so groggy and out of it I could barely stagger down to the galley for breakfast. The ship was rolling heavily, pots and pans clattering, dark green water sloshing over the portholes as the *Aurora* plunged bow-on into the waves. I ate breakfast without much enthusiasm and went off for a nap. I was due another tablet (or two) but I decided to forgo it. I didn't know whether I'd be seasick or not; I'd never had much to do with boats. I just knew that I didn't want to travel to Antarctica on downers, curled up on some sofa in the lounge like a doped cat. I let the drugs wear off, nibbled experimentally at lunch, took a turn around the deck afterward, breathing in the cold, fresh, salty air, and found that I was fine. And so I remained for the rest of the journey—warding off the occasional queasy morning with a stomach-settling bowl of corn flakes, before tucking into what became my usual breakfast of eggs, bacon, pancakes, and plenty of coffee. I never missed a meal.

Day followed day of heavy gray rollers, increasingly cold winds, empty horizons, vast skies, and albatrosses. This was distance, real distance, not the kind they make in nautical miles.

The journey to Mawson is said to be the last great necessary sea voyage left to us these days—necessary in the sense that anyone who wants to go there faces a long, gray, rolling 3,000-mile voyage across some of the world's loneliest and roughest stretches of water; there is simply no other way to do it. You can't fly. You've got to go by ship. Nothing to do but battle the heavy seas and falling barometers, bouncing and pitching and heaving your way south, knot by knot, day after day, through cold mist and gales, fair weather and foul, steaming endlessly through the stormy latitudes known as the Roaring Forties, the Furious Fifties, and the Screaming Sixties, just as the old-time mariners used to do.

We put in the time reading or playing Scrabble, sitting up on the bridge or watching videos. There was darts and table tennis too, the pitching and yawing of the ship injecting an element of chaos theory and unpredictability. It was perfect handicapping—in stormy weather a fumbling novice like me could play a game of darts with some of the old pros on board, often ex-Navy types who carried around their own sets of finely crafted competition darts in leather pouches, and have things come out close to even.

They were empty hours, but far from meaningless, for as they passed, at a steady nine knots, they defined the journey. These idle days cast Antarctica's romantic isolation into a new and personal significance, bringing home the fact that traveling to the Antarctic meant an investment in time and, depending on your vulnerability to seasickness, a certain amount of discomfort. In a hurry-up age when you get used to thinking of thousands of miles of travel being accomplished in a few effortless hours on a Boeing 747—time for a couple of plastic tray meals and a "snack"—this old, slow, time-consuming mode of travel makes the globe feel very big indeed, and Antarctica romantically far away.

One of the quirky side effects of the long sea voyages necessary to reach the Australian bases was how scientists' various projects would evolve en route, as they sat around on long empty afternoons discussing their projects and exchanging ideas with scientists from other disciplines. New ideas would emerge, hypotheses to pursue, and occasionally, as I was told, a scientist's project would literally undergo a sea change as the ship steamed south. And if a new piece of equipment was required for the revised experiments, the chances were that one of the tradesmen, who would have been listening in on the conversations, would speak up with some ideas on how such and such a thing could be thrown together out of scrap available at the base. Most of the tradesmen—the carpenters, diesel mechanics, plumbers, and electricians—were either old hands in Antarctica or had worked for years in the bush and so were extremely skilled at jury-rigging anything you liked out of nothing. I sat beside a physicist, a diesel mechanic, and a plumber one afternoon while they put their heads together over a scrap of paper to finagle some arcane bit of laboratory gear whose function I never fully understood, but which, I was given to understand by the delighted physicist, would actually end up better than a similar article bought from a scientific supply shop back in Australia, since what he was going to have would be custom-built purely for his experiment and ruggedly engineered for Antarctic conditions.

We were alone on the sea. We saw no other ship. Just us: our own little world, 300 feet long and 4,000 tons, population about 120, bobbing about in this immensity of ocean. At night I'd lie in bed and picture us from above, a tiny cluster of lights that went out, one by one, as it grew later, until there was only the red and green running lights, and the faint glow from the bridge, as the ship steamed on into the darkness.

Five days out of Hobart I saw my first iceberg—a big tabular job, looking wild and dangerous as we drew near, with those frighteningly large, dark waves booming against it and sending huge clouds of spray a hundred feet in the air. It was breakfast time and when somebody called out that there was an iceberg ahead we all charged out of the galley and gathered excitedly along the railings up on deck to look at it, our breath all frosty in the gray cold. We snapped pictures and listened in awe to the lonely thump of the surf crashing against those cliffs of ice away out here in nowhere. And then it was astern and those of us who were new to that part of the world felt a little wistful to see such a marvel shrink away, our first iceberg, not comprehending yet how much ice lay over the horizon. Could anyone? More icebergs slipped by, port and starboard, as the day progressed, occasionally and notable at first but then becoming more and more common, and by the next morning we were surrounded by ice.

This was the most magical part of the trip, a surreal tableau of floating ice that seemed to stretch on forever. Although there was nothing quite like this in the book, something about these days made me think of my favorite Narnia book, *The Voyage of the Dawn Treader*, and the chapters toward the end where they sail for days through peaceful seas covered with banks of delicate white flowers at the edge of the world.

We stood for hours on the bow, or up on the monkey island—sailor's slang for the deck above the bridge—talking in low voices and trying to grasp and absorb this haunting immensity and the hugest silence and stillness anyone could imagine. Sometimes it felt like we were riding a giant toboggan, the way the hull would boom over the pack ice, cracking it asunder, turning the huge chunks over and making them sparkle iridescent blue and green in the sunlight, then thud down the flanks of the ship. Sometimes the sky was a hard polished blue and the light so clear you could imagine seeing over the curve of the Earth. Other times we throbbed along through a murky gray monochrome world of sifting snows, lowering cloud, ice, and dark, glassy water.

One evening we witnessed the elusive green flash sailors see sometimes when the sun dips below the horizon. Another time we looked astern at a midnight dusk and saw a huge, luminous, silvery moon rising in a pink-and-violet band above the broken pack ice and reflecting in the water.

Wildlife was everywhere: humpback whales, minke whales, and killer whales; fur seals and leopard seals; albatrosses and scores of different seabirds drifting on the wing. My favorite was the snow petrel, a beautiful, pure white dovelike bird that glided above the broken pack ice and seemed to embody the incredible sense of peace and tranquillity around us.

The best moment, though, came when I saw what looked at first to be a school of odd little flying fish porpoising through the water, in quick, darting, silvery splashes, but then they hopped up on an ice floe and I laughed in astonishment as I realized I was seeing my first penguins in the wild. They were Adélies—those little, comical, tuxedoed characters, about 18 inches high, that the cartoonists love. Over the coming weeks we were to see hundreds of them, standing about on icefloes like guests at lost dinner parties. Later on there were emperor penguins, too: stately creatures almost four feet tall with blushes of orange on their cheeks.

It was magic. Everybody felt it—regardless of how many times they had already been down south. To me that will always be one of the nicest aspects of traveling to Antarctica—the way the shared wonder of being together in one of the world's strangest environments draws people together. Here we had a mix of chefs, carpenters, geologists, helicopter pilots, merchant seamen, biologists, diesel mechanics, meteorologists, doctors, and plumbers—people who might not rub elbows much, if at all, in the real world but effortlessly coalesce down here in The Ice to become Antarcticans.

I could have traveled like this forever, steaming endlessly through that surreal dreamscape of ice, but the miles were inexorably adding up; the continental ice plateau loomed high on the horizon like a bank of clouds, and at about two o'clock in the morning one cold and gray day we crunched to a halt in the fast ice about three miles in front of Davis base. The captain gave a long, echoing blast of the ship's horn to announce our arrival, a startling rupture of the peace and quiet that must have jarred awake anybody sleeping at the base, and concluded the first stage of our journey with an exclamation point.

We were all awake on board, crowding the rails, eager to see. I was up on the monkey island, scanning the cluster of buildings with a heavy pair of binoculars I had borrowed from the bridge. This was my first glimpse of an Antarctic base, and as I focused on its stark, bright, modular buildings and polysided radar domes my first thought was that it was just like in the pictures, the inaccessible ungraspable postapocalyptic setting and the sci-fi ambience. And it was just as still and motionless. But then, the wonder of it all, a door opened in one of the little buildings, a tiny dot of a figure emerged and began the long trudge across the vast plain of snow-covered ice and out to the ship. Movement—this was no picture; I was really here.

They began the business of unloading cargo the next morning, lowering it by crane onto a couple of Hagglunds tractors that had driven out across the ice. At the same time the helicopters were broken out and got into action, taking off from the heli-deck on the rear of the ship and slinging loads into the base. All was busy.

I walked in later that day. I could have hitched a ride easily enough on one of the Hagglunds that were shuttling back and forth, but I preferred to walk and to go by myself, enjoying a quiet think as I tromped across the ice. Those buff-gray rocks along the shore were Antarctica, the continent itself, and while the notion of first footfalls seemed faintly anticlimactic now, after all the thrills and grandeur of the past few days, steaming through the pack ice and seeing all the penguins, whales, and seals, I still wanted to make my landing and to do it my way, since fate had given me the opportunity, by myself and on foot, preserving the gentle fiction that I had somehow brought myself here and drawing together, in my mind, those long-ago daydreaming childhood tromps across the snow back in New Hampshire and this present-tense, snow-crunching arrival on the shores of Antarctica.

It was a fine day for it, clear and sunny, with the temperature a few degrees above freezing. I laced up my Sorrell boots, shrugged into my parka, made a note on the board that I was leaving the ship and walking into Davis, and ambled down the gangplank that ran from a bulkhead door down to the ice and set off for town. It was about three miles, although in that telescopically clear light the base appeared to be much closer, no more than a few hundred yards away. It felt good to be walking, though, feeling the hard crunching solidity of ice underfoot and not being hemmed in by decks and curved nautical railings.

But I wasn't alone. Others were out taking strolls too—specifically a chorus line of Adélie penguins, all top hats and tails. Our paths crossed near the shore and we stopped to stare at each other. I'd never seen a penguin so close before, certainly not in the wild, and so I very slowly drew my Nikon out of my camera bag—careful not to move suddenly and frighten the little things—and lowered myself to a sitting position in the snow. They stood obligingly still while I took a few portraits, but as soon as I tiptoed off to one side with an idea of photographing them from a different angle, they gleefully waddled up to my unguarded camera bag and began poking through it.

"Hey—now cut that out!" I strode back toward my camera bag, feeling faintly ridiculous at the scolding tone in my voice. Scolding penguins? A few of the little guys scuttled away before turning and looking reproachfully at me, but the rest held their ground, giving me no more than a curious glance before returning to the more interesting business of frisking my things. So much for skittish wildlife; I stood by while they had a good snoop around, letting them play nosey *douaniers*, and then, customs and immigration cleared, I took my bag and sidled past them and up onto the shore, Antarctic rock beneath my boot soles at last; it felt grand. I hiked on up to the base.

Antarctic bases might have the romance of distance and sublime views out their triple-glazed windows but they are not pretty, more like rough-and-tumble mining camps sprawled in the snow, although Davis was at least colorful, as a result of a recent makeover in which the old zinc-alum huts were replaced by oversize prefab structures in bold red, blue, yellow, and green. Still, it was stark and utilitarian and projected a sense of exile: About 50 people live here in summer, and a dozen or so during winter—enough so that it was not unknown (although not common either) for newcomers to take a look at their barren new "home" and say no, and refuse to get off the ship. After walking around the base's snowy paths (with their guide ropes for finding your way if you were unlucky enough to be caught out in a whiteout) and poking around the buildings—comfortable in a dormitory sort of way—I decided I had much the better deal than the crew we were dropping off here for the winter. This was the end of the line for them. Their Antarctic travels were pretty much over; this is where they'd remain, these buildings, this view, their entire world, until the ship came by next summer to retrieve them. I still had the prospect of hundreds of miles more of steaming through the ice, miles of new coast to explore by binocular, and new landfalls to make.

We drew away from the base a couple of days later. From Davis, we tracked westward along the coast and into the silent ice-strewn waters of Prydz Bay, where we dropped off the Chinese expeditioners at Zhong Shan base and then deployed a team of geologists to Law, a remote field camp in the Larsemann Hills. I went in with them, to spend a few days hiking while the *Aurora* steamed on down to the end of the bay to deploy a cache of fuel drums and food supplies for the upcoming midwinter tractor traverse between Davis and Mawson.

We went into Law by helicopter, taking off from the rear deck of the ship in an exhilarating roar of rotors and downdraft. This was my first glimpse of Antarctica from the air, and although I had been carrying around a pocket-size mental image of vast expanses of snow and ice, an abstraction, nothing could have prepared me for the immediacy of seeing the ship fall away and those infinite white horizons suddenly expanding before my eyes, endlessly, in every direction, unrelieved by anything else and curving into the bluish distance with the shape of the Earth. Here was the infinity of snow I had fantasized as a child. The *Aurora*—our home, our world complete, with its warmth and voices, beds and hot dinners—was revealed to be nothing more than a tiny orange speck in an immensity of white ice and taut blue sky. And then came abstraction again, a mind-boggling thought to tamp the sheer scale of Antarctica back into the realm of the simply unimaginable: All of this, as far as I could, see, was only a small portion of Prydz Bay, which was itself only an obscure indentation on a long and hauntingly desolate coast in East Antarctica, which was in turn only a region of a continent larger than the United States and Mexico combined—and virtually all of it, more than 99 percent, mantled in ice and snow.

We were heading that morning, though, for one of the very few places on the continent that wasn't, a chain of low, stony hills that fringed this part of the bay. They were discovered back in the 1930s, named for a Norwegian named Larsemann, but left untouched and unexplored for another 50 years. And then suddenly, within the span of a couple of years in the mid-1980s, four bases were built in these hills—two by the Russians, one by the Chinese, and Australia's little summer camp called Law, after Phillip Law, the founder of the Australian Antarctic Division. It was all part of a heady land grab in Antarctica, prompted by word that a new treaty was being negotiated to govern mining in Antarctica and establish a formal protocol to divide up the spoils of Antarctica's as yet unknown but bound to be plentiful mineral resources. This was the greed-is-good eighties and interest was high, but there was a little catch for any aspiring government that wanted to deal itself into the game: Under the terms of the Antarctic Treaty, only those countries undertaking active scientific work on the continent can have a voting say in the continent's future. No problem. Suddenly nations that had never before evinced the slightest interest in polar exploration were seized with polar passions, queuing up to count penguins, record temperatures, and measure snowfall. And, not incidentally, to send voting delegates to treaty meetings.

Faced with such a stampede of newcomers, the old-school-tie Antarctic nations scrambled in turn to increase their presence on the continent, to justify their louder voices at the table, and presumably help them score a better deal on the minerals. The rush was on, a base-building boom the likes of which Antarctica had never seen, not even in the halcyon days of the International Geophysical Year, and any stretch of Antarctic coast not covered by ice—and therefore able to be readily built upon—became prime real estate. Australia, an old player in the game and with by far the biggest territorial claims on the continent—Australia claims 43 percent of Antarctica as its sovereign territory—had already set aside many millions of dollars to make over its three continental bases and, thinking that now might be a good time to expand their Antarctic presence still further, remembered the ice-free stretch of coast along the Larsemann Hills just a hundred or so miles from Davis.

In 1986 they sent a team out to survey a site for a new summer camp, to be named for Dr. Phillip Law, and when they arrived discovered the Russians were already building and the Chinese were on their way. In the space of a couple of seasons, these desolate hills went from being virtually untouched and unexplored, having never felt the weight of a human foot, to supporting four Antarctic bases.

Law was simple and neat—a small trim alpine hut, painted green and gold, which was kitchen and dining room and parlor, and close beside it three of those red fiberglass domes, "apples" in Australian Antarctic parlance, which served as bedrooms or for storage. An Australian flag flew in front of the hut, and at one time someone had painted a boxing kangaroo on the door. I'd come here with a team of field geologists from Melbourne who would be spending the next few weeks here unraveling the complex metamorphic history of these hills—this was their summer home, so to speak, and they set about moving in with the comfortable familiarity of a family returning to a much-loved beach house. I slung my pack in one of the "apples" and then went into the main hut. It was musty yet cozy, wooden shelves bright with tinned goods, its alpine feel accented by the decorative Swiss flags left by a geologist visiting from Switzerland the previous season.

It was late in the day. After a bit of unwind, we got busy in the kitchen, threw together a big pot of macaroni and cheese for dinner, and later, when we'd eaten and finished the dishes, we sat up till the small hours over a 12-year-old Islay single malt and a bucket of very much older vintage local glacier ice, and gossipped about the neighbors—how the doctor at the now abandoned Russian base had died of acute alcoholism within a month of arriving a couple of years ago—and the echoes of the would-be mining treaty of the late 1980s. The geologists told me that, undoubtedly, there was much wealth locked up in Antarctica: good chances of oil in the basins off the Antarctic Peninsula, thick coal seams that had been discovered in the Transantarctic Mountains, and platinum deposits in the Dufek Massif, to name just a few. And there was certainly much more, hidden from view beneath the ice—after all, this was an entire continent, bound to have its own Klondike, Ballarat, or Witwatersrand just like every other great landmass. The trouble, of course, was not only finding workable deposits beneath more than a mile of ice, but then extracting it profitably and transporting it cheaply back to the real world. Even if the technology existed to do it, and it doesn't yet, the economics didn't add up. Thus the squabbling over the mineral rights made about as much sense as bald men fighting over a comb. It all came to an end anyway in 1989, wonderfully cynically, when France and Australia suddenly and unexpectedly pulled the plug on the proposed mining treaty—France largely because it was busily conducting nuclear tests in the South Pacific and wanted to find a not-too-inconvenient green issue to embrace and soften its image, while the Australian government was facing an election in which the environment was likely to be a key issue. There are no jobs lost in preserving penguins. And so the mining treaty was replaced by the Madrid Protocol of 1989, which declared Antarctica to be a sort of world park and forbade mining for 50 years (this later part a bit like Huckleberry Finn salving his conscience by deciding not to steal persimmons, happy in the knowledge that they wouldn't be ripe for weeks yet anyway).

We set out with our rucksacks the next morning, hiking up a wind-scoured valley that looked like one of those stony barren passes somewhere high in the Hindu Kush. We were heading for Progress I, the abandoned Russian base a few miles away on a height of land that overlooked the bay. It was another dazzling morning, the sun bright in a flawless sky and the air moist and cool. It felt good to be walking again, and on bare rock too, instead of ice and snow, hearing the reassuring crunch of gravel and the clink of stone underfoot. The landscape was magical, Tolkienesque, with flocks of beautiful white snow petrels nesting in the crags, the bare hilltops strewn with garnets the size of knucklebones, and the level places dotted with jewel-like freshwater lakes—a remarkable rarity in Antarctica—whose water was so limpid and clear it was virtually invisible, like air. The huge hush and the unblinking sunshine and the far-ends-of-the-Earth feeling you get from being in such an otherworldly place, with those pure white snow petrels wheeling about, created an impression of great peacefulness. But then you come upon the remains of one of those very petrels, killed by a skua and picked over so that only the breastplate and the pair of still-feathered white wings remain, and you're reminded at how violent a place this is; they look like the remains of murdered angels. And then when you look around you the big silence seems more conspiratorial than placid.

Progress I turned out to be not much more than a tumbledown shack on a wide and icy slope, with three broken-down tractor engines left in front of it to complete the rustic imagery. The door was loose and creaky, and inside was cramped and dank, decorated with cheap, peeling wallpaper, and strewn with bits of broken furniture and broken vodka bottles. It would have been grim to spend the long dark of a polar winter here, but the Russians had done it, or at least a few of them had. This had originally been conceived as a year-round base but, except for the stunning panorama over the bay, the site had little to recommend it. Fierce winds howled over these slopes, the snows were deep in the winter, while in the spring, when things warmed up a little, runoff from the glacier farther up the hill made things deeply mucky and unpleasant. They abandoned this place after a year, and promptly built another, and altogether larger, base called (apparently without irony) Progress II, a few miles away and down along the shore, where it could also be more easily supplied by ship. That one too had since been abandoned, although for different reasons. We'd hike over and have a look at it tomorrow.

We ate lunch dangling our feet over a ledge nearby that commanded a spectacular view over the bay, with its pack ice and grounded icebergs, and the cliffs and crags and tumbling glaciers along the coast. Afterward we explored a bit, the geologists going about their geologizing, and we hiked back to the camp by a hilly, circuitous scenic route that took up the rest of the day.

I liked sleeping in my "apple." It was a snug little capsule, with its round porthole windows, and when I opened the hatch and poked my head out into the chilly gray Antarctic morning, I felt like a kid who'd been allowed to sleep out in an elaborate tree house. It had that neatness to it. There were breakfast sounds and voices coming from the hut. I wandered over to start the day.

We set off in a different direction than the previous day, following another wet, gravelly valley toward Progress II. It was cold, clammy, and overcast and the shift in lighting changed the tone of the landscape completely, sombre rather than exhilarating, even a little spooky. We arrived at the abandoned base about an hour later, a kind of hush settling over us as we walked past those first few empty buildings. It was eerie in that bluish overcast, an Antarctic ghost town, its broad main street lined with big shambling two-story wooden structures and corrugated-iron sheds. Wooden crates overflowing with rusted machine parts and drill bits were stacked crazily, leaning against shipping containers with broken doors, and "CCCP" painted on them and hammer-and-sickle stenciling. There were coils of wire and spools of cabling lying about, and rusty old fuel drums—some still full of fuel—and loads of broken-down drilling rigs, old tractors, and scrapped caterpillar-like vehicles, a whole junkyard's worth. Some of them were bizarre, fascinatingly so—vaguely futuristic but in a retro sort of way, like a cover illustration of a fifties sci-fi paperback. Two parts Jules Verne juggernaut, one part George Lucas, piled up and oxidizing beautifully in the salty air, they were intriguing enough to make it as pieces of sculpture, eloquent of futility. Like a perplexed visitor at the Tate, I walked around them for a while, exercising my imagination, having fun trying to picture these things rolling off a production line somewhere, vast factory parking lots full of them, and brisk newsreel enthusiasm.

We spent the rest of the morning snooping respectfully around the base. Nothing had been touched, but left pretty much as it must have been the day the place was abandoned—there were shelves of heavy Russian medical books left in the doctor's surgery; pouting Soviet pinup girls on walls and doors and wardrobes in the barracks, together with a lot of empty Stolichnaya bottles; an unfinished game of billiards in the recreation hall, and festoons of Christmas tinsel and the faded photographic gazes of the last crew to winter here—a couple of years ago judging by the date on the group portrait. It made me think of Pompeii, except the eruption here had been political and economic. After the Soviet Union collapsed, there hadn't been money to spare for Antarctic bases. The crew here at Progress II apparently spent an anxious summer wondering when, or even if, a ship was coming to retrieve them, and when one appeared on the horizon, they didn't waste much time: There was still a loaf of bread on the cutting board in the kitchen, an open clasp knife beside it, and unwashed dishes in the sink.

The next morning the helicopter returned to pick me up. I flew out to rejoin the ship, which was steaming slowly up the bay, and while they lashed down the helicopter the captain set a course toward Mawson, still another couple hundred miles to the west. And for the rest of that day and the next, it was more of that slow magic steaming through the ice.

We reached Mawson, or as close as we could come to it in the thick pack ice that year, after a dazzling midnight run through Iceberg Alley, a labyrinth of weather-sculpted icebergs that had run aground. There would be no walking into the base from the ship this time, though, as I had done at Davis. We were still a good 25 miles out. Everything and everybody would have to come and go by helicopter. I caught a lift later that afternoon.

I loved Mawson from the start. It is the oldest still-operating base on the continent, set up in 1954, and the summer I was there they were still using the original zinc-alum *dongas* and wooden huts, all of them huddled together along a deeply snowbanked Main Street that curved up from the frozen shoreline. It was friendly, quaint, and old-fashioned, the sort of thing Norman Rockwell might have liked painting if he'd ever taken on Antarctica—cozy little vignettes like the old carpenter's shed, its ceiling plastered with raffish pinup girls from the swinging sixties; or the Formica-and-stainless fifties-vintage eatery that served as the galley with the parkas hanging on the wall and a swarm of fake, plastic flies clinging to a roll of flypaper some jokester had brought down from Australia (there are no flies, you see, in Antarctica); or the Morse apparatus in the communications hut and a guy on hand, an old-time Antarctic veteran, who still knew how to use it; or the musty trans-Siberian railway carriage that served as the smoker's purdah.

Then there were the huskies: Mawson was the last base on the continent still using dogs and dogsleds. An elaborate wall chart in the old pub on base showed the pedigrees of Mawson's huskies going back to the first teams of Greenland sled dogs brought here when the base first opened. Over the years they'd been a popular means of transportation, used by scientists to visit emperor penguin rookeries farther out along the coast, and to explore the Prince Charles Mountains in the interior, and by the rank-and-file simply to get away from the confines of the base for a few days, bringing along a tent and a few days' rations, a supply of dog pemmican, and have a small taste of Antarctica as it must have been in grand old heroic days.

But no more: all of these things were coming to an end that summer. Mawson's quaint old buildings were going to be shut down and left to the drifting snows, and the base's operations moved up the slope a ways to the new complex of huge warehouse-size buildings, in big, bold colors, just like the ones I'd seen at Davis. They were putting the final touches on them when we arrived. Some of the construction crew would be coming back with us, having finished their 15-month gigs; most of the rest would be taking the second and final ship of the season in another few weeks' time. There was talk of preserving a couple of the more interesting structures, the carpenter's shed, for example, and a donga or two, and bringing them back to Hobart to furnish a museum of olden days Antarctica, but these, right now, were the final days of their active working lives, when their walls would resound with the voices and bustle of expeditioners going about their daily routines.

It was the end of the line for the dogs too.

Under the terms of the Madrid Protocol, the new enlightened postmodern Antarctica would be a sort of nature preserve in which no introduced species, other than humans, would be permitted. The grandly stated objective of all this was to quarantine Antarctica's ecosystem and protect it from imported diseases, and dogs, it was declared, could bring in distemper—but this was a lot of cant, really, because huskies had been working in Antarctica since 1899 without introducing disease, and by now all of them down there had been born and bred in the disease-free Antarctic environment but had been inoculated anyway as an extra security precaution. And anyway the study upon which these distemper fears were based involved an outbreak of avian distemper—not the very different and distinct canine variety—among seabirds in the North Sea. It didn't add up, but then it didn't have to—the dogs it seemed, with their history and service, were political poker chips, and low-denomination ones at that, in the grand games being dealt out far over our heads.

The base commander at Mawson was a former landscape architect named Alan, a jocular man very much, I was told, in the old-style manner of Antarctic base leaders, and he gave a couple of us permission to set off on a short expedition into the interior, to one of the little field huts in the mountains behind the base. It would have been fun to have taken the dogs for a spin, but the arthritic old team simply wasn't up to hauling a sled up the steep flanks of the plateau, so we bundled our rucksacks, radios and emergency gear, and a couple of days' food supplies into the back of a Hagglunds tractor and set off for a backcountry camp known as Rumdoodle.

A Hagglunds tractor will never in a million years have the romance of a dogsled, and the ride is noisy and rough, but all the same I loved the adventurous feel of heading out into the wastes, climbing up and away from the base, seeing Mawson's scatter of buildings dwindle below us to insignificant dots in the whiteness and then ultimately slip from view as we crawled over the ridgeline and rumbled and clanked our way into the interior.

Rumdoodle turned out to be an alpine hut made very, very tiny by an immense wall of rock that thrust up through the ice like a giant incisor, and towered hundreds of feet straight up above its roof. We pulled up beside it and clambered out, the huge silence swallowing up the lonely *ker-chunk* of our doors closing. We all stood still for a moment, listening, and then, hauntingly and seemingly from far away, came the faint cries of snow petrels wheeling and circling in front of the cliffs that soared overhead.

We spent the rest of the afternoon exploring and returned to the hut early in the evening to make dinner and report in on the seven o'clock "sked," the scheduled radio call back to base to let them know we were all okay. The radio operator back at base very kindly read us a few chapters of *The Ascent of Rumdoodle*, W.E. Bowman's hilarious spoof on mountaineering, and kept everybody entertained—including the radio operator—for an hour or so, the book's quirky English humor, and 1950s tone, giving the broadcast the gentle charm of an old-time radio show. We sat up late and then went out hiking again after midnight when the sun was angling low in the sky, softening the colors and warming the tones so that the snowscapes looked creamy rather than just blindingly white. We stayed out until three, drifted back, made cocoa, and crawled into our sleeping bags.

I woke to the growl of thunder, something I hadn't expected, and glanced out the window, but the sky was a faultless cerulean blue. A sudden scary thought suggested avalanche, and I remembered those dramatic cliffs rising straight up overhead behind us and all those boulders scattered on the ice, but it wasn't quite that either—it was an avalanche of cold, heavy air, my first experience of Antarctica's notorious katabatic winds. They spring up seemingly out of nowhere, sudden powerful gusts that whisk across the ice and can easily sweep a 200-pound journalist off his feet, as I learned to my cost when I foolishly stepped outside to feel how windy it was.

After the big silences up on the plateau, Mawson seemed crowded and bustling, a boomtown on the goldfields with helicopters swooping in with sling loads of cargo, and kicking up the dust, and everybody either packing up to go home or unpacking and moving in, construction workers sawing and hammering and welding. There was a big time in the pub that night, everybody playing darts and drinking "homers"—home-brewed beer—of which there was a huge cellar at Mawson, and then spilling out of the pub very late, four o'clock or so, out into that unblinking Antarctic sunshine, off to a nicely darkened hut to grab a quick couple hours' sleep; today was the big day—time to go home.

It was decided to take the dogs out for a final easy trot around Horseshoe Bay, the very last time anybody would ever use dogs in Antarctica, and just about everybody on the base trooped out onto the ice to see it, to be a part of writing that last sentence on a grand chapter in the continent's history. It was more of an epilogue, really. We were 71 years too late to call this the end of the heroic era—that had happened on South Georgia Island in 1922, when Sir Ernest Shackleton died on his ship just before his final expedition began; this was a case of seeing it packed away in a box, with a lot of other no-longer-needed boyhood stuff, and shoved up in a far corner of the attic.

It was bitterly cold that morning, 14 degrees in a hard, clear, blue sky, and it felt far colder with the razor wind blowing across the ice. The dogs in their traces were yapping, puffs of steam coming out with each bark, old but still keen to have a trot. There were only five dogs left now—the sixth, Brendan, one of the oldest, had died in his sleep a couple of days earlier. They were not a very sharp team, stiff and much out of practice, having been kept on base these past couple of years essentially as pets and for occasional little jogs such as this, but all the same they fell into line, more or less, and at a command from the chief dog-handler, a meteorologist named Rob, the empty sled began to slide along the ice on its final slow loop of the bay. Quite a few of us jogged alongside, reaching out and putting our mittened hands on the sled now and then, as though to grasp a handful of history for ourselves. It was a very moving moment, and a privilege, to be there as the curtain fell on such a big part of the continent's history.

The dogs trotted back to base and the helicopter ride out to the ship and the long journey home to a green and summery place they had never been before. After their harsh lives on the ice, it would be like going to heaven.

They held the handover ceremony in the spacious common room of the soon-to-be-completed Red Shed, the sleek dormitory where the incoming crew, and future crews, would spend their winter. There were the usual speeches, the outgoing station leader thanked his crew and shook hands with his incoming replacement. Polar medals were awarded to the wintering crew, and a special set of polar medals, crafted by the diesel mechanics, were awarded to the dogs, who were also given a rousing cheer. There were tears too.

Afterward we all filed out to where the helicopters and their pilots were waiting to whisk us away, back to the ship, back home. I felt myself hanging back a little, not wanting to leave Antarctica, for the grand trip to be over, for the magic to end. I planned to keep my head down, hold off, and go back on the last possible shuttle, but as the rotors began to whine, and somebody yelled: "Who's going first?" I heard myself speak up, and then I was edging my way through the crowd, flushed of face, with a heightened awareness of the Antarctic rock beneath my boots and knowing that it might be for the very last time, and then I scrambled into the helicopter, glad to be leaving on the first flight. When it came to it I couldn't bear a long good-bye. My last memory of Mawson was a circle of brightly parkaed human dots, waving.

It was about a 20-minute flight out to the ship. I looked through the window, taking in the immense whiteness below for one last time, and then, catching a glimpse of a tiny orange speck in the distance, watched it grow into the *Aurora*. The pilot touched down on deck just long enough to disgorge his passengers, then lifted off again in a roar of rotors to return to base for more. This shuttling must have gone on for a couple of hours, given the distance and the number of people and dogs to be brought out to the ship, although it seemed to take just a few minutes. And then the mechanics were dismantling the helicopter, stowing it away, like a Christmas tree coming down, removing its blades so it could be slid into the hangar on the heli-deck, and lashing it down with heavy canvas webbing. Up on the bridge the captain was busy consulting his charts and weather reports and making ready to put the ship about. He put us on a course of almost due north, to get out of the pack ice as swiftly as possible and into the open ocean, where we would make better time.

I loitered on deck for a while, leaning against the rail and looking out at the miles of ice and sculpted bergs as we steamed north. I'd wanted to stay to see the very last of the ice slip astern, but suddenly I felt very tired. I'd been working on two or three hours' sleep a night for weeks, seldom in bed before three o'clock in the morning yet always first in line for breakfast, not wanting to miss a second of my time down here—really living each day, for once in my life—but now, with heavy curtains of anticlimax draped all around, it was catching up with me. I shuffled reluctantly off to bed. I woke about 18 hours later, and when I came up on deck all I could see were the cold, gray heavy rollers of the Southern Ocean, not an iceberg in sight.

It was a long and stormy passage back to Tasmania, much rougher than the outward leg of the journey, with the Furious Fifties and Roaring Forties really strutting their stuff. We had a couple days of force 11 winds and mountainous seas, with swells up to 70 feet. I watched its fury from the bridge, gripping a rail with white knuckles and shifting my balance as best I could to meet the sudden rolls of the ship; the inclinometer beside me was showing us rocking and rolling at anything up to 45 degrees. At times we were actually surfing, riding the huge, dark mountains of water that rose up behind us, and then plunging into the trough of the wave with a shuddering jolt that sent tons of glassy green seawater booming over the bow, and even splashing onto the windows of the bridge, a good 70 feet up and a hundred feet away. I watched it all with a landsman's horrified fascination, standing there for hours, holding on, hypnotized as though by a snake, unable to tear my eyes away, exhilarated by it all and yet vaguely uneasy about what it might do next. But then, that's what gave it spice and savor. And when that storm petered out, other lesser squalls took its place; altogether it was a rough ride home.

We were a fairly quiet lot, partly because of the weather but mainly because of the sense of anticlimax, the growing awareness that the great adventure was drawing to an end. Those who'd been down there for the past year were shifting their mental gazes away from Antarctica, and the clutch of fellow expeditioners and base routines that had been their world, allowing themselves for the first time in months the luxury of thinking about family and friends, finally letting in the drafts of the homesickness they'd rigorously shut out over the winter. The ship was neither here nor there; they just wanted the voyage over.

They had an Army psychologist aboard, Lt. Col. Nick Reynolds, whose job it was to debrief and counsel the returning winterers, and since the day we first landed at Davis he'd been taking each one aside for long private and apparently very personal interviews. He was a nice guy, and popular too, willing to roll with the punches (or the snowballs) when his wise-acre subjects turned the tables, like the day at Mawson when he was standing on the ice, talking with one of the helicopter pilots, and he looked up in surprise to see he'd been surrounded by 30 or so expeditioners in a near perfect circle. As they began closing in, packing snowballs with very deliberate intent, someone called out: "What's troubling you, Nick? Do you feel sometimes that people are out to get you?"

Before anyone is allowed to winter in Antarctica, they have to undergo a thorough psychological examination—to see if you're crazy enough, as the old joke goes—because once you are down there, once the last ship of the summer has sailed home, you're there for the duration, sealed off from the rest of the world by an impenetrable barrier of ice as effectively as if you were on another planet—or in a maximum-security prison. You can phone home (or e-mail, these days), but you can't visit, and nobody can visit you. No letters, either. A lot can happen in a year: birthdays, anniversaries, family members get sick or even die, babies take their first steps. And all you can do is hear about it over the phone. Lives move on, following the natural course of day-to-day events, except for that of the cloistered expeditioner in Antarctica whose "real" life has been put on cryogenic hold for a year. It is all too easy for them to emerge from the ice, blinking innocently and expecting that nothing has changed in their absence, unable to comprehend all that has gone on or, for that matter, for those they'd left back home to understand the life and experiences they'd had in Antarctica.

Everybody, even those of us on the out-and-back voyage, was going to feel some form of arrival shock, Nick explained, in a group lecture to all of us just before dinner one evening, the ship rocking, as ever, on the heavy seas. Very soon now we'd be stepping back into a bustling suburban world of cars and trees and crowds on the sidewalks, and it was going to feel strange after the scentless sterility of Antarctica. Such a sudden immersion back into the "real" world would affect us all in unpredictable ways, unique to each of us, he said. An electrician from Davis stood up—towering at six foot nine—and told how the last time he returned from wintering on The Ice he'd been so thrilled by the color and smell of roses in a garden that he'd knelt down right there in some complete stranger's front yard breathing in great, deep, appreciative sniffs. Not surprisingly the sight of a shaggy, bearded, seemingly crazy giant practically devouring her roses so alarmed the old woman who lived there that she called the police. Another old hand piped up with a story of a fresh returnee from Mawson who'd been arrested in Hobart after driving away from a gas station without paying; he wasn't being dishonest, it simply hadn't occurred to him to pay. He hadn't had to use money in so long, being accustomed to the cash-free economy on the base.

We'd all changed a little ourselves too, inside and out, in all manner of subtle and not-so-subtle ways, as Antarctica left its imprint on us. Some changes were quite visible, as plain as your face, in fact: Most of the male winterers had grown impressive ZZ Top beards, which, together with the aging effects of a year in Antarctica's cold, dry climate, made them look about five years older than the fresh-faced crew that departed Hobart the previous season. (I'd seen the "before" shots). One guy, returning from Davis and not wanting to give his wife too much of a shock when he stepped off the ship in a few days' time, shaved his off. The transformation was incredible—so much so that although I had been sitting opposite the guy at breakfast more or less every day now for the past fortnight, I didn't recognize him and, figuring him for one of the returning expeditioners we'd just picked up at Mawson, and whom I'd somehow not yet met, I actually introduced myself and asked his name.

There was a girl named Sam on board, a biology undergraduate coming back from Davis, who'd had, I'd been told, gorgeous waist-length red hair when she went down to Antarctica, but in one of those impetuous mood-of-the-moment things, at a party on her last night at the base, she'd joined in with some of the guys and had her head shaved. It had seemed funny on the night, I guess, swept along on the effervescence of a good time, and her radical new look was no big deal at all among her tribe at Davis who knew only her Antarctic persona, but all that was over now, all the contexts were gone, the tribe soon to be dispersed for good, and as the days passed and Hobart drew near, she became increasingly self-conscious, rubbing her hand over her stubble, and plainly wondering how to explain all this to the people back home. What were her family and friends going to think when she strode down the gangplank?

I felt a little sorry for her, stuck in a moment of time, a lost context. Guys with beards could always shave them off, and in 20 minutes return to their old recognizable selves, but unless the *Aurora* turned into the *Flying Dutchman*, and magically wandered the seas for another year at least, there was no way on Earth Sam was going to walk back into her old life looking anything like the person who'd left it.

Long, empty days passed agreeably. We put in the time pretty much as we had on the way out—watching videos, playing Scrabble and Trivial Pursuit, table tennis, or just sitting up on the bridge watching the restless gray seas and endless empty horizons. Somewhere out there in the big bottomless Furious Fifties they held a darts tournament. It went on over a couple of days. All the big-gun much practiced ex-Navy players from the bases, as well as the *Aurora*'s shrewd-eyed crew, brought out their leather cases of beautifully flighted and weighted darts, and I heard how over the past winter the guys at Davis and Mawson had had a darts tournament, by radio, with the Americans at the South Pole, and it was boasted that the winner here might justifiably call himself (or herself) the darts champion of Antarctica (or at the very least the darts champion of East Antarctica).

Who could resist a shot at a title like that? I signed up and began to play the preliminary rounds. And incredibly enough, began to win, with chaos theory and the rocking of the ship working in my favor, much to the groaning disgust of those players who were genuinely good. Their expertly lobbed darts thumped in just shy of their mark, while my cack-handedly thrown ones struck gold—not always, but often enough, and I survived round after round, winning by the skin of my teeth right through the quarter finals and then semis. It was ludicrously fluky, like seeing a coin tossed and coming up heads eight times in a row, or catching a glimpse of a ridiculously long ash on an airily waved cigarette: You know it's got to fall any second, but you're fascinated to see how long it can last. And so I made the finals.

Up to that point the matches had all been conducted informally: Players would meet up at a time convenient to both, play each other, and record the results on the bulletin board. The final, however, was an *event*, held on a night of heavily rolling seas, and when I stepped into the cramped, windowless room way down belowdecks that served as the pub on board, I found it jammed with fellow shipmates and expeditioners, a huge Australian flag decorating the ceiling, and a small space in the middle of the room with a clear view of the dart board on the wall. I edged in, nervous. My opponent—a meteorologist and former submariner—was waiting, with his fancy leather case of darts, looking rueful and nervous too, probably more so than I because he at least had something to lose—face. I didn't.

We started poorly, both of us jittery, but then we hit our respective strides, and before I knew it, all I needed was a double 20 to win. All he needed was double seven. I stepped up to the line, swaying in time with the motion of the ship, took elaborate aim—I was getting the pose right by now even if the skill wasn't there to match it—and then lobbed my dart, thump, seemingly bang on the money. A gasp went up. Heads crowded in to see the board, and then a laugh: The sweet tide of justice had finally started to roll. My dart had hit the plastic surround on the board and scraped past it, just outside the double 20. There wasn't even the thickness of a cigarette paper in it. Missed it by that much. I grumbled aloud and extravagantly about my bad luck but was guffawed down. No sympathy. And I never had a second chance, either, just the big Cadbury chocolate bar they were giving for second place, because the other guy's dart flew straight and true, into the double seven. Game over. Big cheers. Karmic justice had prevailed. All the same, I could still crow that I was the second best darts player in East Antarctica. And I did.

Christmas came and went. We celebrated with a bacchanalian musical revue (memorable acts including one of the helicopter pilots playing a mean blues guitar, a trio of female biologists driving the audience wild as they mimed "Mustang Sally" in cat suits they'd made themselves out of PVC trash can liners, and a grotesquely lecherous Santa Claus), followed by a round of lusty carol singing and a huge feast. The next day, Boxing Day, marked the start of the traditional Sydney-Hobart yacht race. We read about it on the telexes pinned up on the board, just as we had the cricket scores all summer, and realized we'd be steaming up the Derwent about the same time as most of the yachts. We were getting close now, another couple of days; you could feel it in the air when you went out on deck, the softness and what felt to us like warmth.

I woke to the spectacle of storm-lashed rocky spires and a dark mountainous coast out my porthole—it was Tasmania's wild and rugged Southwest Cape, a gloomy, misty, primeval wilderness so forbidding that early mariners marked this bit of coast as "Transylvania" on their charts, and it is still one of the wildest landscapes in Australia. Except now it seemed a reminder of our return to civilization, almost literally just around the corner.

We were pitching and rolling heavily in yet another storm, the same big southerly buster that had been wreaking such havoc on the Sydney-Hobart yachts. It was no fun on an icebreaker either. We'd planned to have an outdoor barbeque that afternoon, but the trawl deck was awash with about three feet of seawater from the dirty great waves booming over the rails, and nobody was very hungry anyway. As we turned up the mouth of the Derwent, and into smoother waters, a pilot boat brought out the customs and immigration people, and the rest of the afternoon was filled with bureaucratic formalities, and the business of turning in our parkas and boots, a poignant parting with our Antarctic personas (we were allowed to keep our sledging caps), and ticking off checklists. A few more beards were gone now, shy, grinning, fresh-faced familiar strangers popping up on deck as we assembled along the rails to watch as we steamed into port. Hobart was waiting, the same pretty little maritime city nestled at the foot of Mount Wellington, the low line of pubs and hotels along the waterfront, the old warehouses on Battery Point, the glint of cars moving along the streets. Back here nothing had changed, nothing at all. The *Aurora Australis* drew alongside Macquarie Wharf, where a crowd was waiting. The ship's horn gave a welcoming blast. Ropes were cast. The gangplank dropped. We were home.

The rest of that day passed in a blur. I remember coming down the gangplank, shaking hands with the first mate, and turning to see an unsettling mass of eager unfamiliar faces, all straining to get first looks of friends and relatives. A couple of my friends, Ben and his sister Phoebe, were there to meet me.

"Hey! So what was it like?"

Until that moment I had been observing this whole arrival scene with as much detachment as if I were watching a newsreel; it was interesting, that's all, another interesting and emotive thing in a world of interesting things that had been happening to me and around me lately. But Phoebe's cheery greeting and welcoming question, and my sudden obligation to respond, broke the spell, thrusting me personally into the picture, and bringing home the concomitant reality that it was all over, my grand adventure ended. Suddenly I just felt overwhelmed, choked up, unable to speak, and finally, after a couple of deep get-a-grip breaths, stammered in a husky voice: "It was the best thing I've ever done."

I turned away, to escape their quizzical eyes and to cast a lingering farewell glance at the ice-scarred prow of the ship that had been my home these past few weeks, thinking it curious and sad to see it surrounded by so many unknowing strangers along a drab concrete wharf, picturing it in my mind's eye as it had been down south, when we were booming along seemingly endlessly through desolate broken pack with the pale polar sun overhead, or as it looked jammed in the fast ice in front of Davis with the Adélies waddling past in the foreground, or the minuscule orange speck we were thrilled to see from the helicopter, 3,000 feet up, a tiny mote lost in that dazzling immensity of ice and sky that appeared to stretch on forever. One image seemed to trigger another then another and an ever expanding collage of sensations and impressions began welling up. I dragged my eyes away from the big orange ship and back to the faces of two good friends who'd been kind enough to come down here to pick me up.

"C'mon, let's get out of here."

We stopped off at a grocery store on the way back to Phoebe's place to pick up a few things for spaghetti bolognese. We sat around the table that night and I tried to tell them all about it.

Antarctica touches everybody who goes there in different ways. For me it had been like being a child again, recapturing at 35 that precious sense of wonder that a child takes for granted—but better even than that, because at 35 you know just how rare and fleeting such a sense of wonder is, and how extremely fortunate you are to have a second bite at that cherry. Youth, as the old song goes, is wasted on the young. For seven weeks I'd led an extraordinary life of icebreakers, helicopters, dogsleds, and adventure at the outermost edge of the world. Everything around me had been new and astonishing, unlike anything I had ever seen or experienced before; every day brought fresh wonders—and was appreciated for it. I can truthfully say I hadn't wasted a second of my time down there, but had lived every moment and returned with a child's joyfulness and enthusiasm for life, and able again to see the beauty and wonder around me in the jumbled-up real world that had gone unnoticed before. Antarctica's simplicity had etched it all into high relief.

I resolved to keep this sense of wonder and perspective alive now that I was back, never yield this rare fleeting second chance I'd been given to see the world anew, but I might as well have tried to preserve a particularly beautiful snowflake as an Antarctic souvenir. It's been my experience that as soon as you make any new and noble declarations, the fates pose a little quiz to test your resolve; say that you're never going to let such and such kind of person affect you again, and you can be sure the tides of life will throw another such person into your life to give you the opportunity to put your new resolution into practice. Claim peace and tolerance, goodwill, perspective, and a renewed sense of wonder for yourself, as I did, and you'll soon find yourself thigh deep in a maelstrom of life's exquisitely tormenting little things—slowpokes in the fast lane, lawn mowers that refuse to start, stubbed toes, spilled coffee down your freshly ironed shirt three minutes before you have to go out the door—trying to exercise your grand intentions and floundering. What had been so apparent and easy in Antarctica's clear air is altogether trickier in the thicker atmosphere up here—the difference between juggling one ball and juggling five.

And so the grand Antarctic-inspired resolutions faded, together with the surprise bout of hay fever I experienced on my sudden return to the dust and pollen-laden air of a South Australian summer, and the shipboard friendships I'd made aboard the *Aurora Australis*. We kept in touch for a while. A bunch of us got together over a barbeque in Melbourne a few months later, and the station leader at Mawson called me up once, out of the blue, a few months after that and we had a grand old chat, not so much about Antarctica but about what we were doing then, which made our chatter somehow better, more natural, an oblique rubbing of the thumb over the imprint Antarctica had made on our lives. But lives move on, the circumstances that brought us together were gone and we all drifted apart on our own separate paths and soon lost contact.

Over the years Antarctica receded to the very pleasantest of memories. At night I often dreamed I was back there, impressionist dreams where the lines were blurred, the details swirled around like cocktail ice, but the essence of the place, its crystalline magic, boundlessness, and romance perfectly sharp and clear and penetrating. I often wished I could go back. It seemed incredible to think that I had seen my last Adélie or emperor penguin—they had been so vital a part of the backdrop—but unless I found a way to return to The Ice, that's the way it would be. That's where they lived; they didn't live anywhere else. And my going back to Antarctica again seemed very unlikely. And in a way it seemed greedy even to try; the wheel of fortune had favored me once, been outrageously kind, in fact. It would be a testing of Providence to go back for more. It was someone else's turn now. That was only fair.

And anyway, did I really want to tamper with memory? What was there to gain? Another trip south on the *Aurora* would only compete with the first, and that one had the unassailable advantage of having been my very first trip to Antarctica, and however fabulous a second voyage might turn out, it had no hope of exceeding the first. No way. At the very best it might just—just—match it. Chances are, it wouldn't. And what would I be left with then? My memories of that first journey—imperfect or idealized though they might be—were too precious to jeopardize like that. I wanted them safe, nicely cellared in the attic of my mind, there to age and improve with the passage of time. I let go the idea of returning to the real geographical Antarctica, but went often in my dreams.

And then one day, years later, I received a phone call from an editor at National Geographic—the kind of telephone call I used to dream about when I was a kid—asking me if I'd like to spend a summer traveling all around Antarctica—the Ross Sea, the Transantarctic Mountains, the South Pole, the Antarctic Peninsula—and write a story. The brief would be to travel the breadth of the continent, visiting bases and field camps, and talk to everybody I could find—scientists, cooks, cleaners, even the children who live on some of the bases these days. There'd be a trip on a Russian flagged research vessel doing a krill survey in the Scotia Sea, and a few weeks on a chartered yacht exploring the remotest pockets of the Antarctic Peninsula. I felt my knuckles whiten on the telephone and said yes in a heartbeat.

CHAPTER THREE

Forms, Forms, and More Forms

In Shackleton's day, voyages to Antarctica began in elegant Edwardian drawing rooms, with the explorer-to-be whiling away his evenings making nice with the gouty old gents at the Royal Geographical Society or lingering over port and cigars with adventure-minded baronets who might be induced to write out a check. Those were the days, a by-gone world of steam engines and viceroys and slow boats to China and Marlow's blank spaces on the maps.

I'd been reading all about how it used to be in the slew of books on heroic age polar explorers that had begun appearing in the stores lately: new editions of Apsley Cherry-Garrard's classic *The Worst Journey in the World*, Shackleton's *Heart of the Antarctic*, glossy picture books filled with the glorious black-and-white photography of Frank Hurley and Herbert Ponting, and brightly written histories and biographies of the main players, chiefly Scott, Shackleton, and Amundsen, but particularly Shackleton, the lovable Irish rogue who was enjoying an early 21st-century renaissance as the ultimate polar hero.

I love books and reading, and with my own big adventure to The Ice pending, and to regions where I'd be following largely in the footsteps of these great explorers, this seemed the perfect time to reacquaint myself with the bold tales I grew up on. So I bought big and trundled home with armloads of paperbacks with crisp snow-white or ice-blue covers.

And then I read them all while putting myself through the calvary of arranging a trip to postmodern Antarctica, and as I read I found myself growing ever more wistful. No doubt about it—the past century was certainly a cruel one for the romance of travel. No more airy spins of a library globe, lace antimacassars, and art nouveau luggage labels; my grand tour of the ice was taking shape around a thick packet of application forms, long late-night telephone calls to bureaucrats in Washington, and tedious hours sitting in public hospital waiting rooms surrounded by racks of brochures on quitting smoking, diabetes, and scabies. Fortunately, at least, I had a hefty stock of escapist adventure stories to help me pass the time.

Nature may abhor a vacuum and do whatever it can to fill it, but it is nothing compared with the abhorrence politicians and their governments feel toward unregulated and un-deeded lands where human beings might operate free of supervision. Antarctica may be the world's last unclaimed continent, but few places on this Web-shrunken Earth of ours are more tightly bound by red tape, restrictions, occupational health and safety regulations, and environmental protocols than an Antarctic base, particularly, I was starting to discover, a U.S. Antarctic base. The U.S. Antarctic Program (USAP) is by far the biggest operation on the continent, overseen by the National Science Foundation on a budget of many, many millions of dollars and run by a U.S. huge defense contractor, with the U.S. Coast Guard and the 109th Airlift Wing of the New York Air National Guard providing logistical support. And since it was with the Americans I'd be traveling, at least down to McMurdo and the South Pole, it was their bureaucratic red tape I had to untangle. And as I cast my eyes over the mound of triplicate forms, approvals, and medical questionnaires required to visit one of their bases, I felt more like I was falling into some vast corporate–military machinery than planning a journey to what is purportedly the world's last great wilderness.

Some of it was positively Kafkaesque. I noticed in the handbooks I had been issued that, for example, if I were to walk past a seal dozing on the ice, and it so much as raised its head to look at me, I would technically be guilty of "interfering" with wildlife, a felony conceivably punishable by hefty fines or even imprisonment. Similar guidelines require a distance of at least 15 feet to be maintained between humans and penguins at all times, a seemingly reasonable bit of environmental sensitivity, but hardly one the insatiably curious penguins are likely to observe. I thought back to those nosey little Adélies at Davis all those years ago, poking their beaks into my camera bag and nearly tripping me underfoot. I'd thought of them as comical little douaniers at the time, but now I saw they had the power of having me chucked in jail. This raised the cartoonish specter of my being chased about the ice by a gaggle of 18-inch-high Adélies, slipping and sliding as I struggled to stay out of the calaboose.

The same laws that forbade "disturbing" wildlife, forbade helping them in any way too. The orphaned emperor penguin chick the guys at Mawson had rescued the year I was there, then raised and later successfully—so far as is known—

released back into the wild would by law have to be left to starve today. (In fact, later in this particular assignment the photographer took a picture of just such an abandoned seal pup, its face crusted with snow as it lay starving on the ice. When the photo ran in the magazine, readers wrote in, outraged that the photographer would not have gone to the creature's aid and the letter's page editor was obliged to explain that the photographer would have been breaking the law—committing a felony, no less—had she done anything else.)

I was perplexed to learn, in preparing for my trip, that in order to visit a particular seal colony in the South Shetland Islands I would need to apply for a permit to "take" wildlife. When this news came in the mail, together with a request for my credentials and curriculum vitae, I thought there had been a mistake; someone must have confused me with some other, more scientific, Smith who was planning to capture and tag local marine life for research purposes. And so I scribbled off a lighthearted note saying I had no plans to take any of the wildlife anywhere. A friendly but firm response came by e-mail informing me there had been no error: Under the strict guidelines of the 1991 Madrid Protocol on the Environment, anyone observing and writing about the wildlife in certain sensitive locations is deemed to be "taking" them.

Chastened, I dutifully sent off details of my itinerary, credentials, and curriculum vitae, as requested, thinking that this was surely as sophisticated an abstraction as anything the medieval Catholic Church might have had to say about murder in the spirit or theft by desire. But then environmentalism is the religion of 21st-century Antarctica, and it is very high church and fundamentalist in a way that would have warmed the heart of Torquemada.

In my naiveté I had also somehow assumed that because NATIONAL GEOGRAPHIC magazine had already presented its proposal to the National Science Foundation, and had received approval in principle for visits to the various bases under its aegis, that this was all a done deal.

It never occurred to me that as an outsider I might merit special and frosty scrutiny by the U.S. authorities. E-mails, conference calls, even personal assurances by various editors failed to convince, and eventually the magazine was obliged to fly me to Washington for an hour-long conference with the mandarins at the U.S. Antarctic Program in the hope that a face-to-face meeting might break down the barriers. (I learned later that all this was because one of the big chief Antarcticans at the National Science Foundation was in a sulk because he'd wanted a particular writer assigned to the story and the editors had assigned me.)

The make-or-break meeting was scheduled for ten o'clock at NSF headquarters in Arlington, Virginia. I arrived jet-lagged, wearing a tie I'd fitted around my neck at the airport, and looking and feeling like a defendant in some minor court proceeding. It was a beautiful September morning, and as I took the cab across town, seeing the D.C. monuments bathed in autumn sunshine, I wished I were doing almost anything else. As a pleasurable way of putting in the time, I'd say the conference ranked somewhere between applying for a bank loan and an income tax audit, and close to how I imagine a plea bargaining session might run.

The photographer assigned to the story, a pleasant woman named Maria, came to the meeting as well. It was the first time I met her. She lived locally in D.C., had already traveled agreeably with the USAP to Antarctica on two earlier GEOGRAPHIC assignments, and was clearly, as far as the NSF was concerned, "on message" and well liked.

All the while the man I most needed to convince of my sincerity and bona fides stared balefully at me from across the table with what I thought at first was a look of cold fury but might have been only a case of mumps, because the organization's media officer cheerfully assured me later, as he ushered me down the corridor toward the elevator in that glad-handing way public relations people often have, that things had gone exceptionally well. He even effused that it was fortunate I had caught everybody during such a relaxed and friendly interlude, before the stresses and strains of a busy Antarctic summer season could kick in and fray tempers and make them appear surly.

I responded with that breezy to-be-sure, to-be-sure manner journalists adopt when chatting with PR types, and all the while thinking that I found his masters about as frolicsome as Easter Island statues. I stepped back into the warm autumn sunshine badly needing my lunch and feeling a sort of kinship now with Shackleton, who must have weathered scores of such meetings in his endless quest for expedition funds and sponsorship.

But the media affairs man knew his people, as they usually do. I flew home the next day with a vague understanding that I would be allowed to go.

Nobody owns Antarctica, not in a legal sense anyway. Seven countries (Australia, Britain, France, Norway, New Zealand, Chile, and Argentina) claim parts of the continent as their sovereign territory, but nobody recognizes these claims, and all the parties involved have agreed not to pursue them, at least not overtly. So in that sense it is still quite possible to thumb your nose at authorities and travel down there on your own anytime you like—if you have deep enough pockets. Nobody can stop you, not yet, although there are moves afoot by some governments, such as Sweden, to forbid their citizens traveling to Antarctica, even as tourists aboard cruise ships, without obtaining permission. Even then, of course, you could still dodge the rules, as Americans routinely flout their government's embargo against travel to Cuba; it just requires a bit of creative routing and no stamps in the passport, thanks.

But travel in Antarctica is frighteningly expensive. It is a hell of a long way from anywhere else, and everything needed to sustain life has to be brought in, and at great expense. It has always been thus. A recurring theme in the diaries of the old-time explorers was the need to raise huge sums of cash, hence all the tedious evenings over billiards, brandy, and cigars with wealthy industrialists and baronets. The toughest part of any expedition, Shackleton often complained, was the ceaseless campaigning for funds.

While it is a fairly easy matter these days—albeit pricey—to book a cabin on a cruise ship and tour the Antarctic Peninsula, if you want to travel into the interior of the continent, you are looking at some very serious bucks indeed, not to mention nightmarish logistics that can take years to plan through. There are no scheduled flights, fuel costs are astronomical, and you have to arrange your own fuel depots, for nobody down there will sell you any if you run out. The nations that operate bases down there have formed a sort of holy alliance to shut out, as much as possible, independent travelers. It is very effective.

It can be done. People regularly do raise huge sums for ski treks to the South Pole. But tens of thousands of dollars won't even buy you a cup of coffee on the base once you get there. That, as those MasterCard ads might put it, is priceless. For that, and everything else on the base, you need to come into the bureaucratic fold, fill out the endless forms, seek permission, and convince authorities your business is genuine—and of benefit to them.

And so to form-filling. I'd thought the Australian Antarctic Division had required a fairly comprehensive physical exam when I had gone south with them, but theirs was just a sweet wish compared with the probing demanded by the litigious, cholesterol-conscious, corporatized Americans.

In the fortnight following the arrival of a sheaf of forms from Washington, I led the life of a galloping hypochondriac. From not even knowing where my local hospital was, I could now find my way around its labyrinth of waxy corridors, flower shops, and wards as easily as any candy striper. Long afternoons disappeared on hard plastic chairs, filling in the empty minutes with my doorstopper biography of Shackleton and having fun imagining the Irishman putting up with this.

He would have hated it. In fact, he would never have made it through. Shackleton had a dodgy heart and was mighty careful never to let a doctor near him. He paid the price, too, dying of a heart attack in South Georgia Island in 1922 at the ripe old age of 47. The Boss, as he was known to his men, might have been able to get away with setting his chin at a gallant angle and reciting a few lines of Tennyson, but these days the powers that be want blood, and ECGs and a host of medical minutiae.

It was hard to blame them, though. The Americans had just spent millions of dollars rescuing the base doctor at the South Pole in the middle of winter, after she discovered she had breast cancer. They were in no mood for fooling around. And so I was poked and prodded, weighed and measured, my family history charted, and my medical background recorded in minute detail. My knees were tapped with a rubber mallet and I answered queries about depression, mental illness, asthma, and whether I was taking vitamins. I owned up to an allergy to cats and occasional bouts of hay fever. I squinted at the small type on eye charts, and had my heartbeat monitored on a 12-line ECG. There were urine tests, stool tests, a TB test, and a bewildering array of blood tests—total iron, chloride, calcium, uric acid, something called "AST," something else called "RPR," and still another something called "CBC w/diff." There were tests for hepatitis A antibodies, hepatitis B antibodies, and HIV antibodies, and another blood test to measure my cholesterol levels. My blood pressure was jotted down (resentful over simmering) and the spot of tinea on the little piggy of my left foot noted on my chart and a particular brand of antifungal powder recommended.

Nor was my tut-tutting dentist overlooked. I spent two engaging mornings leaving nail marks in the arms of his chair, and another in the hospital's radiology ward having an elaborate set of mouth and jaw x-rays done.

When I'd finished, I dazedly parceled the forms, reports, charts, and x-ray films into a large manila envelope, signed an additional form promising not to sue anybody no matter what, and still another swearing that I had no criminal convictions, and posted the lot to Raytheon's office in Denver. The company doctors would review my results, I was told, and determine whether or not I was "PQ-ed" ("physically qualified") to travel to Antarctica.

Over the course of weeks of form-filling, e-mails, phone calls, and conferences, I became fluent in the telegraphic speech of the USAP. There was PQ, of course, for physically qualified, and NPQ for not physically qualified. Scientists were PIs (principal investigators). I was identified as V-002 (that's visitor number two) on my forms. Naturally everyone, PIs included, had to be PQ-ed before leaving CONUS (the Continental United States) for "Cheech" (Christchurch), the jumping-off point for MacTown (McMurdo Station, the main U.S. Antarctic base). At Cheech we were to report to the CDC (clothing distribution center) to receive our issue of ECW (extreme cold weather) gear.

I practiced my abbreviations, went on a spending spree at my local mountaineering shop, buying cold-weather gear of my own, for later on the yacht, and marked off the days on my calendar.

Two days before I was due to fly to New Zealand I received a breezy e-mail from the nice folks in Denver telling me that they had lost my blood tests and therefore I was NPQ. A frantic trip to the Royal Adelaide Hospital followed, where the pathologists obligingly rushed through the tests and faxed the results through to Raytheon and gave me a certified copy to have on hand to fax again in case these latest results were lost as well.

I boarded my flight the next morning. Six hours later I was shivering in the cold drizzle in front of Christchurch airport, picking at a fresh round bandage in the crook of my elbow, wishing I had my rain parka, and wondering how long it would take for my missing luggage to catch up with me. My inner ironist was thinking how marvelous it was that a trip to Antarctica could still be filled with such adventure and uncertainty. And I didn't even know the half of it.

If all went according to schedule—and assuming Raytheon's doctors up in Colorado checked their in trays, liked my blood tests, and rated me PQ—I was supposed to spend a day in Christchurch being fitted out for my ECW gear before catching a flight to McMurdo the following morning. But the cab driver, who'd asked me what I was doing in town, by way of making conversation, didn't fancy my chances.

"The weather down there has been kind of lousy all week," he said as we drew away from the airport. "Blowing snow, poor visibility, the lot—they've been canceling flights every day. Of course, you never know your luck. The front might have pushed through. I haven't heard anything today."

Huh. I settled back in my seat, deflated and trying not to show it. It wasn't the prospect of loitering in Christchurch that troubled me so much—after all it gave my errant baggage an extra day to find me—but hearing a cabbie grouse about flight backups over Antarctica as though it were a traffic snarl on the expressway wasn't exactly the way I had imagined the great adventure starting.

It made McMurdo Station seem disconcertingly like an antipodean Buffalo, New York—one of those snowy destinations where dirty weather frequently means delays and inconvenienced passengers. One of the greatest things about traveling to Mawson on the *Aurora Australis* had been the dark and stormy sea voyage necessary to get there; ten days of gales and empty horizons, brooding skies and wandering albatrosses that reinforced Antarctica's distance and romantic isolation, tamping it into its special place on my mental map of the world.

Traveling there by plane—breakfast in Christchurch, lunch or early tea in Antarctica—was always going to be different, but I hadn't thought through just how different until I heard that cab driver nattering about the delays and hassles; how they'd all been taking stranded passengers to and from the airport for days now as the flights to The Ice were canceled.

Christchurch has been the classic gateway to Antarctica since the days of Scott and Shackleton. Almost everybody here knows someone who has been down to The Ice. My cab driver, I learned on the drive to my hotel, had been there himself, to Campbell Island, one of New Zealand's remote sub-Antarctic islands, back when he was in the Navy.

Since 1955 Christchurch has been the transport hub of the USAP. More than 3,000 passengers—most of them American—pass through here each summer on their way to Antarctica, some making several trips back and forth. Millions of dollars are spent. Incredibly, during those few hectic weeks at the peak of the summer season, there are more frequent flights to McMurdo out of Christchurch International than there are flights to Sydney.

The town's museums are crammed with Antarctic memorabilia, its gift shops sparkle with glass penguins and postcards of Antarctic scenes, and a monumental statue of Captain Scott posed heroically in his polar gear overlooks a bed of petunias and the Avon River in the heart of the city. Antarctica is big business. When I stopped in at one of the mountaineering stores on Cashel Street to pick up an extra fleece, the clerk behind the counter handed me a catalog and told me not to worry if I forgot anything; just send an e-mail, tell them what I want, and they'd pop it on the next flight south.

"We do it all the time."

CHAPTER FOUR

Ground Hog Day

THE FIRST THING I DID WHEN I GOT TO MY HOTEL ROOM WAS PUT THROUGH a call to the International Antarctic Center, the local headquarters for the USAP. A woman there told me that Raytheon had received my blood test results, were satisfied with them, and that I was now officially PQ-ed. She delivered these glad tidings with the cheery brusqueness of a big-hearted nurse telling a mopey patient that—see?—he wasn't so sick after all. And since I had joined the ranks of the PQ-ed, she invited me out to the clothing distribution center to be given my issue of extreme cold weather gear. There would be a fitting tomorrow at two.

I asked about the weather over McMurdo. It seemed my cabbie wasn't quite as *au fait* on the McMurdo scene as he imagined, something which gave me an odd bit of satisfaction. The weather had been lousy all right, and the schedule was a shambles, but a few flights were getting through. One made it in yesterday. The woman on the phone sounded confident about my going in two days, as scheduled. She gave me the address of the Antarctic Center, and I jotted it down and hung up.

The International Antarctic Center turned out to be a gleaming white iceberg of a complex sitting on a manicured lawn about a half mile from the Christchurch airport. If it weren't for its name, emblazoned in polar-blue letters across a main wall, along with the cheesy logo of an emperor penguin, it could have passed for any of the export offices or software engineering firms you usually see huddled close to an airport.

The cabbie dropped me outside the door of the CDC, where a clutch of U.S. servicemen—all crew cuts, camouflage fatigues, and shiny combat boots—loitered by the topiary, smoking, gossiping, and telling jokes. They were from the 109th

Airlift Wing of the New York Air National Guard, the unit that provides much of the transport and logistical support for the USAP.

I eased my way past them, into a musty front room that reminded me of a small-town bus station. About 20 or so outdoorsy Americans were slouched in a semicircle, day packs slung over their shoulders, listening to a ruddy-cheeked, middle-aged man in a Royal New Zealand Air Force sweater begin a lecture on the clothing allowances we'd be given. Samples of the various items were displayed on the wall behind him: parkas, boots, thermal underwear, fleeces, gloves, socks, and mittens. He paced in front of the display, using a wooden pointer, and murdered his vowels in a thick Kiwi accent.

After he finished we sat cross-legged on the floor and watched a 20-minute video. I was beginning to feel like I was back in eighth-grade gym class. The film's narrator was an American, with one of those deep stentorian voices, filled with authority, the sort of voice CNN uses for its promotional spots. The soundtrack was muscular and energetic, familiar to anyone who has ever sat through a mining company presentation to its shareholders. The sense was one of relentless vigor.

The video ran us once more briskly through our clothing allowance, and then on to details of the flight and eventual arrival in McMurdo, with the voice-over reminding us constantly, at every opportunity—and even creating a few opportunities that perhaps wouldn't otherwise have turned up in the natural flow of dialogue—that the clothing issue was, and would remain, U.S. government property at all times and in all circumstances. No matter how badly worn, torn, or frayed it might be, each item must be accounted for.

By the fourth repetition of this I thought to myself, OK: an idée fixe, and my inner wise-guy began to fashion witty ad-libs. But when I looked around me and saw how seriously everyone was taking this I realized any lighthearted sotto voce by me would have fallen on thorny soil. From pilfering and theft, we shifted into the scarier realm of firearms and illegal drugs, with warnings that both were to be left at home. Roll an edifying scene of McMurdo-bound travelers standing in parade while men in SWAT-style blue jumpsuits and combat boots walk sniffer dogs past them and their duffels.

After a final warning that all gear remained U.S. government property at all times, we closed on a note of institutional levity: Congratulations, we had all been upgraded to "Connoisseur Class." We were treated to a glimpse of the cramped paratrooper-style seating we'd enjoy on the cargo plane. Box lunch included and free earplugs for all. Lights up. Time to try on our gear.

It was like Christmas at the missionary box. Everybody was given two bright orange canvas duffle bags crammed with gear, and they were all arranged in alphabetical order in a long row. I found mine, unzipped it, and began pulling out clean, used, bulky winter clothes. What you were issued depended on where in Antarctica you were going and what sort of work you did. Anyone stationed at the South Pole, for instance, was issued with tougher-wearing parkas in distinctive green and black, since "Polies" were apparently notoriously hard on clothes. Tradesmen were issued heavy-duty Carhartt overalls, and scientists, who might have to work in the cold with finely calibrated instruments, received several pairs of thin thermal gloves.

A visiting writer merited standard issue: two pairs of dense thermal long-johns, six pairs of thick socks, heavyweight fleece pants and sweaters, Gore-Tex overalls, a mountain of gloves, mittens, neck warmers, balaclavas, hats, and a pair of enormous army-style canvas and leather, fur-backed gauntlets that looked like they might have been left over from one of Admiral Byrd's expeditions.

On top of it all was the USAP trademark parka, known as Big Red—a massively heavy goosedown number with faux fur lining on the hood, pockets galore, and a Velcro patch on the left breast where you could stick a nametag. It was designed to keep the wearer snug and warm, even in midwinter at the South Pole where temperatures regularly dropped to −90°F or even colder. And for the feet, a pair of gigantic white boots, made of dense rubber to specifications developed by U.S. Navy cold-weather researchers in the 1930s. They called them bunny boots, and they made my size 14 hiking boots look as dainty as ballet slippers.

We had to try on all our gear. I felt like I was suiting up for a ride in the space shuttle. It fit well, but with so much extra padding around the midriff it wasn't easy to bend over and tie the shoelaces on my bunny boots. The rubber in the boots was so stiff, and the thin waxy laces so slippery, that it was impossible to tie them snugly anyway. When I finished, my feeble rabbit-eared knots resembled the first-time shoe-tying efforts of a preschooler.

I waddled around experimentally, already sweating and feverish under all that insulation. This stuff was seriously warm. It was a relief to take it off. The air felt cool on my skin. I packed the polar gear back into the duffel bags, signed for everything, and stepped out into the clear summer sunshine.

Before leaving, I had to step around to the USAP travel office and hand in my ticket back home to Australia. The idea was that if bad weather kept planes grounded at McMurdo, stranding us at the other end, someone at this end could rebook my commercial flight home. A sensible precaution, I guess, but I didn't care for it overly much, this surrendering of my ticket. The whole morning felt too much like an induction, like I'd just joined the Army or something.

In exchange for my handed-in ticket, I received a pass that entitled me to use the PX—a special duty-free store normally available only to U.S. military personnel, where I could post items at the U.S. post office, or make calls to anyone in the U.S.—assuming there was anyone there I wished to call—at the same rate as if I were dialing from Seattle.

In the room next door, a dozen or so Americans in camouflage fatigues checked their e-mails and surfed the Web. They all knew each other and were perfectly at ease and at home with the USAP's brusque military tone, abbreviations, and regulations.

I drifted outside, across the lawn to the large annex that housed an Antarctic museum, gift shop, and cafeteria. The weather had fined up considerably, with shafts of sunlight coming through increasingly wide breaks in the clouds. The lawn looked bright and springlike. Tourists lined up along the curb in front of the museum, waiting to take rides in a Hagglunds tractor—just like the ones they used in Antarctica—for 20 bucks a pop. Groups were taking photos of each other standing in front of an Antarctic mural, where a plaque marked the occasion that Bill Clinton had visited the center and given a speech on Antarctica and the environment in 1999.

I went into the café for lunch. The bill of fare included Shackleton Soup, Scott Pasta, and Bellingshausen Hoki. I settled on the healthful option of the Mawson Baked Potato and ate it at a table by the window, wondering if I hadn't made a big mistake in trying to go back to The Ice. This was all so different. Antarctica was starting to seem stranger and farther away than ever.

They instructed us in their inimitable style to be at the CDC at 0600 to check in for the flight to McMurdo. I set my alarm for 4:30, but woke up every hour or so during the night. At 4:20 I couldn't stand it any longer and rolled out of bed. I was in the shower when the telephone rang. I answered it dripping and heard a chirpy voice tell me that I could go ahead and sleep in: The flight had been delayed a few hours due to bad weather and poor visibility over McMurdo. Check-in ("chicken" as it sounds in a New Zealand accent) was now set for nine o'clock.

I lingered over a three-coffee breakfast at the buffet downstairs and read the paper. Fine weather for Christchurch, nothing about McMurdo. When I returned to my room the message light was blinking on the telephone. Check-in was now half past two. By lunchtime they had scrubbed the day's flight altogether. We were back to reporting in at oh-six-hundred the next morning.

And so began a *Ground Hog Day* sort of existence where, like the Bill Murray character in the movie, we were all condemned to repeat the same day over and over again seemingly until the end of time: Arise at the click of half past four, shower, field a phone call advising you of the new check-in time, breakfast at the buffet, phone call, lunch, phone call, and start all over again.

However, when I came back after breakfast one morning, the phone didn't ring. I sat in my room, idly flicking the channel changer on the TV and waiting for the expected call to inform me of another delay. The instrument remained silent. Marveling at this development in my life, I packed and headed downstairs, still listening for the phone to ring through the door behind me as I walked down the corridor. It remained silent and there was no message at reception. I checked out.

The cab driver made good time despite the morning traffic. We drew up to the curb in front of the Antarctic Center a few minutes early. The sidewalk was bustling with packs and people. It was going to be a crowded flight.

About the only good thing that can be written or said about the flight to McMurdo is that after you've done it once you can dine out on the experience for years and forever after face even the grimmest economy class seating with complete equanimity, if not downright cheerfulness. It is anything up to a nine-hour haul from Christchurch to The Ice, depending on what type of plane you happen to be flying on. I was lucky in that regard. I had drawn one of the big C-141 Starlifters—an airliner-size cargo jet—that makes the run in around six hours.

It waited on the tarmac at a restricted part of the airfield, looking sleek, dark, and predatory. It had a mysterious-looking bulge over the cockpit—so the captain could wear his cowboy hat, or so the old pilot's joke goes—and only a couple of tiny portholes along its fuselage. I don't know anything about its efficiency or cargo-carrying capabilities, but I had to give it high marks for sheer Walter Mitty style. If you wanted to be whisked away from your daily routine and plunged into a world of glamorous danger, this was just the thing to do it in.

However, I felt neither glamorous nor dangerous as we queued to board, merely flushed and sweaty. In a regulation worthy of Joseph Heller or an episode of M*A*S*H, everyone was required to wear the full set of extreme cold weather gear while they waited for the flight. You weren't required to wear it on the plane itself—just here on the ground, in Christchurch's balmy summer warmth, so you could be seen boarding the plane fully dressed for Antarctic conditions. It was one of the many, many nanny regulations in the USAP—obviously dreamed up by a torts lawyer—to ensure that nobody forgot a mitten or something, as though we were all eight years old and going on a field trip to a ski slope.

We had already been waiting like this for a couple of hours because of doubtful weather reports coming out of McMurdo, and by the time they shuttled us over to the airfield I had sweated off about ten pounds and definitely needed the deodorant for manly men. Now as I saw us assembled on the tarmac, dressed in our bulky red parkas, black windproof trousers, and white rubber bunny boots, all I could think of was that we looked like a conga line of 93 department store Santas that Uncle Sam was about to airlift to the wrong pole.

The loadmaster herded us aboard ten at a time, and crammed us in, side by side and knee to knee along two narrow aisles, paratrooper style on seats made of aluminum tubing and bright orange webbing. Shoulders rubbing together, boots interlocked. Bag lunches were passed down, hand to hand. The hatch was closed and then we...waited.

An hour sweltered by this way before the pilot came over the microphone with an announcement that they were having trouble with the No. 4 engine.

"We should have it fixed in about another 45 minutes," he drawled, before concluding with a note of exquisite sadism: "It's come over a little cool and draughty out here on the tarmac so we'll just keep you aboard."

Time slowed to a crawl. We steamed gently like so many dim sum. The guy jammed in beside me, a builder's laborer named Brian, who was on his first trip abroad, regaled me with stories about his glorious redneck life back in Idaho ("where we just love our guns and our freedom"), drinking and driving, driving and drinking, and shooting and roaring through the mountains in four-wheel drives.

At some point he segued into a long and convoluted narrative about how he recently had to chase off some dirt bikers from a secluded patch of land he owned up a ridge. I was feeling headachy from heat and suffocation and wasn't listening terribly closely until a few snippets—"SWAT team," "liars said I musta been guardin' a drug crop," and "handcuffed me and threw me in jail"—began to jell in my fuddled brain.

"Excuse me, did I just hear you just say you were facing multiple felony assault and weapons charges back home?"

"Damn straight! Twelve counts! Assault, aggravated assault, assault with a deadly weapon—you name it. Got a court date in March. Hell, they even threw in use of a handgun in commission of a felony! Now how's that for a bullshit charge? The prosecutor's asking for 60 years!"

"So how come you're here? I had the impression from all the forms I filled out that you couldn't even have a parking ticket to your name."

"Oh, I'm out on $50,000 cash bond. I haven't been convicted of anything yet. They didn't think I could raise that kind of money, but I had cash they didn't know about. My lawyer got the judge to agree to let me come down here for this job, since it was all lined up and everything. Guess they figure there's nowhere I can run to at the South Pole."

"Sixty years, huh?" I thought back to a humorous little book we had as kids called *What Do You Say, Dear?* It was full of bits of conversational etiquette for odd situations, like a moose coming to tea or a biplane crashing through your parlor ceiling; I couldn't recall if it had any advice for what to say when expressing sympathy for a bloke sitting beside you on a cargo military plane who just told you he was looking at 60 years in the slammer on weapons charges. So I had to ad-lib: "Well, I guess you'll be out before you're 100."

"Oh, I'll beat this bullshit all right, but I'll tell you what—if I don't, I'm not going to do time, no way. I got it all figured: I'll post appeal bond—it's only another ten grand, I checked—and head for South America. Adios, you pricks. And if they do catch me, well, confidentially, between you and me, I got me a lot of cyanide they don't know about, and I'll take it too before I let myself go to prison. I'm not kidding. Why I know a guy..."

They started the engines and the noise drowned out his words. I gave Brian an apologetic smile and tore open my packet of yellow foam earplugs. We took off a few minutes later. I squirmed on my seat and consulted my watch—about six hours to go, a long flight by most people's standards, but if you live in Australia you get used to the idea of long, long flights. Six hours was just a hop, or it would be if the plane wasn't so horribly cramped.

I'd brought a book along to read on the flight—*The Treasure of the Sierra Madre*, by B. Traven. I opened it up and began to read: "The bench on which Dobbs was sitting was not so good. One of the slats was broken; the one next to it was bent, so that to have to sit on it was a sort of punishment..."

Hmmmm.

The hours crawled by as slow as a wet week. Like the down-and-out Dobbs in my book, I soon found that there was no way to get comfortable on these bench seats, no way to do much of anything at all. The best I could manage was a sort of unergonomic slouch that offered the brief illusion of being comfortable but soon left my lumbar muscles in such spasms I straightened up again.

The plane was suffocatingly close, warm, and stuffy. Beside me Brian wriggled out of almost all his clothes and sat there in just his jocks. I tried to read my book. I tried to doze. I fidgeted and nibbled the sandwiches in my flight ration. Once, out of curiosity, I removed my earplugs. The sound in the cargo hold was like putting your ear next to the barrel of a giant industrial vacuum cleaner. With the earplugs back in it was like hearing the same thing only underwater.

I was fortunate in that I was sitting diagonally opposite one of the plane's few portholes—a tiny window barely a hand span across—so I could rest my eyes on the sky's cool blueness and imagine the clean zing of fresh air. After a long while, someone sitting beside the window gestured excitedly, pointed outside, and shouted something about icebergs. A few people passed him their point-and-shoot cameras. He fired off a few offhand frames and passed them back.

I checked my watch: another hour to go. Anyone can do an hour. I kept telling myself that. The engines droned. My legs felt heavy and dead. My back and butt and hip muscles ached. After a long while I glanced at my watch again. Five minutes had passed. Oh Jesus. And then the pilot came on over the intercom. I could barely make out his words, although he must have had the volume set as high as it would go. What I thought I was hearing I couldn't believe. A glance at the dismayed faces around me confirmed it. Visibility at McMurdo, now less than an hour away, had dropped to a mile. Three miles is the minimum. The pilot decided to abort. We were turning back, a "boomerang," in the folksy parlance of the USAP. I could have wept.

At some point in the five-hour-long return journey, with night creeping across the porthole, I faded into a nightmarish doze, my dreams incorporating the drone of the cargo plane, the paratrooper seating, and the haggard feel of having been through a war: I had joined the Foreign Legion; this was Beau Geste in bunny boots.

I woke with a skull-splitting migraine. A muffled voice on the intercom was saying something about Christchurch and 30 minutes. It was dark outside the porthole now, final proof that this whole thing hadn't been a ghastly dream: There was no night in Antarctica this time of year; we were really somewhere over New Zealand. The strobes on the underside of the wing throbbed on and off, like pulses of night lightning. The plane bounced in the thick, choppy air. We touched down a little after midnight and taxied back to the restricted portion of the airfield beside the huge USAP hangars. The airport was quiet. We spilled out of the plane on dead legs, taking great gulps of cool, damp night air. A shuttle bus took us back to the CDC, where we changed back into our street clothes.

A couple of nighthawk cabs, alerted by their dispatcher to Antarctica's latest rebuff, cruised into the parking lot, their headlights raking over us like we were spotlit deer. I hailed one and rode back to my hotel.

The night manager gave me my old room back. It seemed like a year since I'd seen it. I gulped down a couple of aspirin, crawled into bed with the vigor of a man twice my age, and looked through the gauze curtains at the twinkling lights of Christchurch. I felt like I had been dragged through a keyhole. And tomorrow we were going to do this whole thing all over again. And for all I knew, I could be resting my throbbing head on this very pillow tomorrow night as well, having put in another day just like this one. There was no reason why not.

Fortunately it didn't happen that way. We made it down to McMurdo the following day. We left at five o'clock in the afternoon, had a cramped, miserable, but otherwise uneventful flight, and touched down on the ice runway a little after 11:00 on a bright Antarctic "night."

CHAPTER FIVE

McMurdo Welcome

EVEN IN AN AGE OF LONG-HAUL JET TRAVEL, WHERE WE'VE ROUTINELY COME to accept the geographical non sequitur of boarding a flight in Sydney and then getting off again many hours later in the chill of London, or the steamy heat, noise, and bustle of Bangkok, to arrive in Antarctica on the same day you left a balmy garden city in New Zealand is a staggering shock. Nothing quite prepares you for it, even if you've been to Antarctica before and think you know what to expect.

The hatch opens and Antarctica's frosty breath swirls into the hold, cutting the musty staleness and the buttery smell of stale, leftover cut lunches. A moment later you are clambering down the steps on wobbly legs and onto the hard sea ice, dazed and blinking in the intense white light. It's this blinding brilliance that you notice first, ahead of the cold. Even while you're still shuffling along the aisle toward the door, you are surprised at the glow coming through the hatch and illuminating the interior of the plane.

The bitter cold follows a second or so behind. Once you step outside the aircraft, the wind whipping across the frozen wastes of McMurdo Sound stings you like a razor. Numbed fingers fumble at the zips on the parka, left undone for hours in the drowsy warmth of the plane, and you try to remember which pocket has the glacier glasses.

And then comes the sense of space. It is almost overwhelming. A strange, stark, blindingly white world of ice and snow stretches to every horizon. The sky is huge. In an instant you go from being wedged in the hold of a cargo plane to feeling as exposed as a pin on a map. The bewildering rush of sights and sensations, after so many hours of sensory deprivation, is enough to make you forget in an instant the cramped misery of the flight.

We tottered away from the plane on cramped legs, feeling a bit like transported prisoners, particularly with the ground crews in camouflage fatigues yelling at us over the roar of the engines to move along swiftly now, no time for pictures, let's go, let's go....

When I shut them out, though, and just looked into the distance, it was like stepping into one of those glorious old Frank Hurley or Herbert Ponting photographs I'd been marveling at so much over the past few weeks. The classic landmarks were all there: the empty vastness of the sea ice, the histrionic sweep of the Royal Society Range, and, looming above the base, the magnificent symmetry of Mount Erebus, the world's southernmost active volcano, puffing smoke majestically into the clear evening sky and projecting its own raffish menace. Nothing had changed—not out there, anyway.

Behind us the dark gray jet whined and more ground crew closed in, with refueling trucks and baggage carts, like tickbirds on a rhino. We were loaded onto an oversize people mover called Ivan the Terra Bus, which had tires so huge we had to climb a short flight of steps to scramble aboard. I slumped in my seat and looked out across three miles of ice to the low-slung sprawl of MacTown.

As we drove toward it, down a dead-straight road on the ice known as Antarctic-1, the smoky summit of Mount Erebus sank coyly behind one of its lofty shoulders. Ivan the Terra Bus lumbered up a steep bluff, off the sea ice and onto solid ground, and then along a rough-and-tumble main street of prefab buildings, pipelines, and a cat's cradle of telephone cables. A pumpkin-orange shipping container marked "Halloween Decorations" sat discarded, frosted with a few inches of old snow, beside a pile of wood and building materials.

The driver dropped us off in front of the Chalet, a Swiss-style ski lodge of a building that served as the local headquarters of the National Science Foundation. We were ushered inside for our arrival briefing and to receive our dormitory assignments. Once again I felt uneasily like an inductee arriving at boot camp.

It was warm and snug and crowded in the Chalet. We sat on plastic chairs arranged in front of a lectern. The walls around us were plastered with pennants, photographs, and commemorative plaques. Over the next 20 minutes a cavalcade of various base leaders and NSF authorities introduced themselves to anyone who didn't know them already, a rough sketch of the ground rules was laid out, and envelopes containing keys and photocopied maps of the base were handed out.

The meeting dissolved in a welter of inside jokes and catching up. There was nobody for me to catch up with just then; Maria, the photographer I was working with on this assignment, had come down a week earlier and was out at a field camp on the West Antarctic ice sheet and wouldn't be back for a couple of days. We weren't going to be traveling together all that much anyway.

I was assigned my room and drifted outside into the midnight brightness, my breath coming in gouts of steam. The view from the wooden decking in front of the Chalet was stunning: a panorama of the Royal Society Range soaring more than two miles into a taut blue sky. The raking sunlight caught the details in the mountains and gave them a chiseled appearance, softening the hard whiteness of the snow to a mellow creamy color. Somehow those mountains looked as far away as ever.

As I walked up the street toward my dormitory, a horn tooted behind me. Startled, I scooted out of the way as a big new parade float of a pickup truck tooled past me. The driver waved. I waved back. There was something surreal about it all, so unlike the Antarctica I remembered.

My room was in Building 155, a sprawling biscuit-colored complex that also contained the dining hall, shop, hairdressers, and the base TV station. The dorm rooms were all upstairs. They were clean but shabby, and reminded me of a down-at-heel backpacker joint: musty smelling, with cracks in the walls, torn carpets, scuffed linoleum, and punched-out holes in the ceiling tiles that revealed wiring and water pipes. But at least there were no cockroaches; there are no insects at all here at MacTown, latitude 78 degrees south.

I thought of the opening lines in *The Worst Journey in the World*, where Apsley Cherry-Garrard remarks that Antarctic exploration is the cleanest way he knows of having a bad time, before going on to compare life in Antarctica rather unfavorably with life in the muddy trenches on the western front in France during World War I. Mind you, he hadn't had a very good time, as the title of his book might suggest. He had been a member of Scott's last expedition, and spent the rest of his life gnawed by the possibility that he might have been able to do something to have helped save his comrades out there on the ice shelf, and later had been among the party that found their frozen bodies.

I was hoping for a better time myself.

I located my room. It was late, so I turned the key softly and gently pushed open the door in case anyone was sleeping in there. No one was. The room was empty and surprisingly big: two double bunks, a threadbare sofa, a coffee table, a couple of wardrobes, and a corner unit where exposed cables indicated a TV had sat in the past. A heavy blanket had been taped over the window to shut out the round-the-clock sunlight. A corner had slipped, giving me some light to see by. I flicked on the switch, closed the door, and went over to the window to adjust the blanket.

Two of the bunks had already been made and claimed, with backpacks and clothes lying on them. I slung my pack against the bottom bunk next to the window and began to make my bed. I didn't bother unfolding the blanket. It was hot enough to grow orchids in there. I looked around for a thermostat, but there wasn't one. Apparently this was the temperature everyone around here liked. I wondered briefly why anybody would keep such a huge building so warm in a place where heating oil costs more than 11 bucks a gallon. Then I remembered the gaudy red pick-up truck that had purred past me on the main street and the answer came to me: The Americans do it because they can.

I was bone weary from the flight and the long day, but too revved up to sleep. I went downstairs to the dining hall, which was still known as the galley from McMurdo's Navy days. It had recently been refurbished and was as bright and cheerful and modern as the rooms upstairs were dingy and downbeat. They were serving "mid-rats," more slang, a sort of midnight supper for shift workers and night owls. I helped myself to a plate of lasagne and a mug of hot cocoa and read "The Scroll," a silent-screen televised bulletin board of daily announcements, movie schedules, church service times, Alcoholics Anonymous and Weight Watchers meetings, and general station news.

I saw that auditions were to be held soon for a McMurdo production of *Much Ado About Nothing*, which had been specially adapted for Antarctica. Instead of a soldier returning to an Italian villa, the bulletin proclaimed, the local version would feature an Air National Guardsman returning to McMurdo. "Hi-jinks ensue. Hilarity follows. Love is triumphant and a good time is had by all." I finished my lasagne and went up to bed a little after two.

The galley was in full swing when I came down to breakfast, full of voices and clatter, and the inviting smells of coffee, bacon, and eggs. A plane was due to depart for the South Pole that morning. I saw Brian—"Sixty Years Brian," as I had come to think of him by now, to distinguish him from the other Brians I had met—heading off to "bag drag," which was local slang for a flight check-in. He waved cheerily, said he'd see me down there in a couple of weeks and we'd crack open a bottle of Scotch. The offhand way he said it—"See ya at Pole!"—as he swanned out the door made me laugh; the folksy way it brought home just where we were.

I filled a plate with eggs, pancakes, bacon, and hash browns, poured a mug of coffee, and took a seat by the window.

It was getting on seven o'clock, and MacTown was hitting its stride. The workday starts at 7:30. A steady stream of people, in twos and threes, drifted up the street, either coming in for breakfast or heading off, thermal mugs of coffee in hand, for another day at the office, workshop, or lab. It was uncannily like a small-town Main Street somewhere cold.

I finished up my breakfast and went out to explore.

The closed-circuit TV monitor beside the door gave the local weather conditions and told me the temperature outside was around 4°F, with a windchill reading of –22°F. I read it with a detached curiosity while I shrugged into my parka and felt around for my gloves and glacier glasses in its dozen or so pockets. Twenty-two below: no big deal.

But then I pushed open the heavy industrial freezer-style doors and stepped into it, and the razor wind took my breath away. It had been a long time since I had felt anything like this. It was considerably colder even than when we arrived last night, and it had never been anything like this cold at Mawson, the last time I'd seen snow. My cheekbones went numb and rubbery in seconds, and my earlobes burned. I flopped the parka's cavernous hood over my head, thrust my hands deep into its warmest pockets, and trudged down the street, feeling sheepish that I was already negotiating with myself to make this particular morning stroll a very short one. This was Antarctica; what was I expecting?

I was glad I had tucked my map of the base in my pocket. It would be easy to get lost here. MacTown is the nearest thing Antarctica has to a city, with a summer population of about 1,200, a grid of streets, speed limit signs, and a shuttle bus that circulates around the town, out to the airfield, and over to New Zealand's Scott Base, about a mile and a half away. There are a couple of bars, an old-fashioned bowling alley, radio and TV stations, a post office, shops, Wells Fargo ATMs, a church with penguin-motif stained-glass windows. The base commander is a deputized U.S. marshal. Pickup trucks cruise the streets, and lanky guys in jeans and hiking boots and beards growl, "Hey, Dude" to each other in broad midwestern accents.

As I walked those frozen streets that first morning I felt in turn as though I were in an Alaskan mining town, a far-flung Cold War radar base, and the campus of a junior technical college somewhere in the Rocky Mountains. It's not a pretty place; Antarctic bases never are. The architecture is mostly industrial prefab, with a lot of heavy equipment parked around and piles of construction materials stacked in lots, and an exposed network of pipes carrying fuel and water and sewage.

MacTown brings out passions. Some love its frontier camaraderie; others decry its unsightly urban sprawl. America's presence here on Ross Island (and anywhere else it has trodden in Antarctica) has always been full-on, from the moment it opened McMurdo back in 1956. Right from the get-go it was the biggest base on the continent. For a while, back in the 1960s, MacTown even had its own nuclear power plant, a 1.8-megawatt reactor known as Nukey-Poo, but it never worked well and had to be removed in 1972, along with thousands of tons of contaminated rock and soil.

By all accounts, the Americans have done a lot to clean up MacTown since those bad old days, shipping huge amounts of rubbish and scrap back to the States and instituting a comprehensive recycling program. One of the first things I was obliged to do that morning was sign up for the mandatory lecture on how the base recycling program works, where and how to dispose of various types of rubbish, and who to call in the event of any chemical or fuel spills.

I quickly came to understand that McMurdo exists alongside Antarctica rather than in it, as though one and a half square miles have been excised from the continent; technical college, radar base, small-town America—whatever analogy comes to mind, the one place this didn't feel like was Antarctica. Not my conception of it anyway. After all, in Antarctica, you don't withdraw 20 bucks from a Wells Fargo ATM and then swing by the convenience store to pick up a packet of Oreos, a bag of Fritos, and a six-pack of Bud and kick back to watch a Cornhuskers football game on TV. But you can in MacTown. And a lot of people do.

From its frozen streets and multiglazed windows, Antarctica is something that seems to exist "out there," more of a painted-on theater backdrop or window dressing than a real location. You can stand on a street corner, look out, and see the Royal Society Range in all its grandeur, but except for the razor wind that flickers between the buildings, those snowy peaks in the distance and the ice all around them seem no more real or graspable than a postcard—or a daydream.

McMurdo isn't just the largest and most citified base on the continent, it is also the site of some of Antarctica's earliest human habitation—Capt. Robert Falcon Scott chose this same rocky promontory on Ross Island to build his base for the Discovery Expedition in 1902. The old wooden hut is still there, sitting out on Hut Point only a few hundred yards from downtown.

I took a stroll out there after breakfast, hoping I might find something—a sense of Antarctica, perhaps—that seemed to be missing here in town. It was a longer walk than it had appeared at first, and the winds out on the point were bitingly cold and the blowing snow stung. The hut was bigger than I had expected, about 40 feet on each side, with a pyramidal roof and a verandah on all four sides. The architecture was familiar: It looked just like the classic old turn-of-the-century outback bungalow it was. Scott had picked it up as a prefab in Melbourne when he passed through in 1901.

I ran my mittened hand along its sides. A century of blizzards had buffed the wood to a satiny sheen. I had the place all to myself, and when the wind dropped the silence was wonderful. It was midmorning on a weekday, and McMurdo had its collective nose to the grindstone, everyone squirreled away in offices, labs, and workshops. I sat on the verandah, out of the wind, dangling my legs, and looked south, away from the humming activity and urban sprawl behind me and idled away an hour or so imagining what life must have been like for that first expedition here, and why their Antarctica seemed more "authentic."

Certainly they were far more exposed to the harsh realities of the local climate than I would ever be in my overheated bedroom in back Building 155. The old explorers did it tough in that sense. No five vegetarian selections in the mess hall either. But in its day this hut and its environs would have seemed just as much excised from the rest of Antarctica as McMurdo does to me now: This was once a bastion of empire and Royal Navy discipline, with every comfort and convenience the Edwardian age and Edwardian logistics and the expedition's own finances would allow. After all, Scott & Co. didn't come here to be hermits and wear hair shirts, but to advance the glories of the British Empire, and their own careers on what was, in effect, a glorious Boy's *Own* camping trip. Theirs was an age that adored gadgetry, same as we do today. They brought motorcars, hot-air balloons, and gramophones and entertained themselves with magic lantern shows during the long polar night; if they didn't have e-mail, videos, and satellite TV it was only because nobody did.

Amundsen and his men built a sauna at their base, Framheim, over on the Bay of Whales, while they waited to start their race to the South Pole in 1911. The same year Scott had a telephone line installed between this very hut and the new one he had built on Cape Evans, 12 miles away; it was the first telephone link on the continent, and if it didn't work as long or as well as it might, it wasn't for lack of trying. Scott and his men played football on the ice, held church services, performed plays, and published books and newspapers. Later on, Scott was to wax lyrical about his purist ideal of trudging on foot to the South Pole, conquering it cleanly, the doughty British way, man-hauling their gear, as opposed to the Norwegians' morally suspect use of dogs, but when he made these claims, the beleaguered Englishman was only making a virtue of necessity. The motor vehicles with which he'd hoped to drive most of the way across the Ross Ice Shelf failed him, the horses he had brought were shown to be utterly unsuitable for the task as well, and he lacked the Norwegians' skills with dogs and skis, both of which he'd also taken with him and tried, unsuccessfully, to use. And so man-hauling it was, an act of last resort.

But Scott was also a romantic and an optimist, with a wonderful turn of phrase, and handed a lemon he made marvelous lemonade, writing eloquently and convincingly of the nobility of each man pulling his own sled, step by step, through the blizzards and deep snows, across the high polar plateau. He was writing for an audience that was only too willing to be convinced. The final stirring passages in his diary, and his Byronic death (and those of his comrades) only a few miles short of the lifesaving food and fuel at One Ton depot, carried the day. Amundsen and his cool, clinical efficiency might have won the race, and won it rather handily, but Scott's gloriously noble struggle with the elements is what captured the popular imagination.

It still does, to some extent. As I sat there on the verandah listening to the silence, I thought back to those dark cramped zinc-alum huts at Mawson that were being swept out and closed down the summer I was there, and the heavy sighs from veteran winterers that the glorious old intrepid Antarctica was vanishing for good; things could never be the same in the flashy new dormitory hall, the Red Shed. It seemed a reasonable thing to argue, then, but now I began to wonder if perhaps that is giving a little too much emphasis to our simple creature comforts, and a bit too much smug credit to our capacity to change our surroundings. Antarctica—that huge place beyond the boundaries of MacTown and Hut Point—hasn't changed a bit, it is as aloof and implacable as ever. This hut, those frozen landscapes—identical to the rich old glass-plate photographs taken by the early explorers. Danger? You can still die of cold and exposure right there on the main street of MacTown if you are caught out in a whiteout blizzard. Wander off the flagged jogging and skiing trails around the base and you might well tumble into a crevasse and never come out again. The sea ice surrounding the point is as treacherous as ever—anyone planning to travel over it is required to take a special survival course.

No, for all the Fritos, Bud, and college football games available on the base—or for that matter, lest I appear hypocritical, my own happy checking of the cricket scores on the Internet—we do not really occupy any more of Antarctica than our boot soles. And I was glad of that, even as I grew aware that my own boots, my stake on the continent, had grown chilly and my feet numb. The wind had really strengthened in the past few minutes, and great plumes of powder snow blew up from the surface and stung my face. I picked myself up from the veranda and began the trudge back to base, and its welcoming hot showers and plates of food and the gregariousness of the galley, feeling grateful for the untouched wilderness spreading around me and for the civility of the base, and taking a bit of refuge in a line in Walt Whitman's *Leaves of Grass*: "Do I contradict myself? Very well, I contradict myself."

CHAPTER SIX

Downtown MacTown

I REJOINED THE 21ST CENTURY IN TIME FOR LUNCH. ONCE AGAIN THE cafeteria was bustling, full of voices, food smells, and the clatter of cutlery. It was big, bright, and spacious, like the dining hall of a well-endowed college, with salad bars, fresh-baked bread, and a vast assortment of condiments, juice machines, and soft-serve ice-cream makers. Chefs in white jackets and classic checked trousers grilled burgers and carved roasts. Kitchen hands scurried to replenish salad bowls and Jell-O molds.

I took a tray, helped myself to a plate of Mexican food, and took myself off to one of the tables by the windows. I sipped my juice drink and watched the people drifting up the snowy main street, coming in to lunch. All wore blue jeans and parkas and carried well-worn day packs slung over their shoulders. At first glance, MacTown really does appear to be the classless society the people who run the place claim that it is, an Antarctican utopia, with everybody living in the same quarters regardless of their pay and social standing, and wearing the same standard-issue Big Red parka so that it is impossible to tell who is the world-famous scientist and who is the janitor. But people are people. And in here, in the galley, where the parkas were off, and MacTown's thousand-odd residents mingle, they became floating radicals that soon coalesced into their own natural cliques.

It was kind of entertaining to watch. The most intriguing group generally occupied the large round table in the center of the dining room: the circle of middle-aged bureaucrats from the National Science Foundation who run the place. They gathered around every lunchtime and dinner, self-assured, thick-waisted men in jeans and baseball caps and Chamber of Commerce voices, shifting their trays obligingly to make room as their hailed fellows well met sidled up. Their easy jocularity with each other called to mind a group of Rotarians on a hunting trip, or executives on some sort of group bonding exercise, glad to be away from the office and all that buttoned-down, neck-tied formality and yet at the same time slightly self-conscious about being seen in blue jeans and wool shirts.

They seemed friendly enough and welcoming, but very few people outside their circle ever joined them. There was nothing to say you couldn't, their table wasn't reserved or anything like that, but hardly anybody ever did. They projected their own lofty exclusion zone. It was so much at odds with the style of leadership I'd seen at the Australian bases. There, although the officer in charge's word was law and they always maintained something of the reserve of a commander at sea, there was also a strong sense of egalitarianism—the station leader, for example, at Mawson or Davis or wherever always took his or her turn at "slushy" duty, mopping the floors and cleaning the toilets, and generally, out of a sense of noblesse oblige, they'd roster themselves on for the least-pleasant chores, the Christmas Day rounds and such. That kind of thing would be unthinkable here. Toilets? Mops? They had people for that.

On that score it intrigued me how Shackleton could be so much in vogue these days—TV miniseries, biographies, even a human resources management guide to tell today's executives how they could benefit from adopting Shackleton's accessible, consensual leadership style, but when it comes to the running of an actual Antarctic base—an increasingly corporate enterprise these days—the stiff and formal and hierarchical Captain Scott approach should be so closely followed, with its classes of "officers" and "other ranks."

For beneath the cheer, those men of the round table (and they were mostly men) were very much martinets in the Captain Scott mold, or at least the Captain Scott of stereotype. McMurdo was a company town and they are the bosses. They rule with a whim of iron and you crossed them at your peril. You could easily find yourself on the next flight home, and, like the rulings of 19th-century Judge Roy Bean—once famed as the law west of the Pecos—there would be no appeal. Naturally they were much talked about, particularly at the worm's eye level of society in which I circulated, and in the sort of way that younger kids at a strict boarding school might whisper about a stern and distant headmaster, a mingling of fear and awe and something very like affection.

Like schoolkids, a lot of MacTownites fantasized about various acts of defiance. The ultimate: skiing down the flanks of Mount Erebus. It has evidently been done at least once. A guy climbed the mountain—without any authorization whatever (it would never have been given in any case)—lugging a pair of skis on his shoulder and then proceeded to make a cannonball run down its steep, icy slopes. It was dangerous—mind-blowingly stupid, really, given the potential for ending your life in a crevasse—but it had stand-up, blow-away glory written all over it. People often spoke of it.

According to legend, the man who was known as the Mayor of McMurdo, a much feared office tyrant from the NSF and the kingpin at the round table, was waiting at the bottom of the run. There was no scene; just a frosty glare as he waved the hotshot skier on—toward the airfield; his bags had already been packed and loaded onto the plane; he was going home. (The Mayor's lofty and disdainful majesty here in the face of such defiance earned him full points for style in all the versions of the story I ever heard.)

"I gotta say, if I ever decide that I don't ever want to come back here any more, that's the way I'd like to go out," one of the old hands told me wistfully. "Ski Erebus, man; what a way to go."

"This is a strange society,'" Josh Landis, the editor of the *Antarctic Sun*, told me, perhaps a little unnecessarily, as we were sitting in his office after lunch. "Money or the usual status symbols in the real world don't mean a thing down here. The biggest social distinction is mobility—who can get off the base and who has to stay. Mobility gives you status. A general assistant may be one of the lowest-paid jobs here, but since they often get out to the field to lend scientists a hand, they are seriously envied."

But they are not envied half so much as the scientists themselves. Scientists in Antarctica lead fairy-tale lives. Comfortably upper-middle-class at home, here they are aristocrats, with millions of square miles of the world's last pristine wilderness, an entire continent, formally set aside for their exclusive use, with fleets of helicopters, ships and planes, and millions of dollars of resources at their disposal. Over the years some of these academics have carved out private fiefdoms larger than some European countries, returning each summer to the same mountain range, glacier, or island that has more or less become theirs by right of continuous intellectual occupation. By and large they wear their aristocracy lightly, in the gracious manner of old money, mixing easily with those around them unlike the merchant-class bureaucrats who run the bases. Their White South is one of continuous adventure, discovery, and conquest.

One of my roommates was a red-haired geology professor from New Mexico named Rick, who ran a series of seismic monitors on Mount Erebus. (Our other roommate was Rick's best friend from college days, a fellow named Rich, who was an engineer with Palm and who had taken a few weeks' unpaid leave from work to help Rick set up a new seismic station.) I liked them both immediately and hung around with them as they prepared their gear and tuned up their instruments for a season working at the summit of the volcano.

"I love it down here," Rick told me one day, as we drove across town in one of those shiny red Fords to pick up a large, specially insulated box the base carpenters had crafted to house his new broadband seismometer. "Back home you're lucky if you can get the departmental Chevy Suburban for a weekend. Here you can whistle up a Hercules and have them haul you, your team, and nine tonnes of cargo to the South Pole, if that is what your project requires. If you need a special piece of equipment built—like this box—no problem, it's done."

In a few days, after they finished sorting out their gear, Rick and Rich and the rest of the Mount Erebus team would be airlifted to a well-stocked field camp near the summit, to spend the summer in almost monastic seclusion, studying the inner workings of the volcano and receiving helicopter support as required.

It is very expensive. But then science in Antarctica is ultimately done in the name of politics, not altruism; it provides a respectable cover for governments to justify their presence on the continent. And under the terms of the Antarctic Treaty, only those nations actively undertaking scientific research have a say in determining Antarctica's future.

Twenty-seven countries operate "scientific" bases in Antarctica, many of them just cynically going through the motions in order to claim a spot at the ruling table. To its credit, the United States—as well as Australia, Britain, New Zealand, and a couple of others—actually takes its treaty obligations seriously, investing hefty sums of money and logistics in cutting-edge polar research. All its projects are peer-reviewed, and published in reputable scientific journals, or they just don't happen. It makes for a happy situation all round: Washington has impeccable credentials for its massive presence, while us lay folk have our sense of wonder piqued by far-flung discoveries and revelations that would never be made otherwise. And, of course, the scientists have golden opportunities to venture to far off corners of the world, and lead the kinds of adventurous lives that their colleagues back home can only dream about as they bicker over who gets the Chevy Suburban on which weekend.

A quick glance at the catalog of projects going on that summer showed the Americans had scientists traversing the West Antarctic ice sheet, scaling the summit of Mount Erebus, fossicking for meteorites on the blue ice fields in the Allen Hills, cracking rocks in the Transantarctic Mountains to study continental drift, making aerial radar surveys over Vostok to chart the lake hidden two miles beneath the ice, monitoring the penguin and seal populations along the coast of the Ross Sea, and probing the outer reaches of the universe with radio telescopes at the South Pole.

Alas, no society is made up entirely of aristocrats. Scientists account for no more than a quarter of McMurdo's summer population and hardly any of its winterers. The vast majority of MacTown's residents are the cooks, cleaners, motor pool mechanics, plumbers, electricians, carpenters, dishwashers, power plant operators, clerical staff, typists, hairdressers, storeworkers, accountants—everybody you need to run a small town. Their White South remains a quirky existence of dormitories, canteen food, regulations, acronyms, and insider jokes.

Most seldom, if ever, leave the immediate confines of the base, tethered there by ten-hour-a-day job commitments, a myriad of safety regulations, and controlling bureaucracy. If they are lucky, loyal, and attract the benevolent notice of their masters, they may at some point in the summer be rewarded with a quick trip to join the penguin researchers at Cape Crozier or visit scientists at the field camp in the Dry Valleys—a 45-minute helicopter flight away, a "boondoggle," in local-speak. But things don't always work out that way. It is not unknown for people to spend a summer at McMurdo, leave, and go home again having still never seen a penguin in the wild.

But the opportunity just to be here, to plant your boot soles on Antarctic rock, see the pristine whiteness and cloudlike mountains spreading out from your dormitory window, and claim McMurdo Station, Antarctica, as your address, however briefly, is a powerful draw card, as I well understood myself.

Josh Landis—a journalist, like me—gave up his rent-controlled apartment in New York City's trendy West Greenwich Village to take a three-month posting at the *Antarctic Sun*, MacTown's local paper. A girl from Juneau, Alaska, who'd been on the same flight as me had come more than 12,000 miles just to be a janitor here. "I would have taken any job at all," she told me. "It may only be cleaning toilets, but those toilets are in Antarctica. That was enough for me."

She'd faced stiff competition for her job, too; MacTown's other janitor was a lawyer from Chicago. The job of dishwasher at the South Pole attracted dozens of applications—the successful applicant was a musician. Not everyone comes south looking for rollicking adventure either. McMurdo's monastic isolation and simple lifestyle make it an attractive retreat. One of the warehouse workers, a lawyer named Jeff, came here as a restorative after spending the previous four years handling death penalty cases for the capital crimes unit of the Albuquerque public defender's office.

"That was the most soul-draining work I could imagine," he told me. "I had a number of very difficult cases that came to a conclusion of sorts in the past year and I knew I needed to step away for a while. So I quit and applied for a job down here. This is a fine place to slow down and sift through some of the experiences I have had over the years. The scenery and the weather is a constant reminder of the wonder of life."

There is a popular saying around MacTown that people come here the first time for the experience, the second time for the money, and the third time because they just can't make it anyplace else.

"So where's your locker?" a technician named Phil asked me one night as we were sitting up late over a bottle of single malt. His question was breezy MacTown-veteran slang for "Where do you call home?" Many of the old hands like to describe themselves as "bipolar," spending their lives flitting between U.S. Arctic bases in Greenland during the northern summer and Antarctica during the austral one. They keep their worldly goods and chattels in a storage locker somewhere stateside at a place where they once had roots.

"Oh, it's not for everybody," Phil explained. "You either like the institutional life—sleeping in a dormitory, eating canteen food, wearing issued clothes—or you don't. It's as simple as that. I happen to love the life, myself."

As the man said, it's not for everybody. One day when I was coming in to lunch, I noticed a large poster beside the entrance to the dining hall that mimicked the cinema advertisements for Independence Day, except this one had a huge flying saucer hovering, menacingly, over McMurdo Station instead of the White House. The words above it trumpeted the news that aliens were coming. It gave a date and time.

From its lighthearted tone I assumed some sort of alien-themed party was coming up. I overheard a lot of the sniggering table talk at lunch about the imminent arrival of UFOs and aliens, and that afternoon even the DJ on the radio station also put in his oar, chuckling over the airwaves at jokes about aliens taking over our minds. By the next day I was starting to feel really out of the loop and over breakfast asked a girl from the motor pool about it.

"Haven't you heard?"

It turned out that one of the staffers was claiming that his brain had been taken over by aliens, and at the appointed hour a spaceship was going to arrive here in McMurdo to take him away. Opinions were divided about what was really going on, with about half convinced he was "doing a Corporal Klinger," from the old TV series M*A*S*H, feigning craziness in order to be sent home, having decided that coming to MacTown was a big mistake and wanting to get out of his contract. Others maintained that, no, he really did believe that aliens had captured his brain and would be coming along soon to whisk him away.

I was plumping for the former, hoping that this was all just a bit of fun, because when zero hour finally arrived, I caught a glimpse of him, seemingly bewildered, in front of the hospital building, surrounded by medics and gawking bystanders, some of whom were wearing alien masks. It looked disturbingly medieval and made me think of bear-baiting.

MacTown was nothing if not engrossing. Like Peyton Place it seemed to expand until it became a world all on its own, large enough, in this case, almost to subsume the huge continent around us. Sometimes it seemed seedy and hard-boiled. Like when you walked into the men's room and saw a large and empty cardboard carton with a sign taped to the bottom: "Sorry, fellows. The condom box gets refilled on Tuesdays. If it's an emergency ask at medical." And then you would count the days on your fingers and marvel that it was only Friday and already the box is empty, and there was still a long weekend stretching ahead.

It was a place where people wore T-shirts that read: "Party till the Sun Goes Down" (a heady concept in a place where the sun doesn't set for months on end), where empty Scotch bottles in the recycling bins often had a series of time-and-tide lines marked on their sides, revealing how quickly the level of the contents had dropped. It was a place where women were jokingly rated an "Antarctic-10": beautiful enough here in MacTown to stampede the bar, but only a plane ride away from being ordinary.

At other times it felt like a folksy town out of Sinclair Lewis. Stop on a corner, look lost, and someone is certain to offer you directions and more than likely will go out of his way to lead you where you want to go. Receptionists were invariably helpful. And in the dining hall the head chef, a large, easygoing man in his checked trousers, could always be found making the rounds of the tables, like a proud restaurateur, seeing to it that everyone was well fed and satisfied.

I had breakfast pretty regularly with a guy named Greg, a soft-spoken African American who worked nightshift in the power plant and was one of the nicest people I've ever met. He was in his 50s, with a couple of kids in college back in Colorado, and had worked on various overseas contracts for much of his life. He had taken this one last offshore job in order to build up a nest egg for his retirement. (By a quirky bit of legalese, Internal Revenue Service grants Antarctic workers tax-free status, provided they claim on their return to have been in New Zealand's Ross Dependencies rather than simply putting "Antarctica" as their residence.)

Before he left for his year at MacTown, Greg and his wife had bought twin copies of a large collection of novels, which they read together, although 10,000 miles apart, and then e-mailed each other daily to discuss the books they were reading, a part of their lives they had in common, as well as their daily routines, which were so different.

As I settled into MacTown's rhythms, I began to notice the little ways its residents sought to distinguish themselves, to assert their individuality in the face of omnipresent authority. Like kids often do with their school uniforms, they devised different ways to wear their parkas, or sewed patches onto them, or stuck ornamental pins in their caps. Some attached elaborately woven tassels to the zippers of their parkas. I acquired one of these myself, a two-toned purple and violet knot fashioned by "Commander," one MacTown's veteran carpenters, and attached it to the zipper of my heavy New Zealand sweater.

"Each of us has our own particular style of making these," he explained, when he gave it to me. "Anybody who knows this place can look at that and tell you who made it, just by the colors and weave and knots." (And sure enough, years later at an Antarctic base on the other side of the continent, I met an American who glanced at it and said: "Say, did Commander make that one?")

Sometimes when I stood on the edge of town and looked out at the austerity of our surroundings, MacTown felt like a fortress town under siege, and in a sense it was. It was surrounded by crevasses and sea ice that could turn treacherous.

MacTown has its own hydroponic greenhouse for growing vegetables, as well as a post-apocalyptic two-year supply of food waiting in its warehouse, just in case the base should have its supply lines cut off for any reason.

We conducted our day-to-day business according to a series of Extreme Condition weather ratings. Condition III was the norm, and under this rating, you could go where you liked around the base. If winds picked up to 48 knots, or visibility dropped to less than 1,300 feet, then Condition II rules were imposed: Only absolutely necessary, work-related outdoor activity was permitted and then, of course, only on the base grounds. When the weather deteriorated still further—to the point where winds were over 55 knots, visibility was less than 100 feet, or the windchill rating was colder than –100°F, then a Condition I was declared and everyone was confined to quarters.

Human nature being what it is, though, it wasn't enough just to be in opposition with the elements; sadly, even down here, in the otherworldly isolation of Earth's last wild place, there seemed to have to be an "other." It is as though we couldn't be an "us" without a "them," not even here.

I sat at lunch one day with a table full of New York Air National Guardsmen, all southern drawls and camouflage fatigues and trouser legs tucked into spit-shined combat boots. The 109th occupied a privileged position on base, somewhat like that of the varsity football team. They were treated to special rooms in the dorms, each with its own TV and refrigerator, and always clubbed together, projecting a vigorous crew-cut esprit de corps, instantly familiar to anyone who ever walked into a jocks' frat house at an American college. A lot of them even looked the part, with enormous biceps and prodigiously deep pectoral muscles from long off-duty hours spent pumping iron in the base weight room.

Their outlook on life tended to be just as muscular. I was treated to a novel perspective on Antarctic politics: the view from the bench press. Swelled by the obvious might and reach of the U.S. Antarctic Program, they boasted loudly through mouths full of cheeseburger about how the boys of 109th Airlift Wing all by themselves could "kick the shit out of the entire New Zealand Air Force," and bragged that Americans owned Antarctica, lock, stock, and barrel ("it's our continent"), and how nobody could set foot on the place "unless we let 'em."

I testily mentioned that I had already come to Antarctica with the Australian Antarctic Division and couldn't recall anybody seeking U.S. permission to do so.

"Don't matter. If we didn't want you Aussies to be down here, you wouldn't be here. No offense, but that's just the way it is."

He didn't mean any offense either and no doubt would have been stunned at my over-sensitivity, had I expressed my umbrage. It was simple. The United States, as the grandest nation on Earth, held all the cards down here—surely that much was obvious—and with an admirable generosity was happy to share the place with others. Why quibble?

I realized these particular swaggering goat-ropers were hardly official mouthpieces of U.S. policy, and for that matter they were not even typical of other Air National Guardsmen I subsequently met, nice blokes some of them, but the fact that we were even having this conversation was saddening. Why did they need to talk about kicking the shit out of the Royal New Zealand Air Force? And this, coupled with the corporate hauteur emanating from the Chalet, and the amused condescension directed at the Kiwis who were ostensibly the United States' partners out here (we had actually been advised back at that first briefing at Christchurch to avoid flying with Kiwi pilots and to stick to U.S.-trained fliers wherever possible), created an ugly parochial impression that was hard to dispel.

I'd had enough of MacTown—far too much, in fact—and wanted badly to get out into Antarctica, the real Antarctica of the untroubled white spaces and piercing blue skies and the haunting desolation that had so captured my imagination the first time around.

But first I had to graduate from Happy Camper School, the polar survival course that everyone is obliged to take before traveling into the frozen outback. I had been waiting for the next class to begin.

I went around to a small, cramped backstreet office, just off Beeker Street and up a flight of wooden steps, and signed up. A pleasant woman named Dawn took down my details and told me to report to the Byrd Field Center the next morning at nine with all the warm clothing I could find. When I came outside again I noticed a couple of those shiny red pickup trucks parked in front of the building, tethered to their parking bays by heating cables that kept their engines warm. They made me think of horses reined up in front of a Yukon saloon.

CHAPTER SEVEN

Happy Camper School

THE BYRD FIELD CENTER SITS ALONE ON A HILLSIDE, NEAR THE EDGE OF TOWN, just off the road that snakes over the ridge toward New Zealand's Scott Base. I trudged up there a few minutes before nine o'clock with my roommate Rich. He was in his late 30s, a brilliant engineer with a degree in music as well, and had a dry sense of humor and razor-sharp irony. It was his first time in Antarctica, although he was no stranger to snow and ice and wintry outdoor survival, having already climbed Denali in Alaska. But nobody, no matter how experienced, who hadn't previously taken Happy Camper School, was permitted to travel into the field.

We slung our packs by the door, kicked the snow off our boots, and went inside. Warmth and a redolence of freshly brewed coffee filled the room. I found an insulated plastic mug and poured myself a wake-up shot. There were going to be 14 of us in class: scientists and carpenters who would be building or refurbishing remote field camps, and a couple of hard-working McMurdo staffers who were being rewarded with the training that would permit them to get off base.

Our instructor was a professional mountaineer named Thai, a walking geography lesson who was half Vietnamese, half Italian, born in Hawaii but living in Alaska when he wasn't guiding his clients up peaks in the Andes or the Himalaya. He was wind-burned and fit, with an easy grin, a manner that inspired confidence, and a ready command of his subject. He obviously liked people, and I guessed he was a popular guide. We sat in a semi-circle and he led us through frostbite, hypothermia, and dehydration and explained that we would all be sleeping outside tonight to put our soon-to-be-acquired knowledge into practice.

I sipped my coffee and tried to look eager—or at least willing. My years in Australia had thinned my once thick New England blood, and I was feeling the cold down here much more than I had expected. Everybody else in the room seemed to be fresh from places like Minnesota or Alaska or somewhere high in the Rocky Mountains, where this kind of weather was just another wintry day. In fact some of them had been laughing that very morning that it was colder back at home, where it was winter, than it was here at MacTown. As for me, I'd taken a peek at the Australian weather on the Internet, when I'd tapped in to check the cricket scores, and saw that it was 110 degrees back home in Adelaide. That's what I was used to.

I hadn't particularly enjoyed the freezing walk up here from the dorm, and behind my pinned-on smile was quietly dreading the prospect of spending the next two days—and a night—outside, no matter how good the sleeping bag that they'd issued me was.

After he finished, we went outside and loaded our gear into two Hagglunds tracked vehicles. In addition to our personal packs and the heavy duffels of camping gear we'd each been issued, there was a mountain of ropes, snow saws, ice axes, and survival kits. I noticed glumly that the weather had deteriorated a bit since we'd been inside. The sky had come over heavy and gray. A cold, gusty wind was blowing plumes of snow. Thai was enthusiastic. "You're lucky! Looks like you guys might have a lively time of it out there tonight!"

It was a bouncing, lurching 45-minute ride, past New Zealand's Scott Base to "Snow Mound City," a wide-open, lonely, and windswept spot on the edge of the Ross Ice Shelf where Happy Camper School students practiced building igloos and emergency shelters. As we approached, I could make out the remains of the snow walls built by previous classes, the blocks crumbling and half buried in the drifting snow. It was spooky and desolate. They looked like my idea of ancient ruins along the Silk Road slowly being consumed by the desert.

The tractor shuddered to a halt. We scrambled out, hopping onto the crusty surface and looking dazedly around. The world out here was a dreary monochrome: gray sky, dull ice, the low-slung profiles of Black Island and White Island, and behind them the dark summit cone of Mount Discovery, an extinct volcano rising more than 50 miles away. A feeble yellow smudge of wintry sun filtered through the cloud. Bleak as it was, it felt wonderful to be beyond the confines of MacTown.

"OK, so which way is south?" Thai asked.

We laughed uneasily. Then 14 fingers promptly pointed in 14 different directions. We looked at each other, a few abruptly changing their minds and pointing in a different direction. It looked as absurd as the scarecrow directing Dorothy to the Emerald City in *The Wizard of Oz*. The immense silence of the ice plain swallowed up our embarrassed chuckles. This was a very alien environment, and the consummate authority under which we had lived in MacTown had got us completely out of the habit of thinking for ourselves. No need to know where south was; somebody in authority would tell us if we ever needed to know.

"It's this way."

Embarrassed hands dropped quickly, although I took a certain quiet—and wholly unjustified—pride in the fact that I actually hadn't been too far off. The only reason I had pointed in the direction I had, though, was the eye-catching prominence of Mount Discovery. It had drawn me the way a card conjurer can make a child choose the joker. I could have been pointing due north for all I really knew.

We unloaded our packs, survival gear, and boxes of sledging rations, piled them onto plastic surfboard-size sleds, and man-hauled them, Captain Scott-style, a couple of hundred meters across the lumpy, wind-packed snow to where Thai was going to have us build our shelters. We had a chocolate break, and then school was in session.

Our first project was to erect a couple of so-called Scott tents. These are old-fashioned, pyramid-shaped tents made of heavy canvas and similar in style to those the early polar explorers used a century ago. They weigh about 90 pounds each, are tall enough for someone my height, just over six feet, to stand up in, and unfold like a giant umbrella. Properly pitched, they can withstand even hurricane-force winds – "Herbies," in MacTown slang – that can come out of nowhere and howl across the ice.

Thai showed us how to hoist it, plant its heavy-gauge steel legs firmly in the surface, stake down its sides, and pile up snow around the base to prevent wind from getting a fingernail grip underneath. We tensioned its guy lines to anchors, known as "dead men," that Thai showed us how to bury securely in the snow. When we finished pitching it, the taut lines and cheery yellow fabric made the frozen monochrome around us seem far less forbidding.

Perhaps it was because of the spirited humanity it suggested, or the dash of color, or maybe simply because it offered a welcome sense of scale. I thought of those happy passages in *The Worst Journey in the World* where Apsley Cherry-Garrard describes the setting up of the camp at the end of a day's march, giving it that wonderful sense of hominess and inclusion you'd feel in a candlelit mealtime scene by Dickens. I could see his point, my willingness to be poetic on the matter helped along by the fact that I'd been too busy and absorbed to notice the cold much at all.

Next we turned to building snow shelters. This was glorious fun, like being a kid again and creating the best snow fort in history (at least it was if you grew up in the big winters of New England like I did). Except no backyard or playground ever had snow like this to work with, unfathomably deep and wind-packed and as carvable as soft stone. We quarried it with a long-bladed saw, gently prying loose the chunky Styrofoam blocks with a shovel. They fitted together snugly. Piece by piece our castle grew—waist high, then shoulder high, completely shutting out the wind. Behind its snowy masonry there was plenty of room to pitch a couple of mountain tents. We were just getting into it, and laying plans to carve out shelves and tables and add crenellations to the walls when Thai called a halt and directed our attentions to another form of shelter: the snow cave.

This required more sweat and less artistry. To build them we threw all of our packs into an enormous pile and then spent the next half hour burying them under a huge mound of snow, 14 of us going at it like coal stokers, pausing occasionally to pack down the snow mound with the backs of our shovels before adding more. Finally, when the mound was so deep and thick and solid that you could thrust the entire length of an ice axe shaft into it and still not touch one of the bags, we began to excavate. Two of us dug down into the crust beside the mound, making a U-shaped tunnel that came up under the pile of bags. We disappeared like badgers, kicking out crumbs of snow behind us, found the packs, and began passing them out of the hole. Eventually, when the last rucksack was dragged out, we were left with a snug, dark bluish cavern, large enough to sleep four. It was a fun day all round.

It was late in the afternoon when we finished. Thai retreated to the field instructor's hut, about a mile away, and left us to experience our first night camping out in Antarctica, American-style.

Rich and I had been tipped off by an old hand to go for one of the Scott tents and we did, commandeering one with almost embarrassing haste and setting ourselves up for the evening, arranging packs, spreading out sleeping bags, and boiling a billy for cocoa on the two-burner Coleman stove. The tent grew warm and comfortable. We kicked off our boots and poked through the ration box, which was crammed full of freeze-dried dinners, instant soups, thin salamis, biscuits, noodles, and chocolate.

I dined that night on three mugs of split pea soup, a few of those toy salamis called Slim Jims, and a double helping of Black Bart Chilli. Rich went with the pasta option. The whole scene reminded me of camping out in the backyard when I was a kid.

We stayed up late, swapping stories, cracking jokes about bunny boots and the god-awful flight down from Christchurch, and sniggering over McMurdo's bustling, overweening, pompous officialdom. I hadn't had such a fun sleep-out since I was about ten. And like kids on a backyard campout, we turned in very late, but with the dazzling polar sunlight still filtering through the sides of the tent.

You would reckon that a nation that ships down a fleet of bright red pickup trucks for tooling around its prize Antarctic base would provide some top-flight camping gear—and you'd be absolutely right. The overnight gear the U.S. Antarctic Program issues to its field parties is lovely: a billowy oversize goosedown bag rated to –50, a pair of heavy-duty thermal mattresses, a warm fleece blanket, and a camp pillow. I slept far more comfortably than I had back at the base, even more comfortably than in the Hyatt Hotel back in Christchurch, despite the fine dusting of frost on my sleeping bag where my breath had frozen during the night. It was like being in bed at home on Sunday; I didn't want to get up, and I surely didn't hanker to go back to McMurdo. I could see why they called it Happy Camper School.

I untied the frosted canvas "door" and poked my head through the opening, and saw that the day had dawned even drearier than it had the previous one. Mount Discovery had faded into the smudgy horizon, still visible but faint. The wind was down—at least here at sea level—but an ominous lenticular cloud, as sleek as a flying saucer, occupied the sky where the summit of Mount Erebus should have been.

It would have been very unpleasant up there, but where I was kneeling in the snow just then felt very nice indeed. For the first time since those final icebergs slipped astern of the *Aurora Australis* seven years ago, I felt like I was in Antarctica, not just looking at it from the edge of MacTown, but actually in it, surrounded by its haunting majesty.

We ate a leisurely breakfast and struck the camp, finishing just as Thai rumbled up in the Hagglunds. We packed the gear in the tractor, and then, since we were all feeling hardened and outdoorsy, followed it on foot, a mile back to Thai's hut for the morning's lessons.

The field instructor's camp was an Army surplus hut called a Jamesway, an arch-shaped structure made of rubberized canvas stretched over an arched wooden frame and recognizable to anybody who has ever seen an episode of M*A*S*H. (In fact, this particular Jamesway had actually been used on the set of the old TV series.) Over the coming weeks I was to see a lot of these Korean War-era relics. When the Army decided to discontinue them, the U.S. Antarctic Program snapped up every one it could get its hands on. They made perfect field bases: cheap, flexible, portable, and surprisingly snug. This one had a wooden floor, a couple of bunks, an oil heater, a field kitchen, and a semicircle of plastic chairs for classes.

We sat sipping hot drinks and munching on muesli bars while Thai took us through the mysteries of using and maintaining field radios, and fashioning antennas out of different lengths of wire, depending on the frequency we wanted to use. We practiced priming and lighting mountaineering stoves and discussed various crisis scenarios.

For our final exams we had to work out a spontaneous rescue plan to retrieve a lost team member (Thai) in a blizzard, and then put it into effect while wearing white plastic buckets over our heads to mimic the whiteout conditions.

Our scheme was to rope up, 14 of us spread along the length of a climbing rope, and leaving one person anchored at the Jamesway door to make a cautious radial sweep. We must have looked like something out of a low-budget children's show, stumbling over the snow with buckets over our heads (the buckets had smiley faces on them), playing an Antarctic version of blindman's buff. But we passed that test, and others like how to pitch a tent, build a snow wall, light a camp stove, and establish radio communications with Mac Ops.

We rolled back into McMurdo, late in the afternoon, prepped and raring to go back out again into the field. In my case, I had arranged to meet up with some geologists who were already at a remote field camp in the Transantarctic Mountains. I'd fly out in the morning. With that prospect before me, and fresh off the ice, MacTown didn't seem quite so bad. I had a hot shower and a big dinner and packed my bags.

The cocky cheeseburger-loving lads of the 109th Airlift Wing of the New York Air National Guard might well have been able to kick the bejesus out of the Royal New Zealand Air Force, just as they boasted, and no doubt they could have barnstormed through the defenses of Iceland, Fiji, and the Seychelles Islands to boot, and with one hand tied behind their backs, but even they had to admit they were hopelessly outgunned by Antarctica's simple quiet force majeure.

A fresh line of snow squalls had drifted in during the night over the Ross Sea, as softly as a cat on a mantelpiece, dumping several more inches of snow on McMurdo and reducing visibility to just a couple hundred yards in the dim gray murk. It was nothing spectacular, no screeching blizzards out of the Captain Scott legend, just a soft, steady fall of big, moist flakes that swirled in the air and blanketed the station like a scene from a Currier & Ives Christmas print. It made it seem almost pretty.

Certainly it was peaceful. Low visibility had once again brought everything here to a standstill. All flights were canceled; the airfield was silent. Nobody was going anywhere for the foreseeable future. McMurdo was on track for its snowiest November on record. More than 16 inches had fallen so far, and the month still had another five days to run. The record was 21 inches, set back in 1971.

I shrugged into my parka after breakfast and headed up Beeker Street to the Crary building, a sprawling beige complex where the scientists have their labs and offices. It was named for Albert Crary, an American geophysicist who, I was guessing, was probably the same Crary honored by the Crary Range, a chain of mountains I'd seen on the map, near the Executive Committee Range.

The air felt cool and soft, just around the freezing point. Tumbleweed snowflakes clung to my sweater where I'd left my parka unzipped. Everything was quiet; there was only a lone figure in the grayness ahead of me, in blue jeans and parka with a tatty rucksack slung over his shoulder. For a moment there I was back in college, circa 1977, trudging off to the academic quad on a wintry morning. The feel was the same, a little bittersweet perhaps, even if McMurdo looked nothing like the ivied 19th-century campus in Ohio where I studied geology a quarter of a century ago. The telling difference was that the ponytails and beards I saw around me now were largely streaked with gray; people my age were professors with graduate students of their own. It was like falling asleep and waking in my 40s.

It got a little eerier still. When I got to Crary I dropped down to see Rick at his office in the lower ground floor, to see how his seismic detector was coming along—they'd been having a few problems calibrating it—and the gentle melancholy of the weather got us wandering off down memory lane, talking about our respective pasts. We'd both studied geology, although he'd obviously pursued it much further than I. He told me how he'd become interested in rocks when he was a kid, spending his summers hiking in the White Mountains in New Hampshire.

"Where?" I asked.

"A tiny little place you've never have heard of."

"Try me."

He named a village just a couple of miles from where I grew up. His mother had been a counselor at a boy's camp there and he'd spent almost every summer in the woods. Rick was about my age, a year younger, and he knew all the local swimming holes and the hiking trails, and better still, he knew them as I did, recalled through almost the same prism of years; he remembered where the candy counter used to be at Tices, an old country store that burned down years ago; and Harry White at White's Garage, a tall, lean, weathered mechanic who had been a crony of my grandfather's; and Mount Chocorua, the granite peaked mountain that rose above our meadow. He'd been up it many times. It had been one of his favorite hikes, as it had been mine, and the trails he'd taken weren't the popular tourist ones, but the little backwoods paths we locals used. We could well have bumped into each other; given how frequently I used to go up the mountain back then it was more than possible, it was likely.

Those same trails, and the same pink granite ledges, had steered both of us toward geology, almost simultaneously, but where he had gone on to become a geology professor, I'd wandered off to follow other, flightier, paths into journalism. He was even teaching in New Mexico, a place I had lived in briefly in my early 20s, enjoyed hugely, and had contemplated moving to before I decided to up stakes and migrate to Australia. As we reminisced, with the snow drifting past the windows, I found myself wondering what my life might have been like had I stayed in the United States, and if this chance encounter with Rick mightn't have been a glimpse into my own parallel existence.

The big low-pressure system seemed to have parked itself over our part of the Ross Sea, with those soft snow flurries continuing to filter out of those low sooty skies for several more days. The planes and helicopters were all grounded; life on base slowed to a crawl.

Crary was a pleasant place to while away the snowbound days. The library had a rich collection of Antarctic material, as well as a bank of iMacs and PCs for surfing the Web and checking e-mails, and a spyglass that commanded a view out over the airstrip and Royal Society Range—or at least it would have if the weather had been clear. But the clouds stuck to the ground like glue, and the most you could see were a few dark, smudgy outlines of Hercules cargo planes sitting idle on the ice.

Crary's offices and labs were filled with equally idle scientists, staring glumly out the windows, hoping for a break in the weather and feeling precious summer field time tick away. Normally by now they would be scattered all over the continent. For anyone who wanted to learn about Antarctica, Crary at that moment was a virtual chocolate box of polar experts. I went door knocking.

One of my first drop-ins was to the meteorite hunters—a team of geologists who spent their summers scouring Antarctica's blue-ice fields looking for telltale bits of black rock. (Antarctica is one of the world's great meteorite hunting places, the ice being like a sheet spread beneath a cherry tree: Anything you find on them had to have come from above.) A couple of years ago they made history and headlines around the world when they picked up a chunk of Mars that had been chipped off the red planet by an asteroid's impact long ago and eventually tumbled to Earth after many eons of drifting through space.

I knocked on the door and was surprised to recognize the weathered face and graying ponytail of a man named John who'd sat nearly opposite me on the second flight down from Christchurch—the one that made it through. In my boredom on that flight I had taken to assigning lives and characters to the faces around me, and John, I'd decided, with his weathered features, ponytail, ironic eye, and general look of sinewy outdoorsy toughness, was a carpenter, probably from somewhere like Alaska, an aging hippie who'd read Kant and Sartre in college, ran to a hard line of cynicism, and had gone into carpentry as a way of making a living in a bullshit world. I had it all worked out.

At least I got the outdoorsy toughness bit right: He was an accomplished mountaineer who had scaled Makalu, one of the world's highest and most dangerous peaks, and he'd skied solo across Greenland. He lived in the backcountry, the Rockies rather than Alaska, and for all I know he may have read Kant and Sartre, along with his geology, but jaded and cynical, he was not. He approached his search for meteorites with the bright-eyed enthusiasm of a boy on a treasure hunt, and for the next two fleeting hours he talked happily about prospecting for stardust in Antarctica (and ambitions to search in Greenland, the Sahara, and Australia's Nullarbor Plain) and showed me collections of iron-nickel nuggets he'd been cataloging, and all in a way that, as with Rick, sent me back down memory lane to the boyish pursuits that had once nudged me toward geology.

I spent another afternoon drinking coffee in the library with a scientist named Norbert, a surface radar expert with the U.S. Army Cold Regions Research Laboratory, who was supposed to have been out on the West Antarctic ice sheet beginning a summer-long traverse as part of the International Transantarctic Scientific Expedition but had suffered a series of migraines and had caught one of the resupply flights back to McMurdo to get them checked out, and now as a result of the big snows couldn't get back to rejoin the team.

The idea behind the traverse was to study climate change, particularly over the past 200 years. Polar ice makes a wonderful archive of Earth's atmosphere. As snow falls, tiny pockets of air are trapped between the flakes. Over the ages, the weight of accumulated snow turns the lower layers into ice and compresses these pockets of air into tight bubbles, forming tiny, perfectly preserved samples of atmosphere caught in a moment in time. By analyzing these bubbles, scientists can detect changes in carbon dioxide levels, gases, and atmospheric pollutants from volcanic eruptions or human activity such as Cold War atomic weapons tests or Chernobyl.

It was all very worthy, and the journalist in me dutifully jotted down the dire indications of rising temperatures, and how the rapid melting of the West Antarctic ice sheet—an unstable mass of ice larger than Mexico—could raise sea levels around the world and redraft the maps.

But what captured my imagination was the traverse itself: days and weeks spent traveling across an utterly featureless existential void of white ice and blue sky, hundreds of miles from the nearest human settlement, navigating by radar and GPS. He showed me pictures of the long tractor-drawn caravan, a weird mix of *Mad Max* and the Silk Road, with its cavalcade of sleds, mobile living quarters and labs, and drill rigs, with outriders following along on snowmobiles. A radar unit, fixed to a tire on a 33-foot-long boom to the lead tractor, led the way, sniffing out crevasses, while a Plexiglas outhouse on skis—known as the Polar Pooper—brought up the rear. It even had the classic half moon carved on the door.

Slow clanking travel into an endlessly receding white horizon might have been more intriguing in the prospect than reality. The doctors had cleared Norbert to return, but he hadn't been all that anxious to go, delayed it a couple of days and now it looked as though he might have missed his chance—something he didn't seem overly troubled about.

Down by the fishy-smelling labs in the rear of the building, I dropped in on marine biologists and video technicians who were editing footage taken from a miniature camera harnessed to a seal's back that demonstrated the almost creepy stealth with which a hungry seal could approach an unsuspecting Antarctic cod, slipping up to within a few inches of the fish's belly before making a perfectly timed lunge.

In another office, a biology professor told me how he had brought down an expert in supermarket-style bar coding to help him tag a sample group of emperor penguins at Cape Crozier. A microchip, similar to the sort used to register pets, was inserted into the penguin's shoulder and a computerized weighbridge and scanner set up near the entrance to the colony. Each time one of the tagged penguins came or went, its ID number, weight, and the time was logged, allowing researchers to monitor the success and duration of their feeding forays. It was an Orwellian sort of deal for the penguins that called to mind the institutional presence endured by MacTown's human residents.

Not all of the scientists were bogged down by the heavy weather, or worked in far-flung locations around the continent. Some did their fieldwork within easy sight of MacTown.

I was loitering in a corridor at Crary one afternoon when a Danish researcher named Kim hurried past, then paused to ask me if I'd like to come fishing. He was rounding up volunteers to help him catch some specimens. I said sure, scampered back to my dorm to get some heavier clothes, and a few minutes later I was in the back of a Hagglunds with half a dozen other scientists-for-a-day, rolling out across the sea ice away from the base.

Most of the volunteers were from the motor pool or were clerical staff, on their rostered days off. Science is a recreation as well as vocation down here. We parked about two miles offshore. Kim began to assemble the augur while we sorted out hand lines, hooks, and bait.

The ice was more than ten feet thick here. The augur bit required to penetrate it was so long that he had to stand on the roof of the tractor to start the hole. We stood and watched, hunched up and arms folded, our backs to the wind. The angry buzz of the augur's two-stroke engine grated in the stillness.

He drilled the hole and shifted the Hagglunds forward to drill another. The holes had to be quite small in diameter so light wouldn't filter down and attract the seals; hungry seals would ruin our prospects of catching anything.

We were fishing for Borch, as Dr. Seuss as that sounds. Borch are a silvery-gray fish, about eight inches long, and interesting to science because of the remarkable antifreeze agent in their bloodstream that keeps them supple and happy in Antarctica's frigid waters.

We baited our hooks and hunkered down over the holes like Eskimos. It was miserably cold out there. More than once I looked longingly back at the base. As the afternoon dragged by I thought of the last time I'd been ice fishing, about 30 years ago, when I skipped school with my best friend, Jack, to go out on Great Hill Pond, and then spent my stolen hours with my teeth chattering and wishing I was sitting in a warm algebra class.

Then as now, the fish weren't biting. The only one who caught much was Kim, who fished bare-handed so as better to feel the nibbles. His hands were a mottled cherry red, but he hardly noticed or cared; his Nordic blood seemed as impervious to cold as that of the Borch he was studying.

We caught a dozen fish between us—Kim accounting for nine—plunging each one immediately into a nearby bucket of seawater to prevent it being snap-frozen in the sub-zero air; their antifreeze apparently didn't work as well as Kim's did out of water. We finished late in the afternoon, rolled up our lines, and lumbered back to the base in the Hagglunds. The Borch went to their new home in the bio lab's aquarium; I went on to the welcoming warmth of the base.

And so the days slipped by fairly agreeably, even if time was starting to hang a little heavy on my hands, since like the scientists I too was looking at the clock and watching my summer field time ebb away. I spared a thought for the people who must be stranded up in Christchurch, and remembered with a shudder the dreary routine of hanging around hotel rooms or over at the Antarctic Center waiting to find out what was going to happen and when, and never knowing. The record delay, I learned from one of the old hands, was 16 days.

Christchurch seemed so close at hand at times, a common denominator that linked all of us. Like the cabby back at the airport, I too was beginning to think of the distance between "Cheech" and MacTown as just a simple hop; we were just two communities connected by a plane ride. Sometimes I wished I was back there, something I never expected to feel in Antarctica. But then, with the exception of that first icy shock when I stepped off the plane, and that overnighter doing Happy Camper School out on the ice shelf, I hadn't felt much like I was in Antarctica even yet. I still felt as though I were in limbo, although at a lofty position from where I could at least see, or better imagine, the great White South.

Various dreary melodramas about town played themselves out—a spat between journalists at the *Antarctic Sun* caused one to resign in a moment of pique and take up duties as a janitor; a graduate researcher was sacked ingloriously from her post and was waiting for the next flight out of town; and then there were the mutterings from the newcomers among MacTown's support personnel who had come down to the ice expecting Shackletonian adventure and were only now realizing that this was it: an office job in a hard-bitten company town, but with a great view out the window when the weather was nice.

For those who wanted to get ahead there were classes offered in typing and computer skills and personal investment. Playing the stock market is a popular pastime here. With constant Internet access and long empty evenings, when Wall Street is opening half a world away, a year at MacTown provides the perfect opportunity to parlay tax-free earnings into a tidy investment portfolio. There is plenty of time to research stocks on the Web and pick likely winners, and the local gossip is full of stories of average Joes who have made it rich playing the market from here. The computer room just off the dining hall was usually crowded with people checking e-mails, market reports, the weather back home, or the college football scores.

Thanksgiving Day came. The chef turned out an epic spread that actually felt homemade—no small feat when you're cooking for more than a thousand—despite being handicapped by the fact that most of the fresh veggies earmarked for the feast were still up in Christchurch, waiting on pallets to be loaded into cargo planes whenever the flight schedule started up again. There was turkey and ham and all the traditional trimmings, and a few nontraditional ones as well, such as Antarctic cod. And then followed the very traditional groaning sprawls in bed, or in front of the TV and a football game.

A couple of days later I scored a dinner invitation for barbeque night over at New Zealand's Scott Base. It was about two miles away, along a well-graded road that skirted the coast of Ross Island. I walked most of the way, hitching a lift the last few hundred yards from the shuttle bus that linked the two bases.

The New Zealand base was much, much smaller than McMurdo: just a simple, modernistic pistachio green complex that housed about 50 expeditioners during the summer. I had glimpsed it when we drove out to the ice shelf for Happy Camper School. From a distance it had merely looked tidy. It felt homey and personal up close, much like the Australian bases I knew. I liked it immediately.

I went into the vestibule, took off my boots, and hung my parka on one of the hooks. Something about it, whether it was because it was a Kiwi station and I felt a sort of trans-Tasman familiarity with the culture there, or whether it was simply because it operated on a human scale, reminded me of Mawson base, although the two stations didn't resemble each other at all physically. It had the same open-handed gregariousness and egalitarianism, where the station leaders took their turns doing "slushy" duties—doing the dishes, mopping floors and cleaning the toilets—along with everyone else.

Dinner was the classic barbie: grilled chops, steaks and snags, beetroot, salads, bread and butter, and a bowl of ice cream for dessert. There weren't half a dozen selections available for the main course, or a carvery where a capped chef waited with a bone-handled knife, or a separate buffet for vegetarians with the latest in California cuisine; there didn't need to be. It was nice for once to have something simple and modest and familiar.

Rick and Rich came over after dinner, and we sat up late in the Scott base pub afterward, gossiping with the Kiwi scientists and helicopter pilots. It was a relaxed and pleasantly beery evening. I felt like I had found Antarctica again, the one I remembered and had begun to doubt existed. The three of us walked back to MacTown at around midnight. The sky was lifting and patches of blue sky were opening up between the clouds. The stubborn weather pattern was finally breaking.

One of the New Zealanders said he'd heard flight operations would be starting up again in the morning. Sure enough, a message was waiting for me back at the dorm telling me to report to the heliport in the morning for my flight to Darwin Glacier.

CHAPTER EIGHT

Primal Landscapes

I FOUND MY WAY DOWN TO THE HELIPORT A LITTLE BEFORE SEVEN. I weighed myself on the scales there and jotted the figures down in the manifest book, found a helmet that fit my head, and wandered into the hangar, where the chief pilot—a wiry, silver-haired Vietnam veteran named Jack Hawkins—sorted out his paperwork ahead of our flight. The hangar had the customary macho ambience of aviators' hangouts everywhere, tools and spare parts piled around, "God Bless Texas" painted on the ceiling, and a pair of wall-mounted clocks set to the time at McMurdo and Lafayette, Louisiana, where the helicopter contractor was based. As I soon discovered, the birds these guys flew are "helos"—pronounced hee-low in a fine southern drawl—not "choppers."

I was carrying a gift-wrapped bottle of Scotch, a token Rich had asked me to pass on to Jack, the fallout of a boozy evening a few nights earlier in Gallagher's when Rich's leftish Seattle perspective on matters like hunting, shooting, and gun control collided volubly and colorfully with Jack's ardent Lone Star State point of view. Passions had run kind of high by the time the bar closed down, and Rich had felt chagrined the next morning. Jack hadn't been offended—he'd bounced around the world too much for that—although he was pleased to receive the Scotch and promised to put it to good use.

We loaded up the helo and took off about half an hour later. As MacTown's industrial sprawl fell away beneath the skids, the snowy magnificence of Antarctica took over, spreading infinitely into the horizon. The base resumed its true perspective, tiny and wonderfully insignificant in the face of such grandeur.

Violent storms on the surface of the sun were playing havoc with radio communications all across Antarctica, which meant that Jack had to relay messages back to McMurdo via a Hercules cargo plane that was making a run down to the South Pole. If it had been winter right now, and dark, we would have been treated to a spectacular display of the *Aurora Australis*. As it was, the solar burst was just another operational headache. Listening in on the casual grumbling of the pilots, buglike in their dark-visored helmets, and that vast crystalline desert spreading out to every horizon, made me feel as though I had slipped into an imaginatively filmed postapocalyptic movie. The southern drawls of the voices on the radio and the "God Bless Texas" Hawkins had on his helmet seemed just the sort of corroborative detail George Lucas might have dreamed up.

We were flying southbound over the Ross Ice Shelf, a monotonous plain of ice larger than France, heading toward a field camp on Darwin Glacier, a broad frozen river flowing through a range of mountains about 200 miles away. According to the altimeter, we were flying more than 6000 feet up, but you had to take that on trust. There was nothing on the white, featureless snowscape below to give any indication of how far we were above it; we could have been 100 feet up, we could have been 100,000, there was no trustworthy perspective other than the cockpit instruments. Nor was there any sense of speed or motion.

"It says we're traveling at 74 knots, but I feel like I've been hovering over the same spot for half an hour," Hawkins remarked after a while.

The peaks in the distance seemed to be painted on the horizon. This was my first glimpse of the big mountains in Antarctica's interior, the vast Transantarctic range that stretched across the continent. It was exhilarating just to be alive. I drew a folding map of Antarctica from my day pack and spread it on my lap to see where we were headed. Incredible as it seemed just then, with such a wild sweep of mountains spreading into the violet distances all around, our entire journey that morning, including everything I could see through the window, would all have fitted inside a two-inch circle on that poster-size map. I thought back to that first helicopter flight I'd taken off the *Aurora Australis*, over Prydz Bay, on the other side of the continent—another vastness, seemingly infinite, yet connected to this vastness by an almost astronomical sweep of ice.

All of this was a just tiny portion of a frozen wilderness, covering millions of square miles, that had lain untouched and undiscovered at the bottom of the world for all but the last finger snap of time. And it was empty the way nothing else in this world is empty. Nothing lived out there—no animals; no trees, grass, or even moss. There is no soil, no insects, no worms—only a sterile void of snow, ice, and jagged shards of rock.

Antarctica's interior may be drier than the Sahara, as cold as Mars, and nearly as lifeless, but it wasn't always like this. I was heading for a field camp at 80 degrees south where paleontologists were peeling back 270 million years of history to a time when all of this was a damp green wilderness of forest and tundra and part of an enormous landmass called Gondwana. According to Rosie and John, a couple of geologists I had met over dinner when I first arrived at McMurdo, what I was flying over now would have resembled parts of Alaska or Scotland's western isles or northern Norway, a postcard wilderness with glaciers occupying the valley floors and cold, rushing streams with ferns and leafy trees along their banks. Now it was a vastness of ice and rock, deathly still beneath a bright and empty vault of sky.

We reached the camp about two hours later, coming at it through a lost world of towering cliffs, shimmering walls of ice and dark stony peaks. Although I knew by the passage of time and the fact that mountains were looming up all around us now that we must be getting close, I had already lost the expectation of seeing human handiwork that we all unconsciously carry around with us, and so I didn't even notice the camp at first. And when I did, I thought it was just a smudge on the window. It was so tiny. It was the first real indication of human scale I'd had since we had lifted off from McMurdo.

The rotors throbbed, the airspeed indicator read steady 70-odd knots, and the speck slowly grew larger until it resolved into a Jamesway and a cluster of bright mountain tents. A ski-equipped DC-3 was standing on the ground beside them, having flown in a half hour earlier to drop off fresh food and fuel. A clutch of tiny figures, bright in red parkas, were unloading boxes from the plane's rear hatch and stacking them on the snow. Another figure was hauling a loaded sled away from the plane, rope over the shoulder, toward an old Army hut 100 yards away. They heard the helicopter approach, looked up, and waved.

We landed on a wooden platform beside a cluster of fuel drums and bundled our gear out of the cargo cages on the helicopter's struts. I looked over at the DC-3, stylish and silvery, parked at a rakish angle and casually projecting Bogart adventure against a backdrop of wild, frozen mountains.

I slung my backpack by the door of the Jamesway and helped them finish unloading the DC-3. Its pilot was a lanky New Zealander named Max who vaguely resembled James Coburn and had been flying around Antarctica for years, mostly operating out of South America for a charter firm that offered logistical support for private expeditions and flew documentary filmmakers around the continent. This year though he was flying on charter to the USAP, a novelty both for Max and the Americans, whose officials are notoriously hostile to any form of private enterprise in Antarctica. But they'd wanted to see if this specially refurbished DC-3, fitted with turbo-prop engines, could fill the niche between helicopters and the lumbering heavy-duty military LC-130s when it came to resupplying field camps, and so Max was having the summer of his life. After years of frosty rebuff and having his radio calls ignored, he was finding himself persona grata for once.

"I had to fly to the South Pole the other day, and I heard them radio down from McMurdo that I was to be given every courtesy and assistance. I never thought I'd live to hear those words from the Yanks!"

We stood admiringly by while he taxied away in a blizzard of prop-blown snow that totally obscured the plane. It was a stylish exit. After a dramatic pause and crescendo of engine noise, it reappeared, shooting out of its snowy mist; hard, bright, and shiny. It skimmed the surface of the glacier at over 120 miles an hour, its skis cutting up little puffs of snow, before rising gently. He banked and circled the camp before setting off over the ranges, back to McMurdo. We watched the plane shrink, a silvery glint in an empty sky, and then vanish. The hush that fell over the glacier was profound.

I spent a few days at Darwin Glacier Camp, packing a lunch in my rucksack every morning and going out with the geologists who were spending their field season sampling and mapping a particular strata of café-au-lait-colored sandstone dating from the Permian era—about 270 million years ago. There were three geologists staying there, together with two general assistants, who cooked and ran the camp, and a professional mountaineer, who handled crevasse crossings and technical climbing situations.

Most days, the scientists would commute to their sites by snowmobile, but they were also given helicopter support for a few days each week to get them up onto otherwise inaccessible aeries and crags higher in the mountains. I had come out on one of the rostered helicopters—there were two assigned to Darwin Glacier that week—and the camp was filled with the extra voices of pilots and helicopter maintenance crews.

It was a nice, comfortable camp, with the Jamesway at its heart and a little suburbia of mountaineering tents spread out along the ice where we all slept, and a floorless Scott tent that served as a latrine, with a deep hole dug in the ice and a portable toilet seat over it. The helicopters sat on their two wooden platforms; snowmobiles were parked beside the Jamesway, together with piles of rations boxes and assorted field gear and everybody's ice axes thrust in the snow outside the front door.

The Jamesway itself was cozy and homey, with a big table in the center that was generally cluttered and amiably crowded at mealtimes, the occasional deficit in chairs being made up for with upended ration boxes. The rough wooden tabletop was covered with Antarctica graffiti—impromptu poems, drawings, nicknames, and little stories, and littered with geological maps and condiment bottles and specimens and stained coffee cups.

The kitchen was in the rear, together with the radio. A pot of melting ice was always simmering on the stove, ready to be made into coffee, and the pantry shelves were bright with labels. Jamie, one of the general assistants, was a qualified chef, and we dined well on satays and elegantly prepared pasta dishes.

We put in some sociable evenings. One night one of the helicopter support crew—a smoke jumper named Brian, who was with the U.S. Forest Service back in the real world—kept everyone entertained by teaching us how to tie one-handed bowline knots. The warmth and clutter and laughter in the canvas hut provided a fascinating counterpoint to the bright, silent emptiness outside. It gave the camp a wonderful sense of place, dispelling any loneliness a glance at the map might have suggested.

The geologists—Rosie, John, and a graduate student named Paul—decided to take advantage of the helicopters to get up to a ledge on top of a towering rock face, more than a thousand feet high, that overlooked the Hatherton Glacier. It was about a 20-minute flight from camp through the mountains. The view from the clifftop was stupendous: the glacier a river of ice carving a lazy bend between two huge massifs, and vast cloudlike snowfields stretching into the distance, broken up by nunataks—sharp, exposed rocky nubs that look like bishop's miters or jagged incisors—that jutted above the ice.

This was my first time in Antarctica's mountains and I was awestruck, unable to drag my eyes away from their untouched wildness and the captivating thought that no human eye had ever seen these mountains, any of them, or even guessed at their existence, until 1903, when one of Scott's advance scouting parties passed through, named them the Britannia Range, and then left them to their perpetual slumbers. Nobody returned for more than 50 years, and even today few people have ever been up in these mountains. Exhilarating as it was to stand at that clifftop, there were still grander things to come.

A couple of days later, after breakfast, I noticed Rosie and Tim, the mountaineer, poring over a map and deep in conversation with one of the helicopter pilots, a gentle giant from Louisiana named John. On the flight back from our usual clifftop, Rosie had spotted an interesting outcrop very high up, near the summit of another mountain, much farther out, and she wanted to know what the odds were of our getting up there.

It didn't look particularly promising. The winds were gusty enough on the ground and would probably be even more so at almost 9,000 feet, which was roughly the altitude of that intriguing ledge, and there was no telling if there would even be a safe place to drop us off up there. But John was willing to make a recon flight to check it out, and after breakfast the four of us set out, packing our rucksacks along in case it was possible to make a landing—as well as our survival bags, emergency tents, and extra rations in case the winds picked up and we found ourselves stranded up there for a while.

It was like flying to the hall of the mountain king. Sheer, dark cliffs of colonnaded dolerite, thousands of feet high, guarded the summit ridge and made me think of the pipes on an enormous cathedral organ. They were topped with wind-whipped curlicues of snow that resembled confectionery. As we flew toward it, those mauve cliffs growing huge and intimidating in front of us, the helicopter seemed about as significant as a gnat.

The sandstones Rosie was interested in were found along the summit ridge, a knife-edged spine of rock that fell away into heart-stopping plunges on either side. The winds were much lighter than expected; in fact, the air was nearly still, and John spotted a small but flattish shelf on the upper part of the ridge. He sidled carefully up to it and almost kissed the rock with the skids, keeping the engine hot. We baled out quickly, hustling our gear down the slope and covering it with our bodies to keep it from blowing up into the rotors when John took off. Tim signaled us clear. John acknowledged. The staccato rapping of the blades rose to ear-splitting pitch. Dust and ice shards were whipped into the air, stinging averted cheeks. The helicopter climbed and veered away in a single motion, appearing almost to plunge into the void that yawned only a pebble-flick away.

The sound receded quickly. When we stood up and peered over the edge, John was already tiny, swallowed up by space the way a deep well swallows a pebble. Silence took hold. We were alone, high on a mountain that until 60 seconds earlier had never before been trodden by a human foot.

The view was immense. Entire ranges of wild, splintery peaks stretched into the distance. The air was telescopically clear. Everything seemed enlarged and sharper somehow, so that you noticed the fine details that are usually too small to notice: the hairline cracks in the cliff faces, the grooves and curls of the blown snow, the texture of distant rock. The sky was taut blue and you could imagine the Earth curving away from you.

It was surprisingly warm on the ledge, a few degrees above freezing, with the sun's rays radiating off the rock. We shed our parkas, weighting them down with rocks in case the fickle mountain winds picked up, and scrambled about in our shirtsleeves. In the sunny silence it felt as though we had come to break an enchantment. And in a sense we had.

The ridge on which we stood was the remnant of an ancient glade. Chips of petrified wood, as fresh and crisp as newly hewn timber, lay scattered under our boots, and the creamy sandstones bore the imprints of long extinct ancestor of the horsetail bush that had flourished along the banks of an ancient stream. Ripple marks in the same fine-grained rock showed how the waters had once flowed and revealed where the prevailing winds came from more than 270 million years ago.

Rosie interpreted the rocks for my benefit, explaining causes and effects and deftly piecing together a sequence of primal landscapes—a muddy lakebed, a glacial moraine, and, near the top of the ridge, a prehistoric swamp that became a thick bed of coal. She had a nice narrative ability; the landscapes took shape before my eyes and came alive. Although I had studied geology in college, until that moment I had never thought of it as abstract art, or imagined that the principles of sedimentation could offer so vivid a palette.

"This is glossopteris," Rosie explained, after I handed her a curious, circular rock that was banded gray and cream and resembled the stump of a freshly lopped sapling. "It was a deciduous tree that also lived in South America and Australia. Finding it here in Antarctica was one of the things that helped prove the continents must have been linked at one time."

I turned it over in my hand, intrigued by its growth rings and marveling that each one was a tangible marker of a particular summer whose autumn had come more than a quarter of a billion years in the past.

It was one of those magical days, the sort you can store in your mental attic and dig out years later to draw strength or peace from or rekindle your sense of exhilaration and wonder, depending on what your soul needs at that particular moment.

While they got down to the hard business of paleontology, specifically ancient pollens, I occupied myself with scrambling along the ridge, admiring the views and exercising my imagination on those chunks of petrified glossopteris. Eighty million years after this obscure copse of trees died, the supercontinent known as Gondwana began the incredibly slow process of breaking up. Over many tens of millions of years, Africa and Australia separated from the greater landmass, gradually sliding northward toward their present places on the map. Antarctica was then linked to the world only by a tenuous land bridge extending from the southern tip of South America. And when that too finally broke away, about 45 million years ago, it was on its own—an island continent cloistered at the bottom of the globe. Powerful circumpolar winds raced unchecked around it, shutting out any moderating influences on Antarctica's climate. Eternal winter set in.

Our own day on the ridge neatly recapitulated this history. The balmy shirt-sleeve weather of the morning gave way to bitter winds and subzero cold in the afternoon. The sky remained hard and clear. Extravagant plumes of snow blew off the summit's sandstone pyramid, about 150 feet above us. The cliffs looked more forbidding than ever. We had long put on our parkas—and every other piece of warm, windproof gear we had brought along—by the time we heard the helicopter buzzing toward us like an apocalyptic dragonfly come to whisk us back to camp.

CHAPTER NINE

The Ultimate Destination

I FLEW TO MCMURDO WITH JACK WHEN HE FINISHED HIS WEEKLY TOUR OF duty at Darwin Glacier. John flew the other helicopter, hovering about half a mile off our port side, the sight of his helicopter adding a sense of depth and scale to the whiteness that had been missing on the outward flight. A patchwork of low broken cloud and mist covered the ice shelf and briefly threw a question mark over our ability to land at McMurdo, but Mac-Ops reported that conditions were fine, if gusty, over the base. The sky above us was a hard, polished blue and sunlight dazzled on the snowy flanks of Mount Erebus in the distance.

McMurdo's clutter had a homey familiarity when we flew in over it. We set down on the heliport, the rotors churning up a cloud of dust. The weather had been warming up here as summer took hold, and the snow was melting surprisingly rapidly. The streets were becoming muddy in places and the hillsides above the town were revealed to be black and gritty, although they were still streaked with snow. It made me think of a West Virginia coal town in midwinter, although that was weathered volcanic ash we were seeing, not coal dust. I went around to my locker, stashed my field gear, and reclaimed my old room in Building 155. It felt even stuffier after sleeping in the mountains, but I had to admit the hot shower was nice.

The base was bustling, with helicopters buzzing in low and taking off again, and the airfield busy, and everyone playing catch-up after all the weather delays. But it is an ill wind indeed that blows nobody any good, and the seemingly endless snow squalls that had plagued McMurdo for much of the early summer and thrown the U.S. Antarctic Program's schedule into such costly disarray, now did me a wonderful favor. Like Scott, Shackleton, Amundsen, and virtually every other Antarctic visitor before me, I had passionately wanted to reach the South Pole; it's the ultimate Antarctic destination. I had been promised a visit to the base there, but on the understanding that it would have to be a very brief one—probably only a few hours on a day trip with one of the resupply flights, out in the morning, back to McMurdo that afternoon.

The reason was simple: Space at Amundsen–Scott South Pole Station is extremely tight even at the best of times, but much more so now that there was a massive construction project under way to build a new base. More than 200 people were squeezed into the base's already cramped living quarters—iron workers, welders, electricians, plumbers, contractors, architects, as well as the usual complement of scientists and support personnel. Resources were stretched to the limit. Everything was operating on a just-in-time basis: workers and materials flown in as required and then flown right back out again as soon as their particular role was completed in order to make room for the next crew.

But then those troublesome squalls blew in and threw the whole summer's fine-tuned flight schedules so badly out of kilter that the decision makers had to pencil in a new completion date for the project—2006 instead of 2005.

It also apparently freed up a few berths at the base, and some charitable person higher up the chain of command thought of me. I never did learn for sure who it was—I believe it was one of the base commanders at Pole—but he or she has my eternal gratitude. All I knew was that I was sitting in the library over at Crary one Friday afternoon, checking my e-mails, when one of the assistants who worked at the Chalet found me, said she'd been looking all over for me, and if I packed quickly and got myself down to the airfield I could spend the weekend at Pole.

I grabbed my toothbrush and went.

There were nine of us—eight astrophysicists and me—for the evening "sleigh ride," as flights to the South Pole are known. The plane was a wolf-gray LC-130, a ski-equipped version of the Hercules transport plane. These chunky four-engine turbo props are the workhorses of the U.S. Antarctic Program, so useful for hauling heavy loads around the ice that the U.S. government regards them as a strategic asset and refuses to allow their export—a Defense Department restriction, dating from the Cold War days. Only the 109th Airlift Wing of the New York Air National Guard is certified to fly them. They have eight. This one was the *City of Albany*, its name painted stylishly on its nose.

The bus dropped us off at the airfield a bit early. The *City of Albany*'s pilot and crew were still eating dinner in the little prefab galley. Nearby a couple of maintenance men, on their meal break, tossed a football around. Mount Erebus puffed lazily in the background. I slouched against a wall, watching the loadmasters prep the plane for the 840-nautical-mile hop to the end of the Earth, smiling at the thought of the potboiler I'd tucked into my carry-on out of habit. In a few minutes I'd be flying to the South Pole. Tonight I'd be sleeping there. What fiction was I going to read that could compete with that?

We took off a little after seven o'clock in the evening, banking gently over the frozen airfield and heading due south, leaving the familiar landmarks—Black Island, White Island, Minna Bluff, and Mount Discovery—adrift as we climbed to a cruising altitude of 22,000 feet. In three and a half effortless hours we'd accomplish a journey that took Antarctica's original explorers ten years and three expeditions to make, at the cost of enormous sums of money, manpower, physical toil, heartbreak, and tragedy.

Somewhere out on that vast featureless plain of ice, even now, lay the bodies of Scott, Wilson, and Bowers shrouded together in their collapsed tent. So too were the bodies of Captain Oates and Edgar Evans. Ninety years' accumulation of snow had long ago sealed them into the ice sheet; they'd be buried more than 100 feet beneath the surface by now. A few years ago a New Zealand glaciologist, who'd obviously had a bit of spare time on his hands, calculated that given the dynamics of the ice sheet, Scott's body would have reached and passed the site of the One Ton Depot, the food cache they'd strived in vain to reach. In another 250 years or so, as the ice continues its glacial creep northward, the chunks that entomb the men will break off into icebergs and their perfectly preserved bodies will sink to a final resting place on the floor of the Ross Sea.

We were following pretty much the same route Scott and Shackleton had pioneered on their attempts at the Pole: south across the vast numbing monotony of the Ross Ice Shelf, then dogleg through the Transantarctic Mountains along the Beardmore Glacier and over the high polar plateau to the South Pole. It would be a stunning flight, and because a Hercules cargo plane has very few portholes, the crew invited us up to the cockpit to take in the view. We all crowded in.

I found myself talking to the co-pilot, a former B-52 captain and Gulf War veteran named Bryan, who was a nice guy and the very antithesis of those muscle-bound jocks I'd met at lunch that day back at McMurdo, the ones who'd boasted of the 109th's ability to blow away the Royal New Zealand Air Force; but then, Bryan had actually been to a war. He'd left the Air Force a couple of years ago, signed on with the New York Air National Guard, and now divided his time between the Arctic and Antarctic, resupplying U.S. research bases. Although he'd made the South Pole trip more times than he could count—every flyable day during the season—it never lost its freshness or imaginative appeal.

"I can't help but think of Shackleton and Scott every time I make this run," he shouted above the roar of the engines and the foam plugs in our ears. "Imagine man-hauling a wooden sled with hundreds of pounds of gear over that, day after day after day, with next to no food and constantly being cold." He glanced at his ground speed indicator and did a quick bit of mental arithmetic. "You know, right now we are covering as much ground in about three minutes as those guys did on a good day. And they didn't have many good days."

The view out the cockpit window was frighteningly simple: just blue and white, the incarnation of the horizon indicator on the cockpit dashboard. An hour droned by in this same featureless vault of white and blue, lulled by the hypnotic drone of propellers and then a line of high, wild, splintery peaks began to gather on the horizon ahead of us. This was the heart of the Transantarctic Mountains, but these summits were far loftier than those mountains I had explored with the rock doctors out at Darwin Glacier; some of these peaks towered more than 15,000 feet above the ice shelf. I remembered how Shackleton described his first sight of them in his journal—one of my favorite passages in his, or any explorers', writings, a brief perfect mingling of discovery at its purest and the hardships of travel.

"It was with feelings of keen curiosity, not unmingled with awe, that we watched the new mountains rise from the great unknown that lay ahead of us," Shackleton wrote on the night of November 26, 1908, as he reflected on the fact that he and his men were the first human beings ever to have laid eyes on these peaks. "No man of us could tell what we would discover in our march south, what wonders might be revealed to us, and our imaginations would take wings until a stumble in the snow brought us back to the immediate present."

It might have been a kindness that they couldn't have guessed what lay ahead. What would be revealed to them in the course of the next few weeks was that this mountain range acted like a gigantic dam, holding back an inconceivable buildup of ice, millions of years old and more than two miles thick; that the South Pole was to be found on a bitterly cold, windswept plateau, as high as Tibet's but infinitely more forbidding; and that the only way to reach it would be to pick their way up a frighteningly steep glacier.

Ever the optimist, Shackleton wrote at the foot of it: "The pass through which we have come is flanked by great granite pillars at least two thousand feet in height and making a magnificent entrance to the Highway to the South."

Some highway: an endlessly tumbling cascade of ice, treacherous crevasses, pressure ridges, and cathedral-size boulders that looked as though they had been casually tossed there. It went on and on, climbing from near sea level to an altitude of more than 10,000 feet with hardly a break.

Nothing in all the reading I had done about the heroic-age explorers—even their own journals—could bring home their sheer courage and strength of will like the spectacle of the Beardmore Glacier (named by Shackleton for a wealthy industrialist who'd helped underwrite his expedition) and the thought that half-starved men in woolens and crude mountaineering gear had actually struggled up all that while dragging heavy sledges behind them.

It looked steep and scary even from 22,000 feet, in the warm, crowded, noisy comfort of the cockpit. And the reward waiting for them at the top was...nothing, just a flat and utterly sterile expanse of ice that stretched another 250 empty and bitterly cold miles to the Pole.

I glanced at the glowing digits on the instrument panel's GPS display. We were then coming up on 88° 23' south, the highest latitude reached by Shackleton and his party on their attempt at the Pole. The numbers flickered on, blink by blink toting up the seconds, minutes, and degrees of latitude toward the perfect 90. Those abstract figures were the only indication that we were moving at all.

Those seconds and minutes and degrees ticked over at a faster rate than expected and a few minutes after ten o'clock the *City of Albany* hissed its skis onto the ice at Amundsen–Scott South Pole base and for a few exhilarating moments the cargo plane became a 65-ton toboggan, skidding to a halt in a roar of reversed engines and blowing snow. The hatch opened and we looked around us at desolation that was almost overpowering: empty white horizons stretching away farther than the eye could see or the mind could grasp.

The air was thin and sharp, the light blinding. It was a perfect summer day. The temperature stood at –27°F, the windchill was –58°F, and a double halo of ice crystals circled the sun.

One of the astrophysicists on the flight, a wiry guy named Van, couldn't contain his excitement, punching me playfully on the shoulder and exclaiming: "This is it, dude! Ninety south! We're at the damn South Pole!"

The base was familiar from photographs: an ice-blue geodesic dome with a U.S. flag fluttering from a pole on its roof. We entered through a broad tunnel, walking beneath a large sign that read: "The United States of America Welcomes You to Amundsen–Scott South Pole Station." It was dim and cavernous inside, and the air was even colder because sunlight never reached in here except where it glowed through a small, round opening in the top of the dome. There was no floor, just hard-packed snow and ice.

The station leader was an athletic 33-year-old woman from Colorado named Katie. She led us through the warren of insulated steel modules that make up the village inside the dome, and up a flight of stairs into a game room where we sat down for a briefing on the rules and peculiarities of life at Pole, such as the weekly limit of two, two-minute showers. She advised us to take it easy until we acclimatized to the altitude, and to drink plenty of fluids in the desert-dry air. She was suddenly drowned out midsentence by rebel yells erupting from the bar.

"Sounds like you've got some pretty serious drinking going on," I remarked.

"Yes, I expect so," she laughed. "The fresh milk came in on your plane. We've all been looking forward to it."

People back at McMurdo had hinted that "Polies" were a breed apart, sort of like the hillbillies of the U.S. Antarctic Program, and if not quite dangerous, they were certainly weird. Who else would voluntarily spend a winter living in prison cell-size accommodation, with nothing like McMurdo's amenities, sealed off from the rest of the world, without any hope of going home (or anywhere else for that matter), in total darkness and mind-boggling outer-space cold? It sounded like a recipe for madness.

As I walked around that first evening, I had to agree that it was certainly a funky sort of place. The frozen carcass of an Antarctic cod dangling like a piñata from the top of the dome was a good pointer to that. We were an awfully long way from the sea and 9,301 feet up, so it wasn't there to bless the fleet. It had hung there for years, apparently, and for reasons no one was ever quite able to explain, or at least not in a way that made sense to me. But I liked Pole, and not simply because of the romance of its location. Its offbeat residents, rhythms, and quirkiness had a logic to me even if I never did understand that ornamental cod.

Maybe it was because I grew up in an old New England village where everybody knew each other's business going back for generations. Pole had the old familiar feel, with all its comfortable paradoxes. Folks here were at the same time laconic and gregarious, querulous and gossipy, yet quite tolerant, and all of this was overlain by an offbeat sense of humor and self-awareness that the residents of big-city MacTown either lacked or kept well hidden. This was Lake Wobegon on the high polar plateau.

In the few days I spent there I took a turn "driving the Dobson bus," local slang for operating the antiquated Dobson spectrometer (a 1930s vintage gadget that resembles an iron lung), which is used to measure the ozone hole and is "driven" by manipulating a sensitive steel wheel. I made the rounds of the new base with the construction boss—a laconic tobacco-chewing former plumber from Mississippi named Carlton Walker, who turned out to be a logistical genius, juggling more than 800 cargo flights carrying ten million kilos of building materials. I even did some bicycling down there, riding "around the world" with an astrophysicist, pausing to lean on the ornamental pole and savor that incredible ego-boosting knowledge that, just at that moment, the world really did revolve around me.

"Pole's a funny sort of place, but I love it; it's home," Katie said. "I've wintered here three times, met my husband here, and I know most of these people like my own family. I'm only down for the summer this year, but I'd winter again in a heartbeat. The hardest part for me is going to be getting on that last plane out in February."

It was after midnight by the time we finished our briefings, but before I went to bed I wanted to put my hand on the South Pole. Just in case the world came to an end overnight, I wanted to have reached it. I asked where it was and went out to find it. They were well supplied: They had not one but two South Poles here, sitting almost side by side on a rise behind the dome. One is called the ceremonial pole, and it really is the classic red and white candy cane straight out of a child's storybook. It is about waist height, with a shiny mirror ball on the top. The flags of the 12 original signatories of the Antarctic Treaty form a colorful circle around it.

This shrine is where most visitors have their "hero" pictures taken of themselves posing at the bottom of the world. I ran my mittened hand over its polished steel orb, looking at the fisheye reflection of myself standing at the very bottom of the globe with blue sky all around.

The geographic pole—the precise geographical position of 90°00'00' south—was located about 50 yards away and is marked by a plain steel post and a simple sign. Because of the constant shifting of the polar ice cap—about 30 feet a year—this official geographic pole has to be repositioned each summer. They do it in a ceremony on New Year's Day. I went over and claimed the official honors. Somebody told me the next morning that I would have been about the 7,000th person to reach the South Pole. The words of the first were inscribed on the sign. Roald Amundsen, on December 14, 1911: "And so we arrived and were able to plant our flag at the geographical South Pole." And history's most famous second-place finisher, Capt. Robert Falcon Scott, on January 17, 1912: "The Pole. Yes, but under very different circumstances from those expected." History's 7,000th-place finisher just said: "Cool."

If Scott found the Pole a little too well trodden for his taste when he rocked up in 1912 and found the Norwegian flag in the snow and a few ski tracks about the place, he should see it now: the huge blue fiberglass dome, a sprawling construction sight where the next base was being built, a tent city of Jamesways to house the construction crews, an astronomical observatory a half mile a way, and a control tower. Not to mention a bar full of Polies whooping it up on glasses of fresh milk just flown in from a small city called McMurdo, situated where Scott's old base camp used to be.

But what would have stunned poor Scott most of all (and Amundsen too, for that matter) is the fact that at the pole itself both the Union Jack and the Norwegian flag have been relegated to the ranks of bystanders adorning the ceremonial monument together with the flags of ten other nations who signed the original Antarctic Treaty. At the South Pole proper, the geographic pole, the Stars and Stripes waves alone. Looking at it fluttering aloof and heroic against the hard polar sky, anyone who didn't know better could be forgiven for thinking that the Pole was an American conquest, and theirs alone, like the moon.

It was more of an American homestead. In point of fact, the Americans arrived at the Pole a very, very distant third—about 45 years after Amundsen and Scott left the scene—and they didn't make any Homeric odysseys on foot or dogsled to get here. They flew. A U.S. Navy DC-3, named *Que Sera Sera*, touched down in October 1956 bearing an admiral and a team of surveyors. And the Americans came to stay, pegging out the South Pole in the twin pursuits of Cold War politics and Sputnik-era science. There was nothing quixotic about it. They meant business. By February 1957, the new Amundsen–Scott South Pole base was up and running. Americans have occupied the area ever since.

Drifting snow long ago buried that original base, a fate that awaits the present dome as well. It was built as a replacement in 1975 and is showing its age and frailty. Consequently a massive construction project has begun on a hi-tech third-generation installation, one that will be elevated on pylons and will be able to be jacked up over the years to keep it above the encroaching drifts. I'd noticed the bustling around me, and heard the whine of compressors and belt-driven machinery and the beeps of reversing tractors when I first arrived, but particulars like that had been lost in my stumbling awe as I tried to absorb the larger truth that I was really at the South Pole.

Now, with the first rush of blood behind me, I saw that the area in front of the dome was a vast sprawl of heavy equipment, building material, construction shacks, and work in progress. It was very late, but time is no more than a social convention in Antarctica, particularly here at the South Pole, where the summer sun doesn't even make a pretense of setting but circles the sky at the same constant elevation. It is as though it were perpetually noon. Work continues at a harried pace, as busy as an anthill, around the clock during the short summer season. A background hum filled the air like a lost chord.

Summer folk and visitors at Pole live outside the dome in a seasonal village of Jamesways or in futuristic blue modules known as hypertats. The hypertats were named for characters in the Flintstones cartoons: Fred, Wilma, Betty, and Barney. I was in Fred, cubicle number four. It was about the size of a first-class compartment in a Pullman sleeper: It had a bunk, a slender wardrobe, a nightstand, and a reading light. A curtain served as the door, and the big square window angled over the bed had Velcro strips around it so you could seal out the 24-hour daylight with a heavy patch of canvas. It was simple and nice and warm.

I unpacked my backpack, fastened the shade over the window, flicked on the reading lamp, and crawled into bed with the novel I hadn't read on the plane. It was well past two o'clock in the morning by now, but I was too revved up to sleep, or to read either for that matter. I just held the book for form's sake. My mind was trying to wrap itself around the fact that I was really at the South Pole.

I'd made it. I was here. The South Pole—end of the line. I could never be farther south than I was right now, nobody could. I cast my mind back to the time when I was a kid and we'd driven below the Mason-Dixon line and how I thought that had really been something; I'd been south. And now here I was in the heart of the Antarctic, almost 10,000 feet up, and 90° south latitude. The South Pole: the very bottom of the world. Sure, I hadn't exactly arrived through any heroic efforts on my own part, but all the same I was here and the occasion still seemed to call for a quiet satisfied smirk in my mental mirror. I should have known better. These are precisely the kind of hubris-filled moments that catapult you into one of life's humbling experiences. Mine wasn't long in coming.

First a bit of scene setting: the South Pole, as I mentioned, sits on a sheet of ice thousands of feet thick ("Ski South Pole," as the local T-shirts say: "Two inches of powder, two miles of base") where the temperature seldom rises to zero, even in summer, and plunges to –100°F or colder in winter. Obviously there is not going to be much in the way of surface water—every drop of water, whether it's for drinking, washing, or flushing toilets, has to be melted from ice. And with the cost of transporting fuel here being what it is, they try to be as economical with water as possible. Drink as much as you like—they encourage that for health reasons, because of the high altitude and bone-dry, bitterly cold climate—but showers are strictly rationed, as are laundries, and there are few toilets on base. We were told all this, and where everything was, during our induction briefing.

I'd paid good attention and had been particularly diligent in following the advice about avoiding altitude sickness: Eat light, take it easy for the first day or so at Pole, and drink plenty of fluids. During our arrival briefing I had probably downed a good two liters of water and juice, and had stopped in at the galley for another tall glass of juice after my visit to the pole. It seemed to be working like a charm—my gloating about having arrived at the South Pole was marvelously untroubled by headaches or any of the usual symptoms of altitude sickness. Pity my bladder hadn't expanded along with my ego.

I woke with a start at about four o'clock in the morning, absolutely bursting and panicking to remember where the toilet nearest to Fred was, and then recalling it was in another building about 50 yards away—that's 50 yards across the ice. I scrambled out of my nice warm bed, with no time to waste on details such as boots, trousers, parka, or regrets for not bringing my pee bottle with me. Truly, I hadn't thought I'd need it.

Seconds were precious. I bolted through the curtain, down the corridor, and flung open the door, squawking like a scalded cat in the sudden blinding eye-watering glare. My pupils shrank to mustard seeds. I clapped one hand over my watering snow-blinded eyes and plunged into the great South Pole outdoors and the incredible ball-shrinking shock of –67°F windchill, stumbling toward where I remembered the toilets were, dressed only in undershorts, and hopping barefoot across the burning-cold ice and yelping like an apprentice firewalker. I reached the door of the shed where the amenities block was, fumbled awkwardly with the handle, tripped over the sill in my haste, sprawled headlong on the floor, and then scampered the rest of the way on all fours, like a salamander, every last vestige of dignity gone.

But I made it. As I stood there contemplating the barefoot dash back across the ice, to where my warm bunk awaited, I thought of those words of Scott's: "The Pole, yes, but under very different circumstances from those expected."

CHAPTER TEN

Southern Exposure

SALLY'S GALLEY IS THE AFFECTIONATE NICKNAME GIVEN TO THE OLD CANTEEN at Pole, a cramped and crowded little eatery that made me think of an old-fashioned truck stop café along the Alaskan Highway, circa 1975, when I stepped in for breakfast the next morning. Dozens of well-used parkas hung from hooks along the walls, and an amiably gruff crew in Carhartt overalls sat at long Formica-topped tables wolfing down bacon and eggs or breakfast burritos and reading the world news on well-thumbed mimeographs of an abbreviated *New York Times*; the datelines were all two days old or older. I stepped up to the counter, picked up a plate, and ran my eyes over the mountains of eggs and bacon and sausages, pancakes and syrup, and the makings of those oversize burritos. I'd heard that the food was good and plentiful at Pole, but then I guess it had to be. Most of the people around me who were tucking into those huge platefuls of breakfast were about to start nine-hour shifts on the construction site, hanging iron, welding, and hammering in that bitter cold air outside, or, tougher still, carving out tunnels under the ice, for the fuel storage facilities, using those big loggers' chain saws. It was reckoned that each worker down here would put away about 5,000 calories' worth of groceries a day—and even so, most of them would lose 15 pounds or so over the course of the summer.

Scientists, technicians, and visiting writers didn't quite have the same calorific requirements. We loaded up our plates simply because the food was so damn good. I built myself a generously sized burrito and turned my greedy eyes to the pastry rack, which was piled high with fresh-baked muffins, scones, bread, and trays of thick, rich, moist cookies—oatmeal-raisin and chocolate chip were two varieties that caught my fancy. As I cast my longing eyes over them I remembered how generously full around the cheeks my face had appeared last night, when I'd seen it reflected in the mirrored ball atop the barber-striped South Pole. Even allowing for the fish-eye distortion, there was no question but that I'd been putting on weight lately and so I wavered a moment and then took two—just to go with my coffee.

I spotted "Sixty Years" Brian across the floor and waved; he was stoking up for his next shift with the chain saws down in the ice tunnels. I eased away from the counter, casting my eyes around the room, not too unhappy that there was no room at Brian's table, and sat down beside a weathered, sinewy, saturnine-looking man named Carlton, who was the construction boss. He was about 40 years old, a couple of years younger that me, but he looked about ten years tougher, his face deeply lined and tanned by long exposure to the biting winds and the intense solar rays at the South Pole. His eyes were red-rimmed and weary and a two-day growth of stubble darkened his cheeks. He told me, over a cup of hot black coffee, he'd had a total of about ten hours of sleep that week.

"About my average this time of year. Summer's the only time we can get anything done. So we just have to try to fit a year's worth of work into about three months. A couple of weeks ago I worked a 14-hour shift hanging iron in windchill that was 142°F below zero. It was awful, but it had to get done. We couldn't afford to lose that day."

He spoke with a soft southern inflection, which set him apart from most of the other Americans I'd met in Antarctica; they all tended to come from the North or West. But Carlton is a native of Pascagoula, Mississippi. He started out as a builder's laborer, working for his father when he was 11, and later became a plumber. He fell into Antarctic work by accident.

"I was at a bar one night in Mississippi ten, twelve years ago when a guy started telling me about some construction jobs down here. I was looking for a bit of a change. I applied and got a job at McMurdo the next summer. I liked Antarctica, but McMurdo was too big. I applied to work at Pole and found myself a home. I've been coming back here every summer for the past ten years now."

For the past couple of years he has been overseeing the construction project. He invited me along on his morning rounds.

"NASA tells me that this project is the closest thing on earth to building a space station," he said as we strode across the blinding white ice to his office in one of the Jamesways so we could get our hard hats. "They've taken a big interest what we're doing here—it's got a lot of applications for them. This is the perfect proving ground for building a base on Mars. We're at the end of the longest logistical chain on Earth—15,000 miles from the United States to McMurdo to here, and while we can move much of the bulky stuff to McMurdo by ship, the only feasible way to get it the rest of the way to the South Pole is on a Hercules. And that means that every single piece of this base had to be designed to fit into a 38-foot-long cargo bay—pretty much the way you'd have to design the parts of a space station to fit inside a rocket—and then assembled here in some of the most extreme conditions imaginable."

We picked up hard hats and entered a long, dark, steel-ribbed cavern cut deep in the ice, one of several such bunkers at Pole, each nearly a thousand feet long and carved out by chain saw. These are where the fuel depots and the base's new one-megawatt power plant will be housed. He flicked a switch. A chain of light bulbs stretched along the walls, illuminating a walkway. We followed it past a long line of ghostly-looking fuel tanks.

"Each one of those represents a plane load."

The air down there was as still as a mausoleum, and very, very cold. My breath came in dense clouds that I imagined I could hear crackling into ice crystals.

A few hundred meters away, in cold, blinding sunshine, ironworkers scrambled over the massive pylons, sunk deep in the ice, on which the new complex would be built. We stopped in at the garage and workshop, where tradesmen were putting in wiring and pipes. Wherever Carlton went, every few paces somebody popped up with questions, unrolled blueprints for him to examine, or presented him with some new problem to solve.

"You know, the first time I ever saw the plans for this place they were sketched on a cocktail napkin in a bar in Denver," he told me, after sending somebody on their way with fresh answers. He paused to take a tin of tobacco out of his pocket, and put a pinch in his cheek. "I had no idea then how it was going to take over my life. Even back in the States I'm working on this seven days a week. Each season's work has to be planned at least a year in advance, down to the tiniest nut and wrench, schedules and rosters worked out, flights arranged, so we can be sure that everything and everyone is going to be here when we need it—not a minute before, and not a minute too late. There's just no time to waste."

He was a busy man; I left him to his scheduling nightmares and drifted back to the galley for a cup of coffee and a couple of chocolate chip cookies as a restorative, and then gave some thought to trying to find the meteorology office. It was surprisingly hard to find, tucked away at the end of a dark and narrow alleyway in the maze of structures inside the dome. I had to ask directions twice, but I found my way there eventually, notepad in hand, ostensibly with the worthy journalistic objective of discussing global warming, but really with a childish curiosity to see how cold it might get while I was here at the South Pole.

The coldest temperature I'd ever experienced was –43°F, according to the battered old thermometer outside our kitchen window one bitter January night back in 1969 when I was ten and dreaming that one day I might go to Antarctica. I wanted to know if I had a chance of breaking my record. This seemed my best shot. I was hardly likely to do it living in South Australia, and Mawson base, even in winter, had never experienced temperatures colder than –35°F.

The weather column in the *Antarctic Sun* a couple of weeks earlier had given me encouragement when it reported a temperature of –84°F for the South Pole, and while it was too much to hope that such a grandiose reading would be repeated this far into summer, –45°F seemed a fair bet.

"I'm afraid the odds aren't good," the senior meteorologist, a guy named Dar, said when I sheepishly revealed the true purpose of my visit. "This time of year it stays a pretty constant –20°F to –30°F, although the windchill is a lot colder. I suppose you're not counting windchill?"

"Nope. Doesn't it get colder at 'night'?"

He shook his head. "There's not much diurnal variation. The sun stays a constant 22 degrees above the horizon. I'm afraid this is pretty much it." He glanced at his computer. "Twenty-eight below zero, right now, with a windchill of –57°F."

"Oh."

Suddenly his face brightened with a new thought. "Hey! Wait a second—didn't I see you going around with Carlton Walker?"

"Yeah, he was showing me around the construction site."

"Did he take you down into any of the tunnels?"

"Sure."

"Congratulations, then! You broke your old record. The air in those tunnels remains constantly at the South Pole's average year-round temperature of almost 60 below."

I went away satisfied, although my new record seemed decidedly bush league at a place where people colloquially dropped the minus when referring to temperatures and spoke casually of winter temperatures in the 80s, 90s, and "when it gets over 100." Dar's own record was –107°F. "Nobody comes down here wanting to record a winter low of –99°F. Everybody wants those magic three-digit readings. The coldest it has ever been here at Pole is –117°F, and we're all just dying to be on hand to record –118°F."

I'd heard tales of spit snap-freezing in the air and landing with a crackle on the ice. Dar laughed and told me that was a bit of an exaggeration. He'd made the bravest of experiments, stepping outside the dome one time when the temperature was "down in the 90s" and urinating in the snow. It froze almost instantly—but only once it was on the ground, not in the air.

I envied his raffish experiences as a winterer. Much as I enjoy being in Antarctica, though, I know I could never take that ultimate step and winter on The Ice. The idea fascinates me—the camaraderie of the base, the sense of isolation, what it must be like to step outside the dome here and see the stars as sharp as needles in the crystal-clear hundred-degree-below-zero night—but in my heart of hearts I know that I couldn't do it. It is something I would like to *have* done, rather than something I would ever really want to do. I'd like to have the cachet and the memories, to have *been* a winterer rather than to *be* one. When it comes down to it the cost is just too high—eight months of your life, at least, and more likely a full year, whether it's here at Pole or McMurdo or Mawson or wherever. Once that last ship or plane has departed, there is no going home; you're sealed in for the duration, for better or worse. There is no changing your mind, no deciding after six weeks that you've had enough, got the gist of what overwintering was all about, and will now move on to something else.

What's more, you'll find it a very changed White South to the one you knew in summer. Summer months in Antarctica are full of breathtaking scenery and glorious outdoorsy travel and adventure—that is, of course, if you happen to belong to the privileged scientific classes or are one of their hangers-on—but nobody goes anywhere during the long polar night. Everything stops. For the most part wintering is simply a matter of garrisoning the base, keeping things functioning, until the sun returns in the spring and outdoor work can resume. For me those long dormitory months, stuck indoors, wouldn't be Antarctica so much as an exercise in human dynamics and close confinement; you could be anywhere, in outer space or a nuclear submarine or a Cold War military bunker. No doubt it would be an interesting experience, but with the exception of those few quirky bits of local color—those mind-boggling temperatures outside, for instance—not a quintessentially Antarctic one, or at least not enough of one for me to want to trade away those months of life for them. I love to travel, to move, to be out roaming and seeing and doing. Life is short; the world is big and full of interesting things. One of Antarctica's great lessons is a renewed appreciation for them—all the sights and colors and diversity around us that we come to take for granted in our day-to-day lives suddenly seem rich and bold after Antarctica's frosty sterility.

I like my Antarctica sparkling white, blue, and violet, pretty and bright. I'm just as happy (almost) to hear about it from those who paid their admission price, did their time. And so I ambled around the base that morning, talking to old hands who'd wintered there, about the indoor Antarctica, of plastic flowers and the video library and the galley and the bar.

People seem to take up smoking at Pole, rather than quit, the station leader Katie told me (the station shop is extremely well stocked), and those who try to remain closet smokers are soon found out; there are no secrets in an isolated community of a few dozen people huddled beneath a dome 176 feet in diameter. The walls have eyes. But along with this group omniscience is an understanding that whatever happens on The Ice stays on The Ice.

It has happened that some people have found out, too late, that they made a terrible mistake in trying to winter here. A few years back one of the kitchen hands up and quit in the middle of the winter, after a series of spats with one of her colleagues. No amount of convincing would induce her to return to work, and of course she couldn't go home, making her resignation more of a permanent strike. The station leader that year was a military man, a martinet disciplinarian known as Colonel Klink to his charges, and irritated by her intransigence he confined her to her quarters, allowing her entry to the galley at mealtimes only and no access to base entertainments such as videos or the library. Or at least he tried to—how well he was able to enforce his maximum security, solitary confinement policy was a matter of debate, but it must have been a deeply unpleasant few months, and at the end of it the woman was presented with an invoice for her food and lodging dating back to the moment she downed tools. She refused to pay. How far it all went down the legal avenues back in the States was also the subject of gossipy conjecture, but everyone agreed that the bill was eventually withdrawn.

On a happier note, the winter calendar is filled with parties, the South Pole season. A few months later I received an elaborate invitation, by e-mail, to a cocktail party at Pole; RSVP. I had to pass on my regrets, but later I received, by e-mail, a nice batch of photos from the event. They were taken outside the radio shed, in the unheated confines of the dome, everyone cheery, huddled together in their bulky parkas, holding their breath in the –90° cold. Breathing creates so much steam at those temperatures that if they hadn't been holding their breaths the picture would have been totally obscured by the mist.

And then there is the South Pole's famous and exclusive 300 Club, admission to which is open only on the coldest days of the long polar winter, when the temperature plunges to –100°F or colder. To join, you and the other initiates must sit naked in the sauna with the thermostat cranked up to 200°F until you can stand the heat no longer, and then out you come, running out of the accommodation block, out of the dome itself, and into the bitter dark outside for a sprint to the ceremonial pole and back—buck naked except for shoes and perhaps a scarf over your mouth to protect your lungs against the razor-cold air. Again, a few months later, when I was sitting in the pleasant green of an English summer, one of the astronomers, a guy named Dana, e-mailed me some photos of the day a bunch of them joined the club—and quite G-rated pictures they were too; there was so much steam coming off the sauna-heated bodies as they dashed into the spooky blackness beyond the portal there were only the haziest outlines of human bodies. "It wasn't so bad going out," he told me, "It only gets tough over the last 50 yards coming back in—you really start to feel the cold then."

Dana also e-mailed me a photo of the last plane taking off from the Pole, and the little knot of soon to be winterers standing outside the dome, waving farewell. There was wistfulness in it, the soft late-season light giving the scene a touch of autumnal melancholy that together with the isolation and circumstances confirmed me in my feelings that I wasn't cut out to be a winterer; looking at that photo I knew I would definitely have wanted to be on that plane. And at the same time it provided a teaser, a hint of some of the beautiful aspects of Antarctica I'd never see.

That soft light—such a contrast to the blinding glare over the Pole in summer—was the beginning of the spectacular three-week sunset the high-latitude Antarcticans enjoy every autumn. As the never-setting summer sun circles lower in the sky, it casts an increasingly gentle glow over the landscape that as the days pass runs through the suite of warmer tones—gold, pink, orange, and red as the sun hugs closer to the horizon, then shifting to mauves and violets and duskier pinks and lavender as it drops below it, and the sky overhead grows deep. It is the longest of good-byes.

And then the stars come out. If there were anything that might induce me to sacrifice eight months of my life confined to an Antarctic base, it would be to have a glimpse of the stars in the South Pole night. To me, nothing is more exhilarating that looking up to see the Milky Way sprawling across the sky in vast stellar clouds. The best I've ever seen it is while camping alone in Australia's Great Sandy Desert, more than a hundred miles from any other person or dwelling. It was magnificent, the swirling galactic arms of the Milky Way stretching across the sky, the Magellanic Clouds, the Southern Cross and the other constellations so thick with stars that you could pick out their shapes only by choosing the brightest. What must it look like from the South Pole at night—10,000 feet up, literally thousands of miles from any dust or light haze, and in the bitterly cold, stable, and bone-dry polar air.

I'll never see it, but had a vicarious glimpse as I wandered through the rabbit warren of scientists' offices in the dome and chanced to look at a bulletin board. Among the montage of postcards, mostly of bright sunshine and palms and European capitals, was a stunning deep space photograph of a dense cloud of stars against a rich black void, with a sinuous wave of what appeared to be green cosmic gas running through it.

"That's beautiful," I remarked and, seeing a German physicist named Stefan sitting at a desk nearby, asked: "Can you tell me what nebula that is?"

He glanced up at the photo and laughed. "That's not a nebula; I took that picture myself just outside the dome last winter during an aurora. See, you can see the buildings along the bottom."

Sure enough, there they were: tiny, dark silhouettes of rooftops and radio antennas I hadn't noticed earlier. It was truly unearthly. For an astronomer, Stefan explained, being at the South Pole is the next best thing to actually being in space.

Astronomers have been working at the South Pole in a modest way since the 1960s, but it wasn't until the Hubble Space Telescope began bringing back those breathtaking images of deep space that scientists began to appreciate the Pole's potential as an Earthbound viewing platform. For all its magnificence, the Hubble telescope is hugely expensive and difficult to maintain, and since there is only the one instrument floating out there, it is difficult to share it around with everybody who wants to use it.

"But the viewing conditions here at Pole are nearly as good as those in space," an astronomy professor named Jeffrey, from Carnegie-Mellon University, told me later that day as he showed me around the futuristic observatory complex, newly erected at the fringes of the base, about half a mile from the dome. "There's no water vapor or dust, and the cold, clear air is incredibly stable; there's no distortion. Compared with other places on Earth, looking at the stars from here is like wiping the mist away from your car window—suddenly you can really see. This is the perfect window into space."

Since 1991 an array of high-tech radio telescopes has been springing up at Pole, exotic bits of technology that look more like modern sculptures than a layman's idea of an astronomer's telescope and bear inscrutable acronym names such as VIPER and DASI and AST/RO and AMANDA.

"The acronym doesn't mean anything, it just sounds good," Jeffrey laughed as he showed me around VIPER. "Its predecessor was COBRA." VIPER was a supersensitive instrument, capable of looking back 13 billion years to the dawn of time, and scanning the cosmic background radiation left over from the big bang and discerning for subtle temperature variations—as small as one 100,000th of a degree—caused by the uneven distribution of matter in the first few moments of the universe. These primeval seeds are what eventually curdled into vast structures such as galaxies, stars, and planets.

Down the hall, a team of astronomers from Harvard monitored a submillimeter radio telescope called AST/RO. It was trained that morning on a stellar nursery, a gigantic cloud of gas and dust where stars are formed in our own galaxy. It was marked on the charts as NGC-6334, but more evocatively known as the Cat's Paw Nebula and located near the stinger of Scorpio's tail.

"We're much too late to study the cloud that formed our sun," Chris, an astronomer from Harvard, told me. "But we can observe the same process happening in other places around the Milky Way."

Still another telescope, known by the acronym DASI, listens to the echo of the big bang, looking for clues to the size and shape of the universe, how it formed, and how it might all end.

The most bizarre is AMANDA—an acronym for Antarctic Muon and Neutrino Detector Array—a gigantic "telescope" that isn't pointed into the sky at all, but consists of a ring of 19 holes bored more than a mile deep into the ice, into which long chains of optical sensors, resembling Christmas tree lights, have been lowered. The object is to detect elusive subatomic particles called neutrinos, using the body of the Earth itself as a giant cosmic ray filter—cosmic rays being absorbed by the rocky mass—and the thick polar ice cap as a kind of lens. These mysterious unstoppable entities—nobody knows if they even have mass—slip through the universe like ghosts yet give off telltale blue flickers as they pass through the ice and from which astronomers believe they can glean information about the birth of black holes, supernova explosions, and the power sources at the heart of galaxies.

As I walked back to the dome for dinner that evening, past the ceremonial and geographic poles, I marveled again at Antarctica's capacity to enrapture and keep its wonders as fresh as the air and snow itself. A century after Scott and Amundsen planted their flags here at the South Pole, what the Edwardian world regarded as the Last Place on Earth has become a convenient low-budget alternative to outer space and stepladder to the outermost reaches of the universe.

Sunday is a day of rest at Pole, even during the frantic summer season, and as I walked to breakfast from my hypertat that morning, past the little suburbia of Jamesways where the shift workers were still sleeping, looking around me at all the heavy construction equipment sitting idle after its week of round-the-clock activity, I found the quiet stillness seemed strangely unnatural. I'd grown rather used to the idea of Pole as human anthill. We played a game of soccer later that afternoon—"Polies" (meaning tradesmen and base personnel) versus scientists.

I was collared for the scientists' side; they wanted some size against the lineup of 210-pound construction workers they were playing against. We won a close match, although I made no contribution to the result. For not only am I a lousy soccer player, with only the haziest idea of the rules and notions of offside, but I lacked the locals' unique skills—the deft ball handling in mountaineering boots, and running and kicking and playing the bad bounces on the ice.

Afterward, Jeffrey—the astronomy professor—and I got a couple of mountain bikes he and another astronomer had brought down for the summer and raced each other around the world at the ceremonial and geographic South Poles—all the while scoffing at Lance Armstrong for making such a big deal about racing around France in three weeks, when the pair of us could cover the world, or at least cross every degree of longitude, in as little as 15 seconds. We raced east to west, west to east, cracked jokes about whether we should stop and adjust our watches for the various time zones we passed through and generally played the Pole for all it was worth, quirky humor wise, before retiring into the dome, cold and wet from spills in the snow, to sit down over coffee and a stack of those thick rich Sally's Galley chocolate chip cookies; like a couple of seven-year-olds at recess, except for the black coffee, maybe.

It was my last night at Pole. After dinner an Australian physicist named Darryn came up and said there were a few cool things around the place I hadn't see yet. He'd checked out a snowmobile and a radio and suggested we go for a drive. I bundled into every bit of warm gear I had; the windchill outside was about –60°F, but when you added the wind in your face on a snowmobile it would be much worse. We set off, ski goggles on our faces, roaring down the ice runway, heading north—naturally—toward an empty horizon of blue and white, where ice meets sky.

The South Pole may have a wonderful resonance as a ne plus ultra travel destination but it doesn't have a lot to recommend it visually. But as with a lot of things about Antarctica, you have to look beneath the surface, in this case to where we were heading: the buried remains of an old C-130 cargo plane that had crashed here in the early 1970s. Nobody had been injured, but the plane was a write-off. They dragged it a couple of miles past the end of the runway and left it to the eternally drifting snows. By now it was buried about 30 feet deep, and adventurous "Polies" had dug a shaft down to the cockpit and made it into a sort of Bohemian attraction.

We had a smooth, fast ride down the graded runway, but past the end of it there was nothing but rough sastrugi (rock-hard ridges of snow, sculpted by the wind) that bounced the snowmobile around like a dinghy on a rough sea.

A quarter of a century of constantly drifting snow had buried the plane wreck so deep that a cairn of snow, left as a marker, was the only way to find it. Nobody had visited the place for at least a year. The cairn looked derelict and wind-worn. A battered old shovel had been thrust into the snow, and a plastic bucket with a frozen bit of rope on it was stuck in the ice nearby. We wrestled them loose and began to dig, taking turns with the shovel. It was hard work in the cold, thin air. Our hard breathing and the scrape of the shovel were the only sounds in that immense silence.

We dug down about a foot before the shovel thumped against something hard. It sounded hollow. It took a few more minutes and some hard scraping to clear away the crusty snow and reveal a trapdoor made of old plywood. I used the blade of the shovel to pry it loose. Darryn curled his mittened fingers around the edge and gave a heave. The trapdoor opened into a dark, cold, and narrow pit that seemed dismayingly deep. An aluminum ladder plumbed its depths.

I sat nervously on the edge of the hole, legs dangling, and dropped the shovel into the gloom, after which I wiggled my booted feet tentatively at the uppermost rungs on the ladder. Feeling committed now that I'd tossed that shovel into the pit, I eased my weight onto the ladder.

A few shaky minutes later I was standing at the bottom. Darryn lowered the bucket on its rope, and I began to fill it with the older and more crumbly snow from the bottom of the pit. There wasn't much room to work down there. I yelled when the bucket was full. Darryn hoisted it, dumped it, and lowered it down again. We went on like this until I had scraped clear a second trapdoor. This one was frozen in and even harder to pry open.

When I did, though, a truly spooky blackness yawned between my feet. It looked as cold and dark and inviting as a grave. I heard Darryn clambering down the ladder above me, bringing the two heavy flashlights. He flicked his on and slid into the pit with the easy familiarity of a local.

"Come on in!" His voice echoed eerily. I took a deep breath and felt for a foothold in the blackness, wondering if this was such a great idea. A moment later I was sitting on cold, hard ice where the seats used to be, looking at a ruins of the cockpit by the beam of a flashlight. It looked ancient, the thick coating of frost taking the place of cobwebs. Military stenciling gave it a creepy, secretive, apocalyptic feel. It was like something out of *X-Files*—the part where you yell at the TV screen: "Scully, don't go in there!"

I was just thinking that when I heard a rustle, turned, and saw Darryn's boots disappearing into a narrow opening, about 16 inches high, that led to the cargo hold. "You can get back here too!"

I'm not claustrophobic, but getting down on my belly and following him through that slit wasn't easy. It opened up to a long, low cavern that stretched the length of the wrecked plane. It was high enough so that you could sit up. It was bitterly cold in there, deathly still and black, and you could sense the immense weight of the ice pressing down. Flashlight beams cut through our steamy clouds of breath and revealed pipes encrusted with ice, more of that military stenciling—serial numbers, acronyms, and various incomprehensible safety warnings—that seemed as mysterious as runes, as well as the scribbled graffiti of earlier visitors. I saw Peter Hillary's name; one of the Polies must have taken him out here when he skied to the Pole.

Darryn produced a marker and we left our autographs for posterity and crawled back out. Dazzling sunlight and wind and open empty horizons never looked so good. Etiquette required us each to haul up three pails of snow, by way of maintenance. We did that, replaced the wooden traps, and stuck the shovel back in the cairn.

"Come on, let's go," Darryn said, as he clambered onto the snowmobile "There's something else you've got to experience down here."

We drove another few miles farther into the void, bouncing and lurching on the sastrugi until finally the last vestige of South Pole's buildings had slipped beneath the horizon. Darryn stopped and switched off the engine. Silence fell like soft, heavy curtains. I stood up on the seat and ran my eyes along the planet's emptiest horizon, turning a full 360°, seeing nothing but the flat line where white meets turquoise.

Unless you've been out there on that high polar plateau, it is impossible to comprehend such desolation or such stillness. I have traveled through the heart of Australia's Nullarbor Plain, and although this vast waterless limestone cap, 800 miles across, is by any other standard an incredibly eerie and hostile void, it is as lush and lively as the Amazon rain forest compared with the South Pole's emptiness. The Nullarbor at least has its thin desert grasses, meager soil, a few lizards and snakes, rodents, and birds; there are sounds and smells and the sun's life-giving warmth out there. This crystalline desert was truly lifeless, a sterile plain of ice two miles thick and a cold, empty sky overhead, nothing more.

After a few moments I became aware of a faint throbbing sound. I glanced around wondering where it was coming from, but then the penny dropped: The mysterious sound was my own heartbeat. We stood and listened to our breath and heartbeats in the world's loneliest and quietest place. I let it all seep in—the turquoise color of the sky along the horizon, the texture of the sastrugi, the magnificent simplicity—so I could draw on it later, in the noise and confusion back in the real world.

I left the South Pole on Monday afternoon. McMurdo by comparison seemed huge and bustling, and the air felt balmy and soft after the thin frigidity of the

South Pole. In the few short days that I'd been away, a warm had melted much of the snow from the hills around the base, leaving them black and bare, and Mac-Town's streets muddy. Road crews were grading them and the chirp of reversing tractors was everywhere, and they sounded to me like the first crickets in spring.

CHAPTER ELEVEN

The Right Altitude

OBSERVATION HILL IS A 700-FOOT-HIGH VOLCANIC CONE THAT OVERLOOKS McMurdo Station and Scott's old Discovery Hut and was used by the men on those early expeditions as a lookout point because it commands a sweeping view of the Ross Ice Shelf, over which the sledging parties returning from the south would be approaching—or not as was the case with Scott's polar party in 1912. Those of his men who kept a forlorn vigil up here later built a cross on the peak to commemorate their five dead comrades and inscribed the famous lines from Tennyson's Ulysses: "To strive, to seek, to find and not to yield."

I strove up there myself a couple of days after my return from Pole, partly to take an admiring look out over the ice shelf over which I had just come, but mostly for a better view of the gleaming spectacle of Mount Erebus. Dazzling white and shaped a bit like Japan's sacred Mount Fuji, except much more massive, Erebus is quite simply one of the world's most beautiful and evocative mountains: a live volcano at the bottom of the world, puffing smoke and ash into the clear skies more than two and a half miles above the shores of the frozen Ross Sea. It is Antarctica's Statue of Liberty—the magnificent spectacle that has welcomed and awed generations of explorers as they sailed up to this part of the continent and been an encouraging beacon, visible many miles out over the Ice Shelf, for homeward-bound sledging parties as they trudged north, for they knew that their base, friends, food, and warmth would be found at the mountain's foot.

It was discovered in 1841 by the Victorian explorer Capt. James Ross when he and his men became the first humans ever to sail into the vast silent ice-strewn sea that now bears his name. As they sailed along the never-before-sighted coast, on a continent that wasn't on the maps, at a higher latitude south than anyone in history had ever reached, they could hardly believe their eyes when in the midst of all this they came upon an enormous rumbling volcano as well, fire in a world of ice.

Erebus was the guardian of the underworld in classical mythology and a perfect name for the huge, fiery mountain on the edge of a frozen and forbidding continent. The mountain's slightly lower and dormant cousin is called Mount Terror. Splendid names, but it was only lucky chance things worked out so well in that department: However fitting the classical allusions and suggestion of medieval fright, the prosaic truth is that the mountains were actually named for Captain Ross's two ships—HMS *Erebus* and HMS *Terror*. As I climbed back down the hill I thought that romantic posterity could be grateful that Ross wasn't in command of the *Mayflower* and the *Beagle* at the time.

Rick and Rich, my roommates when I first arrived at McMurdo, were somewhere high up on Erebus right now, working with a team of fellow geologists out of a field hut just below the volcano's summit. I was going to join them but first I had to attend "Altitude Class," a practical lecture on altitude sickness and how to recognize and treat it in the field. Attendance is required for anyone working at a high-altitude field camp in Antarctica. (It isn't required, however, for those going to the South Pole, since that is a major base with its own hospital and doctor.)

Altitude sickness is a serious problem in Antarctica, its effects aggravated by the extreme cold, arid climate as well as Antarctica's unique position at the bottom of the globe. The spinning of the Earth makes the atmospheric column swell up and become thicker at the Equator but considerably thinner at the poles. What this means is that while the South Pole, say, is 9,301 feet above sea level, the physiological effect on your body will be as if you were at an altitude of anywhere between 10,000 feet to as much as 12,600 feet, depending on the atmospheric pressure on the day. There was a TV screen in the galley at Pole that along with the temperature, wind, and windchill, also gave the day's "pressure altitude."

On the summit of Mount Erebus the air can feel as razor thin as that on a 15,000-foot peak elsewhere on the globe. McMurdo—and indeed the vast majority of bases around Antarctica—is at sea level, so a helicopter flight from here directly to the Erebus hut, which also happens to be the highest field camp on the continent, can seriously knock you for a loop. Symptoms can range from mild shortness of breath to dizziness and thumping headaches, and ratchet all too rapidly on up to life-threatening conditions such as pulmonary and cerebral edema. The best remedy is to get to a lower altitude quickly. The Americans had been doing a lot of work at high altitude around the continent that summer—mostly at Pole and with the Russians at their remote Vostok base, and had already done a number of emergency evacuations.

Altitude Class was held at Byrd Field Camp, the same venue where Happy Camper School held its introductory lesson. Most of the pupils consisted of carpenters bound for Vostok, about 11,000 feet up on the plateau, where they'd be building a new base to replace the decrepit Russian installation there.

Over the next hour the instructor, an Alaskan mountain guide named Steve, took us through all the nasty eventualities that could await us up there, the need to take it easy and drink plenty of fluids, and then introduced us to Diamox, a drug that is supposed to help prevent altitude sickness, or at least mask its symptoms. I had heard about Diamox already at the South Pole, where it had been urged on new arrivals, although I had passed on it and never suffered at all.

Finally he showed us how to operate a Gamow Bag—a collapsible hypobaric chamber, used in emergencies in high-altitude mountaineering camps where rescue could be hours or days away. It was about the size of a fat man's coffin and made of heavy-gauge airtight fabric. The victim is sealed up inside, while a colleague works a foot pump to raise air pressure inside the bag, artificially lowering the effective altitude for the person inside. It looked about as much fun as being buried alive.

We signed off on the sheet Steve passed around, and spilled outside into the balmy sunshine of an Antarctic spring. The temperature was comfortably above freezing and felt warm. Parkas were unzipped, or even left back on their wall hooks in favor of wool shirts with their sleeves rolled up. There were puddles in the tire tracks on the streets. The high, thin, icy sterility of the mountains seemed very far away.

I hadn't been at all troubled by altitude at the South Pole, had even played soccer and done some vigorous shoveling to get to the trapdoor that led to that buried C-130, but not being troubled once by high altitude is no guarantee that it won't happen next time. It's like seasickness that way. It can happen to anyone, at any time, and being in shape or being a mountaineer doesn't necessarily make much difference. At dinner that night I learned that Jean, one of the geologists up on Mout Erebus, had flown back to town suffering from altitude-induced headaches and nausea that had made life too unpleasant for her to continue working up there. Food for thought to accompany my meal: Jean was an accomplished climber who had summited Mout Kilimanjaro in Africa. I know they said fitness was no real guarantee that you wouldn't get altitude sickness, but all the same when I heard that I wished I'd done a bit more about keeping in shape, held to those long-lapsed New Year's resolutions.

We were late getting away the next morning, with low cloud and murky visibility and mists from the melting snow and ice socking in the airfield in the morning, but by early afternoon it had all cleared away and we lifted off. There were three of us aboard—Maria, the NATIONAL GEOGRAPHIC photographer, a mountaineer named Sarah, and me. We were bound for a little camp on Fang Glacier, about 10,500 feet up the mountain, rather than the geologist's hut nearly 1,500 feet higher: Because of the field camp's extreme elevation and dodgy accessibility for rescue flights, anyone working on the volcano's upper flanks first has to spend a couple of days acclimatizing at Fang.

It was a heady flight, but the weirdest thing about it was how quickly you lose all sense of the mountain. We had a glorious view of it, puffing serenely, when we lifted off, but as we circled around, gaining elevation and drawing ever closer, it simply became too big and ungraspable; it absorbed us. Erebus is what geologists call a strato-volcano, a towering giant akin to those huge volcanoes—Kilimanjaro and Mount Kenya—in the East African Rift Valley. When I'd asked Rick to put Erebus's size into context for me he told me to imagine nine Mount Fujis all clumped together like so much clay, and then I'd get some idea of its sheer bulk and mass. I was imagining it now, to the roar of the chopper blades, as we flew above huge, steep snowfields and over rocky abutments. It was like being an ant and crawling up a mountain in one of Bierstadt's more histrionic paintings. What you could see in front of your face was awesome enough, but what was implied by it all was so much grander still.

It was Shackleton who sent the first party to the summit back in 1908, a hair-raising adventure featuring a team of six Edwardian alpinists, using the crude makeshift climbing gear of the day, slipping and sliding up the mountain, narrowly avoiding crevasses, and nearly perishing in a blizzard. One of the climbers, a young aristocrat named Brocklehurst, succumbed to altitude sickness and had to wait on a lower ledge while the rest of the party gained the summit and became not only the first alpinists ever to conquer an Antarctic peak, but also the first human eyes to gaze down into Erebus's deep smoky crater and see at the very bottom its crowning jewel: a perpetually bubbling lake of molten lava, one of the very few such geological marvels anywhere on Earth.

Their climb had taken several days and nearly cost them their lives; our helicopter ascent to Fang Glacier took about 20 minutes. The pilot dropped us off beside three Scott tents that sat lonely and existential in the middle of a glacier. Except for the meagerness of the air, which we breathed in curious experimental breaths, we didn't seem all that high at first. There were no sweeping panoramas spreading out beneath our feet, no feeling of clinging by our fingernails to the upper flanks of a volcano, just a broad and gently sloping plain of glacier ice stretching out around us and polished sky overhead. One side of the glacier was bounded by a steep, rocky hill that could have been anywhere from a hundred feet high to a thousand. There was no judging scale up here. The summit was hidden somewhere behind this hill, and somewhere fairly close, too, judging by the pall of white smoke that drifted like low cloud overhead.

A formidable jagged spine of rock, which I learned was Fang Ridge, bounded the other side of the glacier, about half a mile away from the camp. What I didn't know then, but learned later, was that Fang Ridge was all that remained of the volcano's original crater rim, which had been blown apart when Erebus erupted catastrophically about three-quarters of a million years ago. Everything above us had been built since then. The smoke and the occasional rumble of thunder out of a clear blue sky was an unnerving reminder that Mount Erebus was still very much a work in progress.

I didn't know, either, not yet, that if I hiked over to Fang Ridge, clambered up a low spot on its wall, and peered over, I'd have found the scary, precipitous view I'd been expecting. As it was I stood by my tent, watching the helicopter shrink to a dot in the sky and feeling slightly disappointed that after so much expectation of being 10,500 feet high on the mountain that all our views still seemed to be generally upward, not out; there were no sweeping vistas. But as I gazed down the length of the glacier, along its gentle slope and let my eyes ramble into the violet distance, I suddenly felt a vague loftiness, the way you can sense the proximity of the beach and the seaside just by the look and color of the air when you are still a few blocks away. Our glacier gave the impression of flowing down and melding with a curiously textured snowfield. It was a while before I realized that the "snowfield" was actually cloud bank spreading away beneath us.

There was nobody at Fang but the three of us. We set about moving in, each of us claiming a tent. Each tent had its own two-burner Coleman stove and a couple of wooden ration boxes crammed with freeze-dried dinners, pasta, frozen meat, chocolate and biscuits, a nest of cooking pots, crockery, and a collection of insulated mugs. Just like Happy Camper School, except we were on our own.

I filled a cooking pot with snow and lit the stove, and while I waited for it to boil, I used a whisk broom to sweep the floor clear of ice crystals, rolled out my sleeping pad and bag and folding camp chair, and arranged a pile of new paperbacks I'd treated myself to before I left Australia. According to regulations, we were to spend 48 hours here, taking it easy, breathing in that crystal-clear mountain air and building red blood cells: tough work, but it had to be done. When I first learned I'd have to cool my heels here for a couple of days of acclimatization rather than head straight to the grand sights at the summit, I'd been a bit nonplussed, but now, settled comfortably in my tent, with a steaming mug of tea and a chocolate bar and a pile of unread paperbacks at hand, and a whole 48 hours of guilt-free sloth stretching out in front of me as unblemished as those cloud banks, I decided that acclimatization was a very good thing indeed and wished that there was some kind of a career to be had in doing it. This was just the sort of thing I knew I'd be good at.

We all had dinner that night in Sarah's tent and afterward walked over to Fang Ridge. It was an easy stroll across the ice, nearly level and with no crevasses to worry about. We had all already made the happy discovery that the day's sudden shift in altitude wasn't causing any problems, beyond a little shortness of breath. And even that was swiftly forgotten once we scrambled up a low point on the ridge and looked out.

This was where the view was. There was no more kidding ourselves we weren't high on a mountain. From here the world fell away from our boot soles in one frighteningly long, heart-stopping plunge, more than 10,000 feet to the shores of the Ross Sea, a smooth blue surface visible between a flock of puffy clouds that looked no larger than the backs of distant sheep. At the same time, it looked close enough, and the slope steep enough, that you could almost believe it possible to lob a rock from here and make it splash. I tried tossing a lump of gray volcanic tuff out as far as I could before peering cautiously over the edge, counting as it free-fell through space. I was up to "six chimpanzee" before it took the first bounce on the wind-packed snow and began skipping down the slope like a bullet, taking what looked like hundred-yard ricochets at a whack, until it finally shattered soundlessly on an outcrop a long, long way below. But as far away as that was, it wasn't even a tiny fraction of the way to the bottom. The sea remained as distant and aloof as a painting. I might as well have tried to hit the moon with a slingshot.

The two days at Fang passed as agreeably as the laziest of summery beach weekends. Nobody felt ill, the food was good and plentiful, the weather stayed clear and mild, the hush over the glacier punctured only by the occasional thundery boom from the unseen summit of the volcano. Between meals and afternoon snoozes, I generally carried my camp chair out to the precipice and improved my mind with books such as Perry Mason in *The Case of the Blonde Bonanza.*

I could have happily built red blood cells for the whole rest of the summer, but all good things come to an end. The helicopter swung around late in the afternoon on the third day to take us the rest of the way up to the field camp. The pilot was John, the same big bearded John who had flown me up to that high rocky ledge in the Britannia Range, except on this flight to the summit camp he was breathing supplemental oxygen. It was a short hop, but a dramatic one with a view of the huge smoking maw of the volcano. The field camp was on a snowy ledge, a few hundred feet below the crater rim. It was a cheerful looking cluster of mountain tents, an old Jamesway half buried in a drift that served as storage shed, larder, and toilet, and a simple timber-framed hut with several snowmobiles parked in front of it.

Like the camp at Darwin Glacier, the Erebus hut had an alpine feel with its rustic old stove and woodsy kitchen, ice axes and plastic mountaineering boots parked by the door, and the shelf of dog-eared novels and magazines for filling in the idle days when the weather turned sour. The superb view of the summit and the spectroscope pointing out the window made me think of those spyglasses they used to have on the hotel verandas in Grindelwald back in the 1920s and '30s when tourists amused themselves watching climbers try to scale the Eiger (and maybe fall off).

This instrument had a loftier purpose: It was trained on the gas clouds that billowed from the volcano. Erebus is by far Antarctica's biggest polluter, an enormous smokestack pouring 30 tons of hydrofluoric acid, 60 tons of hydrochloric acid, 70 tons of sulfur dioxide, and 200 tons of carbon monoxide into the clear Antarctic skies. Those sulfur dioxide emissions alone are roughly on a par with one of America's largest coal-fired power plants.

"It would be nice to know what Mother Nature is doing down here if we are to put man's impact in perspective," the man sitting beside the spectroscope explained, as he jotted down notes and readings.

He was an expatriate New Zealander named Phillip, now a professor of geochemistry at New Mexico Tech, who had spent 30 seasons working on Mount Erebus. He had a droll manner and a baroque sense of humor. His long tenure, mostly here on Erebus, made him something of an Antarctic grandee, and he certainly looked the part: tall, lean, and elegant with a summer growth of dark beard.

After so many years he very much considered Erebus to be his mountain. Over the coming days I was to hear much in a sarcastically humorous vein about a team of scientists who had recently had the temerity to come here, unbidden, with a film crew to field-test a tracked robot that was to have crawled into the crater to conduct a series of experiments. In any event, the thing managed to crawl only a short way down the slope, much to Phil's amused satisfaction. Although not exactly an example of the sort of scientific concord and harmony envisaged by the Antarctic Treaty and the IGY, it was at least open and human.

It was near the end of the working day. The others were all still up near the summit, dots along the ridge. Rick and Rich were out of sight, around the side of the summit cone, working near a precipitous drop-off known as The End of the World where they were installing the Broadband Observatory or Big Orange Box, as the seismic detector was jocularly known, BOB, for short. The scientists might be away, but the field camp was still a hive of activity: a team of carpenters hammering together prefabricated wall segments for a new hut.

Maria, Sarah, and I went off and pitched our tents. By the time we finished, it was time for dinner. We could hear the hum of distant snowmobiles as Rick and Rich returned.

The hut was filled with the aroma of a roast. They took turns with the cooking, and tonight's chef was a young geochemistry postgraduate named Jessie. Being stuck for ideas she had used the telephone earlier that afternoon to patch a call through to her fiancé back in New Mexico and ask him to dig out the *All Around the World Cookbook* from its place on the shelf and read her the recipe for Sunday farmhouse pork roast.

We ate family style, sitting around the large table while Phillip told stories of the good old days when he used to cook his Christmas turkey in a patch of hot ground near the volcano's summit. Erebus had made a fantastic slow-cook oven, he explained; the turkeys came out brown and succulent and tender. But that sort of thing isn't done any more. The environmental do-gooders forbid it these days, at least on that particular part of the mountain. He had tried his volcano barbeque on a different, slightly cooler but permissible, ledge with unhappy results.

"I quickly learned the difference between slow cook and fast rot," he laughed. "When I picked it up, the whole thing fell apart, and for the rest of the summer my clothes stank of rotten turkey!"

We had cake for dessert and made coffee. After the dishes were washed and dried and put away, Rick and Rich and I set out for the crater rim. It was farther away, and a much steeper climb, than it had looked from the window over the kitchen sink.

We took the snowmobiles as high as we dared. It was frighteningly steep going. I rode on the back of Rich's and slid off twice on the steepest bits, once when the machine itself toppled over, and was mightily relieved to get to a ledge known as Nausea Knob where they parked the snowmobiles. From there we had to scramble up the last couple hundred vertical feet, kicking footholds in the snow and slithering on the loose volcanic scree.

It was easy to smell why Nausea Knob came by its nickname. The sharp stink of hydrogen sulfide, hydrochloric acid, and sulfur dioxide, along with the high altitude, made simple breathing here—let alone climbing—very queasy work. But one man's Nausea Knob is another man's perfume. As we hiked higher, Rick told me how he loved the smell of volcanoes; how they always reminded him of his good old postgraduate days studying volcanoes in Italy.

As we neared the crater rim, he paused to offer a friendly word of advice: "By the way, when it erupts, don't turn your back on it. The volcano coughs up some big lava bombs, and you want to keep an eye out to see if any are coming your way, so you can dodge them. Mostly they stay in the crater, but sometimes not. This thing can throw lava bombs the size of a sofa."

By way of illustration, he pointed his ice axe at an odd-looking blackened chunk of rock about the size and shape of a large beanbag chair. It resembled my idea of a meteor. An ominous skid mark streaked the snow above it, suggesting this thing had been both hot and in motion recently.

"Is that what I think it is?"

"It sure is. And fresh too—this would have landed in the last day or so, maybe even from that eruption we heard this afternoon."

He struck at it with his ice axe. Instead of the hard ring of metal on stone I would have expected, the pick sank into it up to the hilt. The rock seemed to deflate. With a twist of the axe he pulled it apart, revealing a soft, gooey center that looked like crystalline treacle. It was still warm. He gave it a friendly poke, turned, and continued up the last few steps to the top.

The summit view from Erebus is truly one of Earth's marvels, a medieval traveler's tale come to life. As I crested the final rise I peeked over the edge at the jaw-dropping spectacle below. A hellish chasm more than 2,310 feet across opened up at my feet. Jets of steam and acrid vapor hissed from charred vents in the rock, far below, staining the sheer cliff walls a sickly greenish-yellow. At the bottom of the pit, partially obscured by swirling smoke, was the famous lake of molten rock.

This wonder of the very ancient world had simmered there for many centuries, continually replenished by springs of lava from the center of the Earth. As I watched, the lake flared into a lurid orange bloom. A huge gulp of liquid rock bubbled to the surface, splashed extravagantly and settled back. The mountain growled, like the deepest chord on a giant organ. I held my breath, half wanting to see it flex its muscles and half afraid it might. The lake settled; a thin peppery crust covered its surface.

"You're looking at one of the very few permanent lava lakes in the world," Rick explained. Just as the South Pole was an open window into deep space and the dawn of time, this magnificent snow-clad volcano provided a living window into what goes on miles below the Earth's surface.

I must have stood there staring for an hour, continually turning away from the crater, to look out over the white tranquillity of Antarctica and then back into the pit again, fascinated by the contrast of this seething fiery pit with the vast dreamscape of ice and snow and cloud spreading out below us. It was like the coming together of heaven and hell. The view of the ranges and glaciers from here was simply incredible. Everything around was in the softest of colors. A band of pale gold shimmered on the flanks of a mountain in the distance; the glacier rolling out beside it was a lustrous milky violet.

It was late in the evening by now, really into the small hours of the morning, and clear enough in the fragile light to distinguish the frozen peak of Mount Melbourne more than 200 miles to the north. And then I turned and looked once again into that seething cauldron.

It was magic. We lingered up there, walking along the rim, looking at the views and watching that lake of molten rock flare and bubble. The mountain erupted once: a mighty thunderclap, an Earth tremor, and a noisy shower of debris that stayed within the crater. A huge moist plume swelled up and engulfed us like a fog. It was warm and pungent. The ground at our feet was thickly strewn with dark oblong crystals of feldspar that were found no place else on Earth, while the loose chunks of rock we walked upon tinkled musically beneath our feet. It was a type of rock called phonolite—named for its bell-like tone when struck—and Erebus is the only active volcano whose lava produces it. The smoke itself contained flecks of crystalline gold.

I spent several days on Erebus, going to work with Rick and Rich each morning as they struggled to get BOB up and running at The End of the World. The idea was that it would transmit its data down to McMurdo and from there it could be relayed on to the seismic labs back in New Mexico. Unfortunately, the Erebus transmitter was interfering with the broadcasts from MacTown's television station, filling TV screens around the base with static when they should have been filled with a weekend's worth of big college football games, and our days were punctuated by increasingly tense conversations via walkie-talkie with the TV station's manager, as the volcano boomed and sizzled above us.

Back at the hut, the others were testing out, and improving, a remote video rig called Lava Cam, which they hoped to establish on the crater rim, to provide real-time constant footage of the lava lake—via the Internet—after they returned to New Mexico. In the evenings we explored the fumaroles—the weird ice chimneys and caverns formed by warm gasses seeping from the ground on the upper flanks of the mountain—climbing down inside them with ropes and axes and crampons. They were beautiful, lit by a cathedral-blue light, and exquisitely sculpted.

Other times we hiked along the crater rim, looking down on the sea of clouds beneath us and at the other peaks rising in the distance, and staring at that lurid sizzling pool of lava at the bottom of the pit. These were days that stay with you forever. They were different from the time spent on that hidden peak in the Britannia Range. That had been haunting, dreamlike, and ethereal. Erebus had moments like that as well, but it also had a hard, edgy reality, with a hint of menace, which was in its own strange way more satisfying.

Erebus was the Old Faithful of volcanoes, Rick explained one evening as we hiked up from Nausea Knob. It erupted up to ten times a day, giving geologists a wealth of data. For the most part they were fairly safe eruptions too—provided you kept a wary eye cast skyward—but the mountain can occasionally turn dangerous.

In 1984 a series of violent explosions rained down large chunks of lava around a second observation hut, higher on the mountain, forcing Phillip and his team to flee. A few years later, in May 1993, instruments on the crater rim detected a massive "steam event"—a burst of superheated steam that would have killed anyone standing on the rim at the time. Fortunately it was winter and nobody was even on the mountain. And then, of course, there was the mute evidence of Fang Ridge, whose jagged rim marks the occasion when the volcano blew its top three-quarters of a million years ago.

Although I had grown used to its thunderclaps, such episodes were never far from my mind when we hiked along the crater rim, with that bubbling pool of lava waiting like a watched pot below. These regular eruptions were called "Strombolian," after Stromboli, the famously active volcano in Sicily, although Erebus bears no other geological resemblance to the Italian volcanoes. Its nearest cousins are the huge East African stratovolcanos, Kilamanjaro and Mount Kenya. Like them, Erebus formed in a rift valley, in its case the drifting apart of the ancient cratonic landmass of East Antarctica from the younger western portion of the continent. But unlike them, Erebus had never grown silent, or stopped creating. It had roared and fumed alone here at the edge of a mammoth frozen continent for many thousands of years.

One of the joys of Antarctica is that even after a century of exploration, conquest, and scientific endeavor, there are still a few heroic age tasks left to do—or rather, redo, as new technology makes older results obsolete. One of these concerns measuring the heights of mountains. A few weeks earlier, when I had first arrived at McMurdo, I mentioned to some of the Mount Erebus geologists that I had seen several different figures for the volcano's elevation and asked which was correct.

"Probably none of them," a geochemist named Jean laughed. "Not precisely, anyway. You know, nobody has ever measured the mountain with a differential GPS yet. There's a science project for you; why don't you do it?"

"Ah, yes, the old differential GPS! Of course!"

"Why not?"

Well, I could think of a few reasons—not the least of which was the fact that I hadn't a clue what a differential GPS was—but I kept my mouth shut. I was running with fast and brainy company here; there's a lot of that around an Antarctic base, and as Benjamin Franklin once said, it's better to keep silent and have people think you're a fool, than open it and remove all doubt. By the time we adjourned, put our trays on the racks by the scullery, it had been more or less settled, that when I came up to their field hut "my project" would be establish the elevation of Mount Erebus. They would have one of the state-of-the-art GPS units up there that would do the job to within a few inches.

Aside from a twinge of apprehension about my own ignorance (which I assuaged by making a mental note to try to find out what a differential GPS did and how one operated such a contraption) I walked away from the galley that morning exhilarated, as though I had just been ennobled. And indeed I had been. I was no mere garlic-and-onions scribe any more; I had a project, a *science* project. That put me right up there in the paint cards of Antarctic society. Scientists, as we all know, are the aristocrats here; the bases, the cargo planes, the helicopters—they all exist just for them. I mean, for us. In fact the entire continent has been set aside, by international treaty, as their—ahem, *our*—fiefdom of peace and research.

And what grand historical company I was going to be keeping. Mount Erebus has greeted and astonished generations of explorers since Capt. James Ross first sailed into these waters in 1841. All the greats have had a crack at measuring its height. Ross did it using a sextant from the deck of HMS *Erebus* and came up with 12,367 feet. Sixty years later when Robert Falcon Scott set up his base camp on Ross Island—a site that soon became the classic gateway for expeditions to the South Pole—he put Erebus's height at 13,120 feet. Using an old-fashioned instrument called a hypsometer, which measures air pressure, Shackleton's 1908 party came away with an elevation of 13,370 feet. Others, less celebrated, have had a go over the years as well. By 1943 the U.S. Navy Hydrographer's Office had settled on 13,200 feet, a figure that was accepted for many years. More recent maps claim 12,444, 12,446, and 12,448 feet, while the U.S. Geological Survey likes 12,333 feet. But now, on the cusp of the 21st century, Smith et al. was going to provide the world with the definitive answer. The thought warmed me right down to the Vibram soles of my climbing boots. I imagined a gilt-framed portrait of yours truly gazing down with a damn-your-eyes sneer from above a mantelpiece at the Royal

Geographic Society, with the bejewelled Order of the Flying Penguin around my neck and several alphabets of letters strung after my name.

First, though, I looked up Jean and in a quiet moment confided that, well, what with my spending so much time on the human genome project, mastering the violin, and fiddling with the unsolved Rubik's Cube that had lain in my desk drawer since 1979, I had grown a little rusty lately on my differential GPS. She understood perfectly, said it was all right and that she and the others would see me through the brainwork. I went away light of heart.

And now on a sparkling December day, with the temperature about –20°F and a stiff breeze blowing, we set off from the hut with backpacks full of gear and weighty batteries, bound for the summit ridge. The highest point on the crater rim was halfway around the mountaintop, necessitating a breathtaking hike along its curved knife-edged ridgeline. Far below, the lava lake bubbled evilly, and wisps of that gold-flecked smoke swirled around us. Off in the distance a frozen world spread out clean and bright and still beneath a piercing blue sky.

We mounted the antennas on the highest crag, hooked up the GPS unit and batteries, and for the next 30 minutes, while we stood with our backs to the wind and admired the view, the heavy yellow box at our feet conversed with nine orbiting satellites. At the same time, another unit back at the hut was doing the same thing.

In a nutshell, what we were doing was a glorified exercise in triangulation, adapting the same principles of geometry used by surveyors for centuries. A fix is taken from a particular point on the Earth's surface—in this case, the highest spot on the crater rim of Mount Erebus—and plotted against the positions of a series of satellites whose orbits, angles, distances, and positions can be pinpointed with space-age accuracy. These sightings would be compared with ones made simultaneously from another GPS unit in the hut, whose exact elevation had already been determined by GPS. Rick, for example, had had to determine the precise position and elevation of his various seismic stations on the volcano—it was just that nobody had troubled to do the same for the summit. Good old-fashioned triangulation would establish the difference in elevation between the two points.

Since the U.S. military unlocked its satellites to give civilian GPS users the benefits of its ultraprecise readings, remeasuring the elevations of famous mountains has been a trendy pastime. In 1999 a surveying party in the Himalaya used this same technology to recalculate the height of Mount Everest and made the gratifying discovery that it was actually a bit higher than previously believed. And so did we on Mount Erebus. Our mountain turned out to be 3,798.22 meters high—that's 12,502 feet and change—a nifty advance on the official U.S. Geological Survey figure of 12,333. Jean later explained the calculations to me. I took it all on board, sipped my Scotch, and nodded sagely, as befitted the man who went up a mountain and agreed that it was high.

Actually I never cared what figure we came up with—higher or lower—for Erebus's elevation; I had a scientist's splendid impartiality on that front. But as those minutes ticked by on the summit I could feel myself growing increasingly anxious as I watched the magic box working—fretting that the cold weather might run down the batteries prematurely, or that our data might be faulty, or that our satellites might slip out of reach. It is funny how science can capture your imagination. I had nothing riding on the outcome, no publications or grant money or career prospects to concern me—I was a true Antarctic aristocrat in that regard—but I could sense the obsessive, possessive, and highly personal nature of science down here. This was "my" project, and as simple and frivolous as it might have seemed compared with the worthier efforts around me, I passionately wanted it to succeed. And when it did I was delighted, as happy as a kid on Christmas. When I eventually flew back to McMurdo, and gazed back at the shimmering white mass of Erebus, I felt in myself a touch of proprietorial pride.

Both Rick and I were booked on the flight to Christchurch the following morning. I spent my last day in MacTown swanning around with him as he tried to sort out the bandwidth hassles with his seismic monitor, whose transmitter was still interfering with McMurdo's television station. He eventually solved it by using an obscure wavelength and setting his transmitter on the eaves of an old warehouse nestled at the foot of Observation Hill.

While he tinkered with its electronics, I cast my eyes around at the stacks of wooden crates inside the warehouse. Most of them were labeled for the South Pole construction site. Looking at them made me think of Carlton Walker, no doubt still red-eyed and stubbly from sleepless days overseeing his project. I wondered what he and the others down there at Pole were doing just at that moment, and pictured in my mind's eye the sprawl of machinery and iron on the barren wastes, the village of Jamesways and hypertats, and the aging dome with Old Glory fluttering from the top.

It all seemed pleasantly close and personal and familiar.

As I looked at those crates it came to me that the South Pole would never again seem quite so far away. Neither would those sandstone ledges in the Britannia

Range, nor the jagged peaks of the Transantarctic Mountains, nor even the summit of Mount Erebus—the strangest and most exotic place I had ever seen. They all belonged to me now; they were part of my experience. MacTown too. They were indelibly etched, the good and the bad, and what had evolved from it all was a richer and more complicated White South.

It was an afternoon for valedictory thoughts. And as we drove back downtown, the dashboard radio in the pickup truck wailing "Get a haircut and get a real job!" I noticed how Rick's eyes kept wandering back to the summit of Erebus, shimmering high and mighty against a polished blue sky. I could see he was still saying his good-byes to the mountain and wondering—as everyone does who is fortunate enough to come to Antarctica—if and when and under what circumstances he would ever be back.

I was lucky in that regard; I knew I would be coming back to Antarctica in a little over a fortnight's time, albeit to a vastly different part of the continent—the Antarctic Peninsula, the 800-mile-long spine of mountains and storm-lashed archipelagoes that stretches up toward Tierra Del Fuego in South America. But there is no easy way to get from one side of Antarctica to another. To reach the peninsula I'd first have to fly back home to Australia, catch another series of commercial flights to South America, and then take a ship.

I flew out on a Royal New Zealand Air Force C-130. It wasn't a crowded flight. There was room enough to sprawl out and sleep on the netted pile of cargo in the hold. It was pleasant, or at least as pleasant as nine hours' fitful slumber can be on a slow, noisy turbo-prop transport.

I woke up when we were on final approach. We touched down mid-afternoon on a fine summer's day, with the air full of rich, subtle, earthy smells that nobody but those of us freshly back from The Ice would have noticed. It nearly had the piquancy of coffee.

The air felt moist and almost tropical. It was good to wear just a shirt with the sleeves rolled up, and not have to worry about a sudden bitter wind springing up. And it was deeply pleasing to be liberated from the U.S. Antarctic Program's Orwellian authoritarian presence; to know that I could do as I pleased, go where I wished, and not require anyone's permission. I felt like a man just released from indenture.

I met Rick for dinner that night at a sidewalk café, and we both took delight in seeing nightfall for the first time in weeks.

CHAPTER TWELVE

Heading for the Banana Belt

IT WAS RAINING WHEN I LANDED AT PUNTA ARENAS A LITTLE AFTER MIDNIGHT. The little airport at the southernmost tip of Patagonia was small and quiet. A late-night glow spilled from the terminal. The tarmac glistened. It was cold, just a few degrees above freezing, but it felt even chillier after the thundery heat of Buenos Aires, where I had woken up that morning.

It wasn't much warmer in the terminal, but at least it was dry. I plucked my rucksack off the carousel, dug out my heavy fleece and caught the eye of one of the blue-jeaned cab drivers loitering by the door and booked him for a ride to my hotel.

The rain had eased to a soft drizzle when we stepped outside. A shaft of moonlight broke through a rift in the clouds over the town. A dull cinnamon glow on the western horizon revealed that sunset hadn't occurred all that long ago, a subtle reminder of just how far south Punta Arenas is.

The driver went fast. We wound through night-lit streets in town and pulled up in front of the Hotel Jose Noguiera. It was a small, elegant place that used to be the mansion of a Portuguese-born wool, timber, and mining baron named Noguiera. The glow of the streetlight played on its neoclassical stonework and ornamental iron. It was quite a place; it surprised me to see such a mansion in a place that I had thought of—for no particular reason other than its lonely place at the tip of South America—as a raw frontier. Punta Arenas used to be a wealthy seaport. It was founded in 1848, just in time and perfectly positioned to make an overnight fortune offering a protected harbor, wood, water, and fresh food to the clipper ships racing around Cape Horn on their way to the Californian goldfields. And from those great beginnings it went on to make even greater fortunes as a prime shipping port during the 19th-century wool boom.

For Punta Arenas the music stopped when the Americans opened the Panama Canal in 1914, a convenient shortcut that meant far fewer ships rounding Cape Horn, but the town is still encrusted with elegant mansions and ornate facades from its glory days.

I paid the driver and went up the steps into the warm light of the lobby. I took a room on the third floor, overlooking the street, and stretched out on the bed, not sleepy, just letting the miles and jet lag seep away.

I glanced at the phone book on the table across the room, with its listings in Territorio Chileno Antartico, and thought about the waters of the Straits of Magellan washing against the waterfront in this raffish old South American seaport.

It had been grand to visit the Ross Sea part of Antarctica, the traditional and historic gateway to the high polar plateau, with its resonance of Scott and Shackleton, but I think I was even more excited to see the Antarctic Peninsula, the wild, storm-lashed maritime face of Antarctica that lay 600 miles south of Cape Horn. The old hands back at McMurdo and the South Pole jokingly called this part of the continent the Banana Belt, because of its damp, moist, and relatively warm summer climate, and the seemingly un-Antarctic lushness of grass, moss, and lichen that clung to life on the rocks and crevices of its island arcs.

The nickname, with its implications of tropical indolence and ease, is a little misleading. Winter temperatures on the peninsula still drop to –40°F, or worse, and the wild storms and fearsome seas that battered the barely charted coasts have claimed far more lives than the bitter polar plateau.

Some of that loss of life is because this part of Antarctica is so much easier to reach and the human history in these stormy waters reaches back so much further. Buccaneering adventurers, privateers, and explorers have prowled the tip of South America for centuries, ever since the ruffed-collar days of Magellan and Sir Francis Drake. Captain Cook sailed through here in the 1770s, nearly losing his ships in the huge seas and terrible storms that plague this part of the world. And although another 50 years passed before anyone is known to have sighted the continent, with a Russian, an Englishman, and an American all claiming the distinction of being the first to eyeglass its shores in 1820, the waters and bleak archipelagoes south of the Cape became well known to sealers and whalers. Throughout the 1820s the islands were scenes of unbridled greed, as British and American sealers, most of them the dregs of society, plundered the fabulously rich wildlife colonies, wiping out millions of fur seals in an orgy of greed and killing.

And when the seals were virtually stamped out, they began hunting the whales. Over the following century, the world's whaling fleets exterminated hundreds of thousands of whales in these icy waters, pushing many species to the brink of extinction, from which they still haven't recovered.

The peninsula's salty human history is a full-blooded counterpoint to that of the high polar plateau, with its thin scentless air and Edwardian exemplars of asceticism and heroic self-sacrifice. Therein is its very human fascination. This part of Antarctica may have showcased some of the worst in human nature—greed, rapaciousness, violence, and cruelty—but, to borrow a cynical train of thought from Orson Welles in *The Third Man*, this was also the part of Antarctica that produced *The Rime of the Ancient Mariner*, Poe's *Narrative of Arthur Gordon Pym of Nantucket*, and *Moby Dick*. And for me this was the part of Antarctica where I would be able to travel independently, on board the yacht *Golden Fleece*, free of any heavy-handed bureaucratic presence.

The *Golden Fleece* and its skipper, a renowned French sailor named Jérome Poncet, was to pick me up on Cape Sherriff, a rocky peninsula on the northern flank of Livingstone Island, which is itself the second largest island in the South Shetland archipelago. And so I'd arranged a lift down there on a Russian research ship, the *Yuzhmorgeologiya*, which was on charter to the National Oceanic and Atmospheric Administration (NOAA) to do a two-month survey of the marine life in the cold Antarctic waters.

The legacy of plunder and exploitation that characterized the earliest days of Antarctic exploration carries on to this day, with big, modern, factory ships netting up thousands of tons of sweet-eating, slow-growing Antarctic fish species—such as the Patagonian toothfish—at a rate that may well exceed nature's ability to replace them. Nobody knows for sure. And so the world's marine biologists are trying to learn as much about the unique Antarctic ecosystem as they can—it is hoped before anything irreversible happens. In 1982 the Antarctic Treaty nations signed the Convention for the Conservation of Antarctic Marine Living Resources to try to extend some form of legal protection to these rich fisheries, but because no one nation owns or controls these waters, catch limits remain more a matter of (dubious) conscience than hard, enforceable law. And so every summer a number of biologists take to the seas. And now I was going with them.

A fresh squall blew in during the night. I woke once to hear rain rattling on my windows. It had settled back to a cool, misty drizzle by dawn, which at those latitudes in January, comes at around four o'clock in the morning. I slept in until eight, showered, shaved, and put a call through to a man named Ricardo, the local agent for the Russian company that operated the *Yuzhmorgeologiya*.

He spoke fluent English and said he'd be around at ten o'clock to take me down to the ship.

I had just finished breakfast when he arrived. He turned out to be a smallish, dapper man in a slate-green sports coat. We drove six blocks to the wharf. Like any canny hitchhiker, I was a little anxious about my lift across the Drake Passage. This is one of the most feared stretches of water in the world, south of Cape Horn, where the Atlantic and Pacific Oceans collide with all the rage the Furious Fifties and Screaming Sixties can muster. Force-ten gales are common. Seas can be huge. The old charts are dotted with hundreds of shipwrecks. An old mariner's adage held that below the 40th parallel there was no law; below 50 there was no God, and below 60 there was no sense. We were going well below 60.

Some cheery know-it-all back in McMurdo had already described the *Yuzhmorgeologiya* to me as a Brezhnev-era rust bucket. In the weeks since, I had painted steadily drearier pictures of it in my mind, imagining a badly oxidized hull and a grubby superstructure stained by diesel exhaust; stuffy overheated corridors that smelled of cabbage, grease, and tobacco; and dingy bunks that reeked of seasickness—most of it mine.

As we drove along the waterfront, I caught sight of a seedy hulk barely afloat in the harbor and my heart sank, but rose again when Ricardo turned instead onto the broad wharf used by the expensive cruise liners. One of those grand ships was in town now, big, sleek, and gleaming white, being readied for a tour around Tierra del Fuego. And berthed on the other side of the wharf was the *Yuzhmorgeologiya*. Not bad, not bad at all.

It was a well-used vessel about the size of a modest freighter with a hull the color of paprika and a Russian flag fluttering among the radar masts. What shabbiness there was about it was the respectable sort that comes from good hard use, not neglect.

Ricardo drew up beside a stack of crates of fresh fruit, vegetables, and groceries that a couple of Russian seamen were hoisting onto the ship. He went over and chatted with them for a few minutes. I got out and ran my much relieved eyes over the ship. Ricardo came back and we went up the gangplank.

The ship was well scrubbed inside. The interior was 1970s veneer, buff yellow with metal trim, and the corridors had a faint redolence of cooking oil and cigarette smoke, just enough to make me smile at the memory of my forebodings.

I followed Ricardo down two flights of stairs, along a narrow metal passage, and through a couple of watertight doorways to a large, busy room cluttered with boxes, lab equipment, and computer gear. About a dozen expeditioners were scurrying about, unpacking and putting things away in an atmosphere of agreeable expectation.

There was a good mix of accents, mostly American but with a sprinkling of Canadian, British, and South African. The man in charge was named Roger. He was a medium-size man with close cropped iron-gray hair, alert brown eyes, and the harried look of a man burdened with the million and one details of getting a seagoing research expedition under way in short order.

Ricardo introduced us and then went up to the bridge to talk to the captain. Roger told me where to find the cabin allocations, adding that there would be an all-hands meeting in the wardroom at two o'clock.

"We're leaving tomorrow morning at eight. Oh, and by the way, lash all of your gear down tightly—anything that can move, tie it down. Things can get really rough out there."

I was assigned to cabin 33, on the upper deck, sharing it with a tall, tanned, and breezy University of California biologist named Kit and a quiet researcher from the National Oceanic and Atmospheric Administration (NOAA) named Brian, who was going to be spending the summer working with penguins and seals on Livingstone Island. They had already moved in, and the cabin was piled high with dry bags and backpacks. Kit had brought along his surfboard and dry suit, hoping to catch a few waves down there off Antarctica's South Shetland Islands as a counterpoint to long days at sea studying plankton.

"Did you know the word plankton comes from the Greek for 'born to wander'?" he asked, looking up from a copy of Arthur Miller's travel classic, *The Air-Conditioned Nightmare*.

I owned up to my ignorance.

"Well, it does. I think that is why I love the little things. They've got the lifestyle I'd like to adopt: wandering the seas."

"Plankton, huh?"

"Sure! Give me the squidgy, gooey things every time. Whales get all the glory. I like the proletariat of the food chain, those amorphous gelatinous things that everybody ignores. They're fascinating."

"Right." While I rolled out my gear, he launched into a humorous and informative monologue about plankton, so full of enthusiasm and quirky fact that I began marveling I had never taken much stock in plankton before.

Clearly this was going to be an interesting voyage. Or perhaps lively was the adjective I was grasping for. Particularly so because I noticed how every little thing in the room was securely lashed and stowed. It looked like someone was expecting the ship to be doing Eskimo rolls.

A few minutes before two o'clock we filed into the wardroom. It was comfortable and bright, with windows overlooking the trawl deck below and a couple of little vases of flowers set on a long table that was covered with a white cloth. This was the officers' mess and where we would dine as well. A stereo sat in one corner, and the fridge by the door was stocked with soft drinks.

We plucked out some Cokes and sat down. The room soon filled. A frizzy-haired American woman who handled the chartering of the *Yuzhmorgeologiya* on behalf of NOAA introduced the captain and the Russian crew. It was an interesting, edgy sort of introduction, full of carefully worded praise for the Russians and the high standards of courtesy, cleanliness, and professionalism they maintained on the ship. I had a sense of much diplomacy at work.

Since the fall of the Soviet Union in 1991, cash-strapped Russian academies have been forced to peddle their polar research ships to Western governments, and even tour operators, at bargain rates in exchange for hard currency. It hasn't always been a happy mix. Smiling service, fresh food, and regular maintenance were not exactly hallmarks of the Soviet way of life, on sea or land, and there was lingering touchiness among the Russians over their fallen fortunes and resentment at the newfound need to cater to Western whims. The well-scrubbed appearance of the *Yuzhmorgeologiya*, I gathered, was something fairly new and owed itself to a large degree of goodwill and forbearance on both sides of the deal.

The woman went on to assure us that if anyone became ill or injured on board, we would all have access, via satellite hookup, to a team of doctors in Seattle, although several old hands remarked later that the Russian doctor we had on board with us was a lot better and more versatile in his thinking than his U.S. counterparts. He was infinitely more popular too. Russian concepts of good health and well-being include such niceties as massage as a form of preventive maintenance. His appointment book was chockablock within minutes.

The ship's captain was introduced. He was almost an ad man's shibboleth of a Soviet naval officer: heavily built, silent and morose, with an impassive Slavic face and a frosty reserve. To be fair, he spoke little English, so it was hard to say what he was really like beyond appearances. Maybe he was a marshmallow inside. Maybe he had watched *Titanic* endlessly on a video in his cabin with a box of Kleenex in his lap, and played Celine Dion on the bridge, but somehow I didn't think so. He looked like he could break ice by smiling at it.

Next the mate stepped up and gave a lecture on safety procedures, mustering stations, and the forthcoming lifeboat drill. He was an athletic-looking twenty-something, with sandy hair and thick wrists and the shoulders of a rugby player. Boxing was the way he liked to keep in shape while at sea, and he generously offered to spar with anybody who felt the need for exercise. It was no doubt well meant, but everyone was far more taken by the doctor's offer of a massage. Although the ship was "dry," the inaugural meeting finished with a bottle of champagne and a toast to success.

We cleared port a little before ten o'clock, a couple of hours later than planned, but then nothing to do with Antarctica runs to clock time. Nobody seriously expects it to. A couple of peninsula veterans told me they once had to wait for six weeks in Punta Arenas while their ship—not the *Yuzhmorgeologiya*—underwent repairs.

I loved the fact that I was going to Antarctica once again by sea, my mind taking a wander down memory lane to the rainy quay in Hobart all those years ago and the icebreaker *Aurora Australis*. I leaned against the railing and watched Punta Arenas slip astern until it was just a mosaic of brightly colored roofs nestled at the foot of some grassy hills. Damp gray clouds scudded overhead. There was something pleasingly windswept and maritime about it all; a watercolor that smelled of sea. I felt good. It was nice to be putting to sea. And I liked the people with whom I was traveling, and the shipboard ambience.

I must admit that if I had been apprehensive about the seagoing characteristics of the Russian ship, I'd been equally apprehensive about the prospect of putting myself back into the Americans' heavy bureaucratic fold, of finding myself on a high-seas version of McMurdo, but as with the ship, the reality couldn't have been more different. Some of the relaxed ambience was simply due to the fact that we were a much smaller and more intimate group, fewer than 20 as opposed to 1,200 at MacTown, and they were far less parochial. Most of the people here had worked together for years and by now functioned almost as a surrogate family. Roger and Valerie, the two voyage leaders, had vastly different management styles from the broody and aloof executives who cast such long shadows over MacTown. Finally, there was none of MacTown's hard, militarized veneer. Although all of the NOAA people on board carried U.S. Navy commissions, none of them wore uniforms. It was all very civil and civilian.

A fresh breeze blew, kicking up little whitecaps, but the ship glided along as steady as a rock. Our course would take us eastward, through the Straits of Magellan and into the South Atlantic, where we would turn and head for Antarctica.

"We'll start feeling the swell when we get to Staten Island," Roger warned, "and then we'll be into the Drake, so be sure everything in your room is battened down by tomorrow morning."

"No worries." My voice was cheery and glib, but I was growing a bit uneasy about the coming roughness. I'd never been seasick at all on the *Aurora Australis*, but that had been quite a few years ago, and now, as we steamed along the Straits of Magellan, I noticed that the scientists around me—veterans all—were walking pharmacopoeias of scopolamine patches and Marezine and were joking about paying the "Drake Tax"—the toll in seasickness and discomfort that goes hand in hand with travel in these petulant waters. All I'd brought along for queasiness was a small packet of crystallized ginger and a tin of English peppermints. Right then it didn't seem much of a tax shelter.

CHAPTER THIRTEEN

Paying the Drake Tax

I SLEPT WELL AND ROSE EARLY, FEELING FINE AS I STEPPED OUT ONTO THE fresh salty air on deck. We'd come out of the Straits of Magellan during the night and were steaming along the southernmost part of South America's east coast. Staten Island, off in the distance, was a brave sight, wild and craggy and bathed in a watery yellow glow from a fan of sunbeams that burst through a break in the clouds. The waters were dark. The ship rolled smoothly but heavily, steaming southwest at 15 knots. Seabirds swooped between the waves.

I tottered up to the bow, an insulated mug of coffee in hand, to savor the spectacle and join the little knot of birders who were out there with binoculars and notebooks recording the wildlife.

It was exhilarating. This was where I wanted to be. The air tasted briny, the birds screeched, and the deck beneath my feet rose and plunged heroically. Somebody yelled "Dolphins!" and we all looked off the starboard bow and saw them arcing through the waves in front of us, the water sparkling like silver off their backs. They seemed to be escorting the ship, piloting it through their personal waters.

I watched them, sipping my coffee and drinking in the moment. Before the morning was out we would have cleared Cape Horn. This was the incarnation of every adventure novel I had ever read. What had been settings for boyhood tales of clipper ships, Spanish galleons, and Elizabethan privateers were now a part of my own story as well.

"Want a pair of binoculars?"

I glanced over my shoulder at the amiable face of a middle-aged man named Wayne, who was the director of seabird research for the U.S. Antarctic Marine Living Resources Program. He was tall and lean, with a stubbly graying growth of beard, and had been coming south every summer since 1976 to monitor penguin populations. It was to his camp on Livingstone Island that I was heading.

"Sure, thanks." I took the offered pair of 7x50s and looped the strap around my neck. Staten Island loomed even more forbidding and fanciful, with its cruel stone peaks and heavy surf crashing against its cliffs, but the magnification also diffused the watery sunlight and made the island seem even more ethereal. It was easy to imagine it through the superstitious eyes of 16th-century sailors. In fact it was hard not to.

After a few moments I lowered the glasses and asked Wayne how the bird-watching was going. I know next to nothing about birds, and had really wanted the binoculars only to look at Staten Island, but thought the loan merited at least a passing interest in what was going on, even if I couldn't contribute intelligently to what they were doing.

"Great! This is a very rich area where we are now," he replied. "The waters along the shelf here are less than a hundred meters deep so you get a local welling up of nutrients. These are rich pickings for them."

As we stood out there in the wind, he pointed out sooty shearwaters, Wilson's storm petrels, black-browed albatrosses, and Chilean skuas—demonstrating a remarkable talent for identifying what were to me no more than swift-moving gray-white-and-black specks.

While he was talking, a fast-moving bird flitting through the troughs of the waves caught everyone's attention. I didn't hear the species name, but half a dozen pairs of binoculars zoomed in on it. Mine too. There was artistry, all right, in the way that bird skimmed the surface, banking hard on a wingtip, pirouetting away from the crests of the glistening black waves just before they broke over it, and then darting along a smooth, glassy trough.

Trying to follow its zigzag course through heaving seas at seven-power magnification while standing on a pitching deck proved to be a transforming experience for me. It didn't make me a bird fancier, but as I panned the sea with those binoculars, I suddenly became conscious of the rise and fall of the ship in a way I hadn't been two minutes earlier. Hitherto unnoticed sensations caught my attention: the gentle pressure on my knees as the ship rose on a wave, and the soft plunging weightlessness and tingle in my temples as it slid down the other side. I discovered a new unit of time: that instant's pause at the bottom of a trough just before the bow begins its next long, slow rise. I set the binoculars beside the anchor winch and took a deep, slow breath.

"I say—thank you so much for the use of those." I spoke with the exaggerated politeness of a drunk trying desperately to feign sobriety. I picked up my mug with numbed fingers. "I…I…I…think I might go back inside and get some more coffee."

Wayne lowered his binoculars from the bird they were all following and glanced over his shoulder. "No need." His voice was affable, coming from somewhere far, far away, somewhere where it was still a lovely morning, not where I was at all. "You can stay out here if you want. I've got to go back anyway and get something from the lab anyway. Give me your mug. I'll bring some more coffee back for you."

I felt a hot flush pass over me, warming my chest and temples. "Oh no, that's quite all right, thanks. I'm going now." I turned about as carefully as though I were made of blown glass and ambled toward my cabin several miles away, careful not to bump into anything and trying to keep my eyes trained on anything level and steady. Seasickness is all about inner ear balance and visual cues. But I had no better chance of regaining equilibrium just then than I had of unscrambling an egg. I picked up pace as I went—no Olympic speedwalker could have appeared more focused or dedicated.

I burst into my cabin at a determined run and spent the rest of the morning doing my taxes, my Drake Taxes. I crept out at noon, very shaky, but nibbled experimentally at lunch and found that it wasn't too bad. By dinner I was as whole as ever and stayed that way for the rest of my time on board. But I never ever, ever went up to the bow again, let alone picked up a pair of binoculars. In my mental map of the ship, that was the dark cellar where you never went.

The Drake was kind. Two more days of easy rollers brought us to the Antarctic Convergence, one of nature's loneliest frontiers, where the cold, dense, nutrient-rich waters meet the warmer but less fertile currents from the north. It is a surprisingly sharp boundary, generally around 60° south. Within a few miles, the air becomes damp and chilly and the water a deep, translucent blue. Flocks of seabirds—albatrosses, petrels, and shearwaters—swoop over the waves, feasting noisily on the rich pickings that well up.

It is a political boundary as well. The waters south of here are considered a part of Antarctica and are protected by the Convention for the Conservation of Antarctic Marine Living Resources. It is essentially a fishing treaty, but unique in that it seeks to manage the ecosystem as a whole rather than just setting catch limits on a few targeted species. So it was here, below the convergence, that the scientists on board the *Yuzhmorgeologiya* were conducting their krill survey. The survey itself was to be carried out in a large empty grid of the Scotia Sea, off the South Shetland Islands, but they decided to do a test run here.

We assembled on the gently heaving trawl deck, letting loose the weighted net and watching as the big drum rolled out cable at 132 feet a minute until, judging by the length and angle of the cable, it had sunk to a depth of nearly 600 feet.

They trawled along for 20 minutes and then slowly winched up the net. Despite the fact that my knowledge of marine biology runs the gamut from A to B, or possibly because of it, nobody there could have been more excited or curious than I was. I've always loved fishing; the mystery of dark water and the wonder of what might take my bait. I spent my childhood—almost from the time I could walk—dropping lines into the brook that flowed along the edge of our meadow. There was only ever one species of fish in it—trout—but that didn't stop the tingling marvel when I watched my line sink into a deep hole by an upturned stump and imagined to myself that anything—frankly—anything might be down there.

Now I was fishing (or rather, helping to fish) at the outermost edge of the world, our net scooping up unseen creatures that dwelled in the darkness nearly 100 fathoms below the surface. This truly was a place where anything might be lurking.

It seemed to take forever to haul in the net, and when its greenish gauze finally broke the surface I rushed to the railing. I'm not sure what it was I was expecting to see—that was the point, I guess—but certainly not an empty net.

"Huh? We didn't catch anything!"

"Sure we did," Roger said.

Then I saw the small plastic canister at the end of the net, something I had mistaken for a weight when it was tossed overboard. "You mean it's all in that white thing?"

"Sure."

"Oh." I tried not to look disappointed. Eager hands around me opened the canister and dumped its contents into a bucket. A fibrous pink sludge spilled out. They whisked it into a laboratory that had been set up in a shipping container on deck and began to sort through it. I followed, a little ruefully.

"Here, take a look at this!" Valerie called over to me. She stepped away from a microscope.

I put my face to its eyepieces and gasped. "My God! What's that?" I was looking at a bizarrely beautiful creature I can only describe as sort of like an art deco grasshopper. It had a clear plasticlike body, with pale pink and blue innards and a snowflake pattern on its abdomen. This was an arthropod designed by the guy who did the iMac.

"It's called Themisto," Kit spoke up. "They make their living by attaching themselves to salps for a free ride and protection."

For the next couple of hours I shifted eagerly from microscope to microscope in the little trawl-deck lab, gawking at the sea monsters we had dragged up from the depths. There were copepods (Greek for "oar feet,"

Kit explained), which use their oversize antennas as oars to propel themselves through the water. And pteropods, "winged foot" molluscs that lost their shells in the distant evolutionary past and now use their creeping foot as a sort of wing to soar through the water. There were larval squids and tiny, shrimplike krill hatchlings with big peppery eyes, and finned transparent horrors called cheatognaths, whose grotesque bristly mouths can detect the slightest vibrations or movements in the water.

"These guys are the predator of the zooplankton world," Kit said. "They prey on copepods, fish eggs, krill larvae—and each other—sneaking up and pouncing."

These creatures, with their spikes, oars, wings, baroque bodies, and voracious mouths, eclipsed anything my imagination could have conjured up, even if they were a bit smaller than expected. And the more I heard about them, the happier I was that they were microscopic. Those cheatognaths and their hideous bristly maws were sea monsters straight off a medieval mapmaker's drawing board.

"We're looking at the abundances as well as the variety of species in each sample," Kit explained. "With the krill, we'll measure the length of their bodies, record their sex, and describe their reproductive state. This helps us estimate the krill population's overall age and demographics, which is vital if you want to manage the fisheries successfully."

This was just a test run. Over the next few weeks the *Yuzhmorgeologiya* would steam a sequence of 100-mile-long transepts through some of Antarctica's best krill-fishing waters, netting samples such as this every 15 miles and using state-of-the-art hydro acoustics to take continuous sonar "snapshots" of sea life—everything from whales to krill larvae—down to depths of 1,500 feet. They would also be studying the chemical and physical characteristics of the water, hoping to use any added knowledge to fine-tune the science of underwater sonar.

But before they began doing all that, they had to drop off Wayne and Brian—and me—at a lonely field camp near one of the old sealer's haunts at Cape Shirreff on Livingstone Island.

Once the trawling gear had been stowed after the trial, the captain turned the *Yuzhmorgeologiya* a few degrees farther on a southerly bearing and, a little more than 24 hours later, the island's bleak and forbidding coastline came into view.

Livingstone Island is part the South Shetland archipelago, a mountainous chain of islands off the northern part of the Antarctic Peninsula. Sublime rather than beautiful, they sweep across the map in a graceful arc, as though they were bending before the might of the howling westerlies that blow continuously at these latitudes. Damp and moody and incredibly rich in wildlife, they were discovered accidentally in 1819, by a British merchant captain named Smith whose ship was blown off course by a storm while he was trying to round Cape Horn.

When he returned with tales of fabulously rich sealing grounds on uncharted islands he sparked a mad rush. Within four years the islands' seal population—more than 300,000 animals—was wiped out and the fortune hunters moved on to somewhere else.

Nature was able to heal itself, even if it did take well over a century. There were thousands of seals dotting the shingle beaches on Cape Shirreff the night we dropped anchor about half a mile off the coast. It was a calm evening, with a soft rain falling and the mountains shrouded in mist and low cloud. For some on board this was their first glimpse of Antarctica. All agreed that it lived up to its haunting, mysterious, and aloof billing.

We could see the camp, a couple of trim wooden frame huts on a rise set well back from the beach, and noticed some figures in bright parkas stepping out the door to wave. They were a team of seal researchers that had been deployed a few weeks earlier. Wayne went ashore that evening with a load of supplies. Brian and I and the rest of the cargo were to come over early in the morning.

I packed my gear, went to bed around 11, and slept even better than I knew. When I woke, the island was nowhere in sight. A nasty squall, with gusts up to 50 knots, had swept in during the night and with the growing possibility of being washed up against the rocks, the captain had given orders to hoist the anchor and back off several miles.

It was raining and cold, but the winds had moderated, and we were proceeding cautiously back toward the cape. The captain, who had much experience in the Russian Arctic but was new to Antarctica, didn't care for either the weather or the shoals around us. When I saw him on deck he was scowling even more than usual.

The island, which had projected a sterile sort of tranquillity the previous evening, now simply looked grim, windswept and treeless, with black volcanic cliffs topped with ice and shrouded with mist and heavy spray coming off the breakers. It was a coast made for tragedy and secrets. I remembered reading how a Spanish man-of-war, the *San Telmo*, had vanished in a wild storm off Cape Horn in 1819 and bits of it were later found wrecked on this same lonely cape. There had been more than 600 people aboard her. There were no survivors.

The captain flatly refused to bring the *Yuzhmorgeologiya* in as close as he had the previous night. None of us relished such a long transfer by Zodiac in those waters, particularly Roger and the other boatmen who would have to make quite a few trips to ferry all the supplies ashore, but the captain was adamant. The anchor chain rattled. The ship heaved in the swell, at rest. The dinghies were lowered into the heavy water and a rope ladder lowered over the side.

"Who wants to go first?"

Not me, no way, but I tottered forward anyway and peeped with infinite caution and fascinated terror over the rail, looking into the sickening swell far, far below, the dinghy dancing on the black deadly water and Roger's upturned face, wet with spray, and the slippery flailing rope ladder that nearly, but not quite, reached it, and felt my stomach do a slow forward roll.

"You're joking, right?"

"Nope! Down you go!"

I went, snugly dressed in my Mustang Survival Suit, but not exactly moving like a pirate swarming down the rigging. That rope ladder was slippery, bounced and jiggled, and seemed to go down forever, hundreds and hundreds of feet. The sound of the wind and the swells crashing against the hull was deafening.

"This is as good as it gets!" Roger yelled to me. A sudden surge had boosted the dinghy to where Roger's head was nearly level with my ankles, but I was too absorbed in my surroundings to seize the moment and had to wait a few white-knuckled seconds for the next big swell. I heard him yell: "OK! Here we go! Go! Go! Go!"

I jumped this time, tumbling into the dinghy as it plunged away. Icy spray splashed my face. I tasted brine. I clutched at the gunwales, smiled feebly, and nodded to indicate I was fairly in. Roger gunned the outboard motor and we were away. I glanced back. The Russian trawler disappeared in the swell. It reemerged, and then sank from view again, all but the tips of its radar masts, as we plunged into another deep trough. Three miles ahead, and partly obscured by mist, lay Cape Shirreff. It was a cold, wet, and miserably rough ride, the Zodiac bouncing hard on the choppy swell, but the waters eased once Roger steered around a rocky arm and brought us into a sheltered cove. He nosed the craft onto the gravelly beach and I splashed ashore, feeling like a smuggler.

CHAPTER FOURTEEN

The Summer House on the Cape

THE RAIN TAPERED OFF, AND BY MIDAFTERNOON A FEW SHAFTS OF PALE yellow sunshine were filtering through the mists, livening up the cliff faces and giving the moody seascape a sort of romantic feel, rather than a threatening one. Between the gentle roll of the surf, the mossy lower slopes around us (the upper parts of the hills and icy mountains were still obscured by mist), and the melancholy cries of the seagulls—a nonnative bird that had allegedly followed the old whaling ships south—this little cove could almost have passed for one of the lonelier strands somewhere in Scotland's Outer Hebrides. Except, of course, for the chinstrap penguins waddling along the beach.

There were six of us ashore to wave away the last dinghy after it dropped off the final load of supplies. We trudged up to the camp feeling agreeably like castaways as another short shower of rain began to fall. I liked the field camp. It was a snug, timber-framed cabin, painted pine green, with a view overlooking the cove on which we'd landed. Decking ran around the outside of it—the terrain here was very boggy—and led to a separate larder and outhouse, its door decorated with the classic half moon.

The interior was pleasingly rustic, with mismatched cooking utensils hanging over the sink, an old gas stove, and a red-and-white waxed cloth on the kitchen table. It was warm inside and had the feel of a much loved summerhouse in Maine. Some of its stylishness was owed to the foul weather that continually besets these islands. The carpenters who built the place were stranded here for six weeks when the ship couldn't get in to pick them up, and so they had filled in their idle days with finishing work and fine cabinetry.

"I really feel like I've come home," Wayne said, looking around the cabin with unbuttoned ease and a welcoming glass of single malt in his hand. This was the start of his 25th consecutive field season on the Antarctic Peninsula. His wife was also a veteran penguin researcher, and although they were not working together this summer—she was on King George Island—they often had in the past, and so the setting had almost a backyard familiarity to him.

Strangely enough, I felt it too. By now I had grown familiar with Antarctic field camps and this had the same comfortable woodsy feel as the ones up on Darwin Glacier and near the summit of Mount Erebus—but it had something else as well. Perhaps it was the location, within earshot of the surf—a familiar "real world" sound—and the haunting cries of the gulls, like seashores back home, and the presence of mosses and grasses. Sitting around the red-checked table, with salmon cutlets poaching gently on the stove for dinner, listening to relaxed banter, Neil Young on the CD player, and rain spattering on the windows, and my stockinged feet stretched toward the heater, made me feel as though I were visiting some old friends. I felt at home too.

After dinner we went for a walk over to the seal and penguin colonies a couple of miles away, out on the tip of the cape. Although the rain had stopped—for the time being—we still wore heavy PVC slickers and gumboots for the ankle-deep muck. It was a beautiful twilit evening. The diffuse yellow glow of sunlight through patches of mist gave the barren landscape a magical quality, the muddy slopes tinged with the green of moss and algae. The dark volcanic crags looked like ruined castles.

We crested a rise. The beach curving out below us was strewn with the blubbery shapes of thousands of dozing seals. Higher up on the hillsides were the pebble nests of nearly 8,000 breeding pairs of chinstrap penguins and several thousand more pairs of gentoo penguins. The damp evening air was filled with cries, squeaks, and grunts, and it reeked with the barnyard stench of guano. Millions of pink splotches on the rocks bore testament to a steady diet of krill. The abundance of wildlife, the wild rocky storm-lashed setting, and all arrayed in diffuse melancholy silvery light made me think of the romantic watercolors painted by artists who used to accompany early 19th-century explorers—it had that untouched arcadian look to it, although Cape Shirreff was anything but untouched. This was one of the beaches hardest hit by the sealers in the 1820s, with more than 100,000 fur seals taken from here in that bloodthirsty decade, and the fact that it was so rich in wildlife now was solely testimony to the marvelous recuperative powers of nature, coupled, of course, with the cessation of hunting.

This lovely arcadian soft-focus glow dissolved a bit—as lovely arcadian glows generally do—as we clambered down onto the beach, with its smells and grunts and squeaks and the unprovoked aggressiveness of the fur seals, for no matter how cuddly they appear in photographs, these are thoroughly unpleasant creatures to be around. They attack, lumbering toward you surprisingly swiftly with an almost bearlike gait, open-mouthed and growling. Fortunately they don't generally press home their charges—point a walking staff at them or clap a couple of rocks together and they will retreat (only sometimes to mount a rearguard action and have a go at your heels as you walk on by). They are big and powerful, easily capable of inflicting a great deal of damage. Mike, the seal senior researcher here on the Cape, knew many of these seals individually, and he led the way, taking us on a circuitous path around the more aggressive males.

The whole reason for the field camp and research season here was to provide some land-based research for the same sweeping marine biology survey being undertaken by the krill researchers on the *Yuzhmorgeologiya*, the idea being to gather the broadest possible sense of life down here and to see how different parts of the ecosystem fit together and relate to each other. So little is known. The seas are too big and wild and inaccessible, the summer seasons so short.

I woke the next morning feeling horribly seasick, and as I sat up in my bunk, with a skull-splitting headache, and looked around at my strange surroundings and realized that I was in a field camp on land. I also realized I'd picked up the virus that had laid low a couple of the biologists back on the ship. I crawled out of bed, and gazed out the rain-spattered window at one of the coldest, bleakest, dreariest landscapes I've ever seen. A big line of squalls had swept in overnight, lashing the Cape with wind and near-monsoonal rains. It drummed mightily on the roof and fell in dense gray torrents until the ground around the cabin for hundreds of yards in every direction became a quivering morass—more puddle than mud. Our "sheltered" cover was sheltered no more; the surf pounded and boomed, dirty and gray, in the strong winds.

I sat at the table, nursing a cup of tea and a violent headache, and thanking God I didn't have to go anywhere that day. We had tried raising the *Golden Fleece* on the radio the previous night, but without success. A woman from Palmer Station, a large U.S. base a hundred miles or so farther south, reported that the yacht had left there a couple of days earlier, but she had no idea where it might be.

I was just saying aloud how glad I was that they'd not yet come to pick me up when there was a knock on the door. We looked at each other; you don't get drop-ins on Cape Sherriff. Brian opened the door. And there stood Maria, the NATIONAL GEOGRAPHIC photographer, dripping wet and spattered with mud. She was with two strangers, both in their 20s, a tall and very fit German guy named Christian and his equally fit Swiss girlfriend, Miriam, who, despite the mud and rain, managed to look as fresh as a peeled egg. They were the crew from the *Golden Fleece*.

"But...but...but," I stammered, doing a fairly good boat impersonation myself, and pointing to the empty sea as though to tell these apparitions they couldn't possibly be here.

"We couldn't get in here, the sea was too rough," Maria explained, "So we're anchored on the other side of the cape. All set to go?"

I shrugged into my parka and boots, picked up my rucksack, and stepped outside into the freezing downpour—and promptly threw up. I dropped my pack. "I ain't going anywhere."

They radioed Jérome the news that I was a bit under the weather. Christian and Miriam kindly carried my pack across the cape and rejoined the yacht, while Maria spent the day with the seal biologists, photographing seals in the cold rain, and I spent the day in the feverish tropics, half delirious, sipping water, listening to the storm blow and gazing glassily out the window at the muck, and the bloated bodies of the seals basking in it, and thinking to myself that this was exactly like that nasty, cold, rainy, muddy circle of hell Dante had envisioned for gluttons.

By five o'clock in the afternoon the rain had eased up a bit and I felt strong enough, or at least willing, to give it a try, and Maria and I slung on our packs and set off across the cape, hiking along the floor of a soggy, mist-shrouded valley where seals lay dozing in the ooze like giant slugs. They raised their heads to look at us, and then settled back. We trudged past them, sinking in up to our ankles, the muck sucking noisily at our boots. We tried to keep to the snow patches, which offered better footing.

The fresh air felt good. At the head of the valley we trudged up a muddy ridge, about 300 feet high, from which we could see the other side of the cape. The *Golden Fleece* was in a sheltered inlet. It looked like a toy, a little blue and white boat with two masts and a chunky wheelhouse. A door opened and a tiny figure emerged. It waved.

We scrambled downhill, our boots sliding in the gravelly mud. The beach was small and black and pebbly. A few whalebones, yellowed by more than a century of exposure, lay half buried in the shingle. We hopped onto the rocks. They were slippery, washed by the constant heavy swell.

A moment later a Zodiac veered into sight around one of the inlet's rocky arms. The man working the outboard was the picture of a rugged craggy-faced Breton fisherman, in yellow slicker and tatty navy blue watch cap. He was in his 50s, dark, medium size, and wiry, with a weatherbeaten face full of Gallic humor and irony.

He skillfully nosed the little craft hard onto the rocks and held it in place by gunning the engine. It puffed thin blue smoke. We jumped aboard. He nodded a greeting and backed away, and we bounced through the spray 100 yards or so to where the yacht waited at anchor. If I had felt like a smuggler when I landed on Livingstone Island, I felt doubly so getting away from it.

The *Golden Fleece* was about 70 feet long, registered in Port Stanley, in the Falkland Islands. It had much sturdier lines than a traditional yacht, with a broad steel hull designed for traveling in Antarctica's ice-strewn waters and a stout wheelhouse that called to mind a small North Sea trawler. It had two inflatable Zodiac dinghies, and a winch for launching them. Maria and I scrambled up the ladder, while Jérome, Christian, and Miriam hauled in the dinghy. The wind caught it and made it swing. Three pairs of hands landed it and strapped it securely to the deck. The yacht pitched uneasily in the swell. Heavy surf rolled against the shoals farther out. We shed our boots and left them in the bay in the wheelhouse, hung up our dripping parkas, and trooped downstairs.

The saloon was spacious and pleasant, with two bolted-down tables and inbuilt upholstered seating, books on the walls, a CD player, and a television. The *Golden Fleece* could carry fourteen people, but with only six of us aboard we had the luxury of space.

Lamb chops were on the grill in the galley, cooked by a woman named Katie. She was French, in her 50s, with short, thick, blond hair and an easy manner. I learned later that she was born in Morocco, had spent years traveling around Central Asia and Siberia, and seemed to be able to turn her hand to almost anything. She was setting a large wooden salad bowl on the table when we came downstairs. "We had all better eat well now because we are going to be navigating tonight and it is going to be very rough."

I remember very little of that first night aboard. I was still running a high fever, and if I'd felt like the land was heaving in a seasick sort of way back when I was in camp, the actual movement of the yacht was truly ghastly. I picked at my lamb chops and afterward, mumbling excuses, stumbled back to my cabin in the stern with a bottle of water and a very uninviting plastic pail. I drew the curtain, tossed my backpack on one of the two bunks in my cabin, and crept into the other, barely able to crawl over the wooden safety sides. I heard the big diesel engine start up a little later, and shortly after that the yacht began to pitch heavily as we nosed out of the cove and into the wild seas off Livingstone Island.

That night I was so sick I was afraid I was going to live. The next couple of days passed in such a feverish blur that even now I'm confused about whether it was two days or three. It stayed cloudy and grim, and the feeble light coming through the porthole hardly varied in the almost constant summer daylight. Time was measured in nightmarish dozes, but whether they lasted five minutes or five hours I couldn't tell.

Sometimes I was hot and sweaty, sometimes I was shivering and cold; sometimes the engines were running, sometimes they weren't. Sometimes the yacht seemed to be flying. Once I flipped completely out of my bunk and landed on the floor with my face unceremoniously in the bucket. It was too good an opportunity to miss....

On the bright side, it was all a curiously liberating experience. I felt so god-awful that I truly didn't care about anything in this world or the next. When I finally crawled out of bed and made my way up to the wheelhouse, we were anchored inside a spectacular ring of reefs and rocky spires near Robert Island, an obscure old sealer's haunt about 60 miles east–northeast of Cape Shirreff. Maria, Christian, and Miriam had gone ashore to photograph a huge cast-iron try pot abandoned by American sealers in the 1820s. Katie was reading a paperback. Jérome was perusing a sea chart of the area, sipping black coffee from a demitasse cup. He glanced up, mimed a look of Gallic astonishment when he saw me, and cried: "It's alive!"

CHAPTER FIFTEEN

The Realtors' Big Three

DROLL, IRONIC, TOUGH, HUMOROUS, AND TEMPERAMENTAL, JEROME WAS also probably the nearest thing there can be to a true Antarctican, having sailed in and explored these waters almost continuously for 30 years, even wintering down here once, freezing his yacht into the ice as the early explorers did, on the coast of Adelaide Island.

"I came here because there were no rules," he said, simply and breezily when I asked him what led him here. "There was no paperwork, no passports, just freedom."

Over the next few weeks, as I lived aboard his yacht, I learned that he'd grown up in a military family back in France and had been sent to military school as a child, from which he dreamed of his eventual escape with his best mate. Both boys loved sailing, and they decided that one day they would buy a boat and sail around the world together. A lot of kids fashion such dreams for themselves—I know I did—but these kids really meant it.

They'd bought a yacht together when they were still in their teens and set out on a course for adventure the moment they had adult freedom and just enough cash to do it. They sailed first into the Arctic. The ice enchanted Jérome, and though they went on to circle the globe, it drew him back. He had seen a bit of Antarctica when they dipped south to visit some of its frozen archipelagoes on their way around Cape Horn. He showed me photo albums of their grand journey—it seemed odd to see Jérome shirtless in the tropics, he seemed so much a creature of the snow and cold. ("Bah! What's there to see in Asia?" he scoffed when I'd imagined aloud about what it must have been like sailing through the Spice Islands, "It's boring. Who needs it when you have all this down here?")

Later he bought a small island farm in the Falklands, where he makes his winter home and spends his summers exploring the Antarctic Peninsula, doing just enough charter work to support his passion. He loved the solitude of the farthest-flung corners of the peninsula, the obscure islands, inlets, and capes where few people, other than him, had ever been—which meant he wanted to go to busy King George Island, with all its many bases, about as much as I desired a relapse of that virus, but the demands of the story called for a few days there, and so he set a course for Maxwell Bay.

It was late in the evening the following day when we sailed into the bay, a postcard-pretty anchorage surrounded by glaciers and mountains at the southern tip of King George Island. The water was like glass. The sky was pale blue and dim because the sun had dipped behind the mountains. A surprising number of lights twinkled along the shore, and this, accented by the blues CD throbbing softly in the wheelhouse, gave the bay an appropriately cosmopolitan feel.

King George Island has always been the busiest pocket of Antarctica. A century ago, this was the crossroads for the world's whaling fleet; today it is Antarctica's Manhattan. Argentina, Brazil, Chile, China, Poland, Russia, South Korea, and Uruguay all maintain year-round bases here, practically cheek by jowl in Maxwell and Admiralty Bays, while the U.S., Ecuador, Peru, Germany, the Netherlands, and the Czech Republic operate summer camps as well. It is the only part of Antarctica ever to host a rock concert or a convention, or to have been visited by a head of state.

There is a reason this 520-square-mile island is the trendiest and most cosmopolitan piece of real estate in Antarctica, but it has little to do with lovely views, let alone science, which in theory at least is why all the bases are here. Its appeal comes straight from the realtors' big three: location, location, and location. King George Island is simply, and by far, the handiest part of Antarctica to get to—only a quick hop by air from South America—making it the easiest and cheapest place for an aspiring nation to set up a base and thereby earn the status of full voting member of the Antarctic Treaty.

It became particularly popular in the 1980s, when the treaty nations were overheard talking quietly among themselves about how to divvy up Antarctica's mineral wealth when and if it ever became feasible to extract it. Suddenly a slew of countries that had never before shown the slightest interest in polar science were scrambling to set up budget-priced Antarctic bases, in order to earn a seat at the bargaining table and hopefully a slice of the pie.

In any event, the mining treaty was scuppered at the last minute, to be replaced by the 1991 Madrid Protocol, which declared the whole of Antarctica and its waters a natural reserve of peace and science, and banned any mineral exploitation for at least 50 years. But the bases remained, and as we puttered up the bay in the soft twilight of a January evening, I had to admit the clusters of topaz-colored lights strung along the shore looked rather pretty.

We dropped anchor that night at the head of the bay, a stone's throw from Chile's Presidente Eduardo Frei base. This is the de facto capital of King George Island and unlike any other Antarctic base I have ever seen. It is essentially a transplanted Chilean village, with a population of 300, including the wives and children of Air Force and Navy personnel assigned here on two-year postings. They live in a hillside suburb of ranch-style houses, painted in cheerful pastel yellows, greens, blues, and pinks. The suburb is called La Villa de las Estrellas, the Village of the Stars.

Chile is one of three nations with overlapping claims of sovereignty over the Antarctic Peninsula. Britain and Argentina are the other two. Even by the Alice in Wonderland standards of Antarctic politics, the two Latin American claims are rather special: God gave it to them.

In 1494 the pope divided the New World into two halves along a line of longitude bisecting the Atlantic Ocean, giving everything east of the line to Portugal and the western half—which included the Americas—to Spain. Since both Argentina and Chile were Spanish possessions at the time, they consider themselves the logical heirs to the old empire's God-given interests, and cited this musty papal treaty as evidence when they lodged their own claims to Antarctica in the 1940s.

Britain had to settle for the secular journals of Captain Cook and the fact that British bureaucrats had filed formal claims for the peninsula as early as 1903. Australia, New Zealand, France, and Norway also claim various portions of the continent.

While none of these claims are formally recognized and all are officially held in abeyance under the terms of the Antarctic Treaty, the various claimants still have fun keeping their aspirations alive. They issue stamps, fly flags, and, in the case of Chile and Argentina, colonize their territories by raising their families here. Here on King George Island, those who still don't get the idea can always tune in to Chile's La Radio Soberania—"Radio Sovereignty"—92.5 on the FM dial.

This displaced little patch of Chile was sleeping when we arrived, or at least it seemed to be. The streets were empty, the spruced-up houses silent in the unblinking summer night. Only the persistent hum of the generator indicated that people lived here. A few penguins loitered along the waterfront.

It had been a long day, and after we dropped anchor we all went to bed. Like the Pinkertons, however, the Chilean Navy never sleeps, and we were treated to a midnight boarding by a Zodiac full of mustached officers in blue sweaters, curious to know who we were and what our purpose was in coming to King George Island. They were friendly enough, and the upshot was an invitation to breakfast at the base the next morning.

They were waiting for us on shore—a welcoming committee of Navy and Air Force officers, a man named Patricio, the base's chief scientist, and Sergio, the grandfatherly 69-year-old head of Chile's Antarctic Program. They were standing beside a plinth, on which a bronze bust of Luis Pardo gazed with cool appraisal at the *Golden Fleece* and beyond it to the open waters of the bay.

Pardo was one of Chile's Antarctic heroes, and justifiably so. He was the commander of the *Yelcho*, the seagoing tug that the Chilean Navy had lent Shackleton in 1915 so that he could rescue the men he had left behind at Elephant Island. It was a bold and magnanimous gesture by the Chileans, particularly in light of the fact that Shackleton's own countrymen—notably the Lord of the Admiralty, Winston Churchill—was disposed to write them all off as a job lot of ne'er-do-wells who should have been decently off at the killing fields in Flanders long ago. But Commander Pardo and the *Yelcho* made it through the encroaching ice and rescued the stranded Englishmen, an episode, it was duly noted as we walked off to breakfast, that clearly demonstrated Chile's long-standing involvement with this part of the world.

We had an elaborate continental breakfast in what felt like a cozy bed-and-breakfast place—with a big old sideboard, nice furniture, pictures on the walls and all the usual old-style boarding house table settings. Frei wasn't one of those speculative bases, slapped up in the boom-time 1980s. It had been around since 1969 and had been built to replace an earlier Chilean base on nearby Deception Island, which was destroyed when the volcano there blew its top in 1967.

As we ate, Sergio told me how he had wintered on that original Deception Island base back in the International Geophysical Year, in 1956–57, when he was a 24-year-old officer in the Chilean Air Force.

"I must tell you the story behind that cross," he told me, calling my attention to a large wooden cross I'd noticed earlier that stood proud on a cliff top overlooking the base. "I built such a cross at Deception Island that first winter and it stood there for years, until the volcano destroyed the base. When I went back there later and looked among the ruins, I couldn't believe it when I found my cross there, partly buried under the rubble but otherwise in perfect condition. It was a miracle.

"I was overjoyed. We took it on board our ship and brought it to this new base and put it up on that cliff where it could look out over the bay. When I came back the following summer, and looked up from the deck of the ship and saw it there, I wept for joy. I even wrote a poem about it; I still have it, somewhere.'"

The elements eventually claimed that original cross, he explained, but a new one had been installed in its place and would go on protecting the base for years to come.

Sergio was made of even hardier stuff than the wood on his cross; he was the longest-serving Antarctican I have ever met, with 45 years of active service under his belt. He was tall for his generation, with humor and irony in his eyes.

"People today can have no idea what it was like that first winter. There were nine of us and when the ship pulled away we really felt like castaways. We lived in tents and were totally out of touch with the rest of the world. Today when I come down here I live in *a house*. I keep in touch with colleagues from all over the world by e-mail and in the evening I watch the same television shows I watch back home in Santiago.'"

It is precisely all these colonizing niceties that has made King George Island an exemplar of all that is wrong with human involvement with Antarctica—at least in the minds of environmentalists. King George Island, and its many bases, raises a lot of passions. And so I asked Sergio what he made of all the changes, particularly the building boom on King George Island and the influx of so many apparently superfluous bases. His answer surprised me. I expected either a head-shaking sadness at the despoliation or, given his senior government position, a defense of the onward thrust of science and civilization and an assurance that the impact on the local environment had been exaggerated. Certainly I expected some form of pro or con on the environment. Environmental impact seems to underlie every topic of discussion in Antarctica, much the way profit or loss is ultimately the root of all business questions, and good and evil is the coin of theology. It is like code neatly woven into a program. But he skipped it completely, stepping right outside the square.

"Take a look around you," he said, "Think of all the bases we have on this island from countries all over the world. Here we have a beginning, a light. On this one little island we have people from all over the world living in perfect harmony. There are no borders or passports here, no politics, no communism, no capitalism, and no religious strife. And there never has been. If anybody here, on any of the bases, were to get into trouble or need help, everybody would offer it, without stint or question. This is precisely the kind of tolerance and human understanding we had hoped would come about all those years ago, during the IGY [International Geophysical Year 1957–58]. I do not know yet how we can learn to export this, to bring this sense of community home with us when we go. But if we can manage it, to bring back this light, just think what a wonderful gift Antarctica will have given the world."

School had let out for the summer, and most of the families on the base had gone "up to the continent" for the holidays, but there were still half a dozen kids here, sledding on a hillside and throwing snowballs at each other. It was the most natural sight in the world, kids playing, but down here in the world's largest winter wonderland it was an astonishing rarity.

And it was wonderful to see. Frei seemed all the richer for their presence, however political their purpose ultimately was in being here. But it was a day for feeling rich anyway. The weather was unexpectedly glorious, with sparkling skies, the bay a lustrous blue, and the frozen mountains all around us gleaming white. The base was pleasingly busy. Overhead, the pilot of a Brazilian Air Force C-130 was practicing touch-and-go landings on the airstrip on a bluff above the town, coming in low over the rooftops, as noisy as a runaway train. Such bold doings were old hat to the kids on the hill. They didn't even bother looking up. I was the one gawking.

"Antarctica is a great place to bring up kids," Maria, the wife of the base's Air Force commander, told me when I stopped by their house for a cup of tea after lunch. "Everything is very family oriented here. It is safe, clean, there are no drugs or bad influences—just the penguins!"

Again we were sitting in the tastefully furnished parlor of her three-bedroom home, the Three Tenors singing softly on a stereo in the background. Outside, her two children—12-year-old Juan Pablo and 10-year-old Javiera—played on their sleds. I could see what Sergio had meant when he emphasized that he lived in a house when he came here; this was nothing like an Antarctic base, it was a suburban house anywhere—Santiago, Melbourne, or Omaha.

"My friends thought I might miss the shopping malls and social life, but really I haven't missed anything. If there is anything I want to buy that I can't get at the supermarket, I can always order it on the Internet.

"As far as the social life here goes, I still play tennis a couple of nights a week in the gymnasium and we have card nights with friends—things people do in small towns everywhere. Everyone here respects each other's privacy. It's really quite a normal life. We are posted here for two years, but I would have no trouble staying for five or ten."

The family dining table was set for a birthday party later that afternoon. It was bright with decorations, tall glasses, and wrapped presents. A cake waited on the kitchen counter. Juan Pablo and Javiera were tumbling into the entryway on the effervescence of a giggle when I was leaving, their mother reminding them to knock the snow off their boots. As I walked down the street I passed a mother pushing a pram through the neighborhood, with a bright-eyed baby peeking through the covers.

It's funny the things that shape your perceptions. In my memory Frei and McMurdo come up as roughly the same size, although my fact-driven brain knows that to be nonsense. The U.S. base is far larger, supplied by huge cargo jets and with a powerful reach that extends anywhere on the continent. But while MacTown might be the nearest thing Antarctica has to a city, it is an edgy adult sort of place; of barroom romances and that jaded loneliness that pervades transient hotels and bus stations everywhere, no matter how cheery the radio sounds. Three hundred people live at Eduardo Frei—but they raise families here, play cards, and watch TV with the neighbors, and Antarctican tennis moms help their kids with homework. That gives it dimensions that far exceed its stature.

Maxwell Bay is nothing if not a close-knit neighborhood. The Chileans sit, cheek by jowl, beside Russia's sprawling Bellingshausen base—so close, in fact, that the buildings of the two bases almost seem to intermingle. The Russians were here first, setting up their facility in 1968 as a major refueling depot for the Soviet Antarctic fishing fleet. The Chileans moved in close beside them the following year, after losing their base on Deception Island. They were Marxist at the time and probably viewed the Soviets as comradely neighbors, a happy circumstance that, as Sergio noted, didn't change despite the various shifts in homeland politics throughout the years.

I hopped across the glacial meltwater stream that marks the boundary between the two bases (and en route crossing a one-hour time zone change; the Chinese had a similar time zone change at their Great Wall base just over the rise) and found myself looking at a signpost made up of century-old whalebones and weathered wood, which gave the distances to Moscow, New York, the South Pole, and a couple of dozen other points around the globe. I was taking all this in when the Russian commander ambled up and offered to show me around.

He was an angular, blond man in his 30s named Oleg, a former radio engineer from a town on the White Sea in the Russian Arctic who had worked in Antarctica for 12 years. He wore jeans and a thin black leather jacket instead of a parka ("I dislike government-issue clothing," he explained), and had an active, alert manner that made me think of an Internet-savvy entrepreneurial Muscovite.

When he learned I had come south on the *Yuzhmorgeologiya*, he asked about some friends of his who worked aboard, and as I filled him in on what limited gossip I could offer, Antarctica began to seem a very small place indeed. And he told me Progress II, the grim and abandoned base I'd seen years ago with the Australians, had been reopened. He told me this as we walked past an ugly junkyard of oil drums, wrecked vehicles, and scrap iron that very much reminded me of the old Progress II.

"All this is going to go later this summer," he said, indicating the junkyard sprawl. Promises had been made in that direction before, but the anticipated ship never arrives. This time would be different, Oleg maintained, adding that the Russians were now working with a British environmental organization to organize transport and get the junk cleared away.

His matter-of-fact air when he told me this was tinged with sensitivity about Russia's image in Antarctica. "I wouldn't want to give the impression that we Russians are just sitting here doing nothing and waiting for foreigners to come and clean up our mess. There are Russian volunteers working on this, too, and I personally worked on removing an old East German base on the other side of the continent. We cleared away more than a thousand tons of scrap. Nothing remains there now but a plaque where the base used to be."

The old part of Bellingshausen base was almost a museum time capsule of Soviet-era Antarctica, with antique sewing machines, battered chess tables, and old-fashioned movie room, with its collection of more than 1,000 old films in metal canisters. Somehow it all projected an air of gloomy banishment.

That too was starting to change. Sawdust swirled, and the whine of circular saws resounded in the corridor outside Oleg's office. Bellingshausen was undergoing a makeover, with the cash-strapped Russians now taking in boarders to make ends meet, offering ready-made accommodations and facilities for foreign scientists whose governments couldn't or wouldn't open a base, in essence an Antarctic B&B.

They had already hosted a group of 20-odd researchers from Germany and Austria, who stayed with them earlier in the summer, and now had their shingle out for more. They weren't the only ones capitalizing on the rekindled interest in Antarctica and the collaborative mood it seemed to inspire.

A couple of days later we sailed over to Argentina's Jubany base, across the bay, where Germany and Holland had built an annex so all three countries could share expenses. A nest of flagpoles in front of the complex reflected the come-all greeting of an international hotel: A welcoming Australian flag flew on my behalf, there was a Swiss one for Miriam, the French tricolor was raised for Jérome and Katie, and Old Glory waved for Maria. The Argentine and German flags, of course, were already flying.

Although Jubany had been established nearly 50 years earlier as an expression of Argentine sovereignty over this part of the world, the *jefe de bas*—a Navy man—took pride in its present multicultural flavor and Antarctica's borderless collegiality, telling me how a team of his divers had recently come to the rescue of a disabled fishing vessel whose nets had become tangled in its propellers out on the high seas.

"So we had Argentine Navy divers fixing an American boat, then towing it to a Russian base for repairs, with the Chilean Air Force flying in parts and people," he laughed. "And the funny thing is, until we were talking about it later, it didn't seem the least bit unusual. This is just the way things are here."

One night we had a party on the yacht. Oleg and couple of other Russians came out with a bottle of Stolichnaya, and a little while later a Zodiac drew up with some German scientists and a pair of Argentine Navy divers. Miriam and Maria weren't there just then, being off visiting the Great Wall Station, where they were having dinner with the Chinese. The saloon in the *Golden Fleece* filled with voices and laughter and languages: English, Russian, German, French, and Spanish.

Jérome broke out a couple bottles of wine, and while he was uncorking them told me that the Koreans, from King Sejong Station, had dropped by earlier that afternoon to invite us over to lunch.

I sat down with a glass of Argentine red and tried to tune in to the gossip. There was plenty of it about. Only a few days earlier the Uruguayans had hosted a town-meeting-style luncheon at their base, inviting representatives from all the other bases on King George Island, and sending their big Navy helicopter around to pick everybody up. The idea was to build on the sense of community in the island, and exchange information on scientific projects. There was even talk of a King George Island newsletter being started up. This strange, frozen little island was like the United Nations, except that it actually functioned.

The Koreans were waiting on the dock when we arrived the next day, cameras in hand and projecting Asian formality and cheery welcome. They drove us up to the base in new Hyundais, and passed around slippers to wear inside the base.

While some of the newcomers who flocked to King George Island in the 1980s did so on a shoestring, the Koreans spent up big, erecting an upscale base, complete with karaoke bar and disco ball, and stocking their laboratories with state-of-the-art scientific gear.

"We had little experience in Antarctica until we came here in 1988," the base's commanding officer, Soon-Keun Chang, told me when we stepped inside. "We considered putting a station on the continent itself, but we realized that would have been much too difficult and expensive to start off with. This seemed a better place to learn our way around."

He was a geologist, but during the long winter on base devoted his time to writing children's books, in Korean, about Antarctica's wildlife, natural history, and heroic polar explorers.

"Antarctica is something new to us in Korea," he said, showing me some of the dozen or so books he had published. "It is important for our children to learn what it means to the world."

CHAPTER SIXTEEN

The Seventh Continent

WE LEFT KING GEORGE ISLAND ON THE BREATH OF A GALE, WITH THE WINDS kicking up to 40 knots, and a heavy swell clattering the crockery in the galley and bouncing me between the two sides of my bunk like a pea in a matchbox. The dirty-gray waters that boomed and sloshed against my porthole belonged to the Bransfield Strait, the rough and moody passage, 60 miles wide, that separates the South Shetland archipelago from the mainland of the Antarctic Peninsula; we were bound for a cluster of islands—Joinville, Dundee, and Paulet—huddled together just off the tip of the peninsula.

It was way too rough to sleep, so I tried to read. I'd discovered a collection of tattered paperbacks in my cabin and found the perfect read to pass the sleepless hours: Shakespeare's *The Tempest*. As the yacht lurched and heaved, I braced myself against a wall of my bunk, but managed only a few pages before giving up. Eventually I drifted off and dreamed of bowling alleys, rodeo bulls, and going over Niagara Falls in a washing machine.

I didn't mind. Much as I'd enjoyed my time on King George Island, the easy sociability of the bases, the cosmopolitan White South, it felt good to get away—liberating, free of polite society and bureaucratic constriction. With the exception of a couple of brief courtesy calls to two Argentine bases, and later on, visits to Britain's Rothera base and the old base at Port Lockroy, we were through with bases now—just traveling with Jérome, letting him show us the rare White South that he knew, as the nearest thing Antarctica has to a true native. Maria had wanted to shoot pictures of masses of penguins, so at the moment he was taking us first to Paulet Island, a tiny speck of volcanic rock where hundreds of thousands of Adélie penguins bred and made their nests, as well as a large population of blue-eyed shags and Southern Giant Petrels.

Jérome had originally planned to take a bolder route, sailing right around the outermost of the islands, past a little cluster marked on the charts as the Danger Islands. I'd liked the adventuresome sound of that. But as the night wore on and the seas grew rougher he altered course and made for the rather more sheltered waters of the Antarctic Strait, the ice-strewn passage between the islands and the peninsular tip.

We were well out of the Bransfield Strait and well into the Antarctic one when I clambered up to the wheelhouse at about half past five in the morning. Jérome was drinking another of his endless demitasse cups of coffee, looking tired but clearly happy to be away from the civilization of King George Island and doing what he loved best: sailing the Antarctic.

He was—and is—a remarkable sailor. At some point in the night I'd been jarred out of my slumbers by a series of almighty crashes that made a landlubber like me marvel that the spine of the yacht could take such a pounding. There were moments when we seemed to be flying, followed by a long, sickening plunge and then a skidding, belly-flop-style, onto a rough swell. It says something of the confidence that Jérome inspired in his seamanship—and perhaps a little of my own inexperience—that I felt only wonder at the power of the sea, and even a touch of grouchy sleeplessness, rather than any sense of danger or terror. I had managed to go back to sleep. And now the sea before us was relatively calm.

In the distance ahead, the dark cliff faces of Dundee Island emerged from the mists. They looked cold and lonely and mysterious. And coming after the wild, stormy night, they felt gratifyingly far away from the cloying tameness of King George Island.

Still, there was human history here as well. Dundee Island—named by a Scottish whaling captain for his home town—was where the U.S. millionaire-adventurer Lincoln Ellsworth took off on the first trans-Antarctic flight in 1935, an epic that took nearly two weeks thanks to forced landings in bad weather. It ended with Ellsworth and his co-pilot having to walk the final 15 miles after his battered Northrop monoplane finally ran out of fuel.

And tiny Paulet Island, just a few miles farther into the mist, was where the shipwrecked crew of the *Antarctic* eked out a miserable winter in 1903, after their ship was crushed and sunk by pack ice. They had been trying to rescue a party led by Swedish explorer Nils Nordenskjold, who had been stranded farther south in the Weddell Sea. A search party sent out by the Argentine Navy eventually rescued the missing men, some of whom had by then spent more than two years living a Neanderthal existence in crude stone huts, subsisting on nearly raw seal meat and trying to keep warm in the cold, wet winters by the smoky flame of a blubber stove.

A low sky was spitting snow when we glided up to Paulet Island. The sea was like black glass. The air was filled with the croaky chatter of hundreds of thousands of penguins. They were everywhere, darting through the water around the yacht, waddling along the shore, and roosting on the countless thousands of pebbly nests that covered the snow-dusted hills. The island was a pointillist study in black and white. It didn't seem possible there could be so many penguins in all the world, let alone on one windswept mote barely a mile across. They looked more like computer-generated extras for a Hollywood wildlife extravaganza than anything real. But the barnyard stench of guano was real enough. A medieval plague port would have had nothing on this place.

We dropped anchor and lowered the dinghy to go ashore. Unlike the castaways from the *Antarctic*, we didn't have Paulet Island to ourselves. A cruise liner, *Clipper Adventurer*, stood nearby and a group of tourists in scarlet parkas was strung out along the beach, their size throwing the knee-high penguins into comic relief.

Because of its huge penguin colony, Paulet Island is a popular stop on Antarctica's nascent cruise ship circuit. About 4,000 visitors make it here each summer. We had known that *Clipper Adventurer* would be near here because Jérome had been nattering to the ship's captain on the radio that morning, but the ship's passengers were stunned to see us. They stared at the *Golden Fleece* as we motored up to shore in our Zodiac. An American-accented voice called out: "You guys came down here on that?"

It was Thomas Cook & Son who first mooted the idea of tourism in Antarctica as far back as 1910, but it wasn't until a Pan American charter flight touched down as a novelty at McMurdo Station in 1957 that the first tourists actually arrived. Another decade passed before regular cruises to Antarctica began to operate. Now it is a trendy destination. More than 20,000 tourists come down to The Ice each summer, most of them by cruise liner from South America. So many ships ply these waters that each night, at about half past seven, the radio comes alive with chatter as cruise directors from the various liners sort out their itineraries for the following day, giving their positions and plans and stating how long they plan to visit each location.

"They do this to preserve a sense of solitude for their passengers," Jérome had explained one evening. "After all, nobody wants to spend $20,000 on a cruise to Antarctica and then spend all their time seeing other tourists."

There were 113 "other tourists" aboard *Clipper Adventurer*, most of them elderly, and all but 4 were American—about the norm for an Antarctic cruise. Wealthy retirees are about the only demographic with the time and money required to travel in this part of the world—in this particular case, a 17-day cruise of the Falklands, South Georgia, the South Orkneys, Elephant and Deception Islands, and obviously, the sprawling penguin colony here at Paulet.

"This is our seventh continent!" a bundled-up woman of about 60 named Karen enthused as she and her husband, Bill, and I picked our way along the slippery rocks toward the ruins of the stone hut built by the castaways in 1903. "We got the idea to come down here and get the last continent from a couple we met on another cruise. This is just fabulous."

They had sold their furniture store back in Columbus, Mississippi, to their son a few years earlier and were now spending as much of their retirement as possible aboard cruise ships; Antarctica had blown them away.

"I'll tell you, those documentaries don't prepare you for what it's like being here in person," Bill said. "You never know what you're going to see down here. Every day it's something different. And the wildlife! The other morning I stepped out of my cabin, and right before my eyes I saw a leopard seal tear a penguin to pieces! The next morning we were seeing whales all around the ship. And now this!" He extended his hand at the hundreds of thousand of penguins spreading in every direction. "It's incredible!"

I liked them, and their fellow passengers, and their happy astonishment at Antarctica's exhilarating space and frosty magic. Such emotional honesty came as a welcome break from the tiresomeness of the scientists, most (but by no means all) of whom affected a lofty, worldly ennui, or else, if they felt a childish wonder and delight at being here, were very reluctant to express it. One scientist I met actually came right out and told me that he was worried that I might portray him in print as enjoying himself down here—which he was—lest any perception of self-fulfillment or pleasure reduce his chances of further grant money. It seemed so sad.

Not so the tourists. They come down here, one and all, for the sheer joy of it and to take in its crystalline beauty, for the thrill of seeing so much wildlife, and the romance of distance, and they make no bones about any of it. They do not pretend that their motives are anything greater than that—or that they are anything less, for that matter.

What's more, unlike scientists, tourists pay their own way, don't intrude on the landscape by building bases, and make no pretense of control or ownership.

Karen and Bill didn't pause long at the Nordenskjold ruin, but went on up the path beyond it, where the bird expert on their tour—an author of an authoritative seabird guide—was leading his charges. I lingered, wanting to get my own feel for the derelict hut.

It had been built out of the heavy black chunks of basalt that cover the island, and from some old black-and-white pictures I had seen, once had a roof of boards held down by stones. There wasn't much left of it anymore but low, guano-spattered walls, 30 feet long by 20 feet wide. Standing there in rain, mist, and spitting snow, with the stench and croaking cries of half a million penguins in the damp air, I tried to imagine what it would have been like to spend a year in that. Or even a day, without the certainty of a warm bunk and a hot, milky drink awaiting at the end of it.

"Many hundred dreams have been dreamed in our island," one of the stranded Swedes wrote in his journal, "but I do not know if they helped to brighten our existence. They grouped themselves around two objectives—food and rescue. Why, we could dream through a whole dinner from the soup to the dessert and waken to be cruelly disappointed. How many times did one not see the relief ship in our visions—sometimes as a large ship, sometimes as nothing but a little sloop?"

While I was squatting down beside its ruined walls, thinking about those people and their dreams, I noticed another tourist wander up, a tall, craggy, dark-haired American who looked to be in his late 50s or early 60s. His name was Nicholas. We fell to talking, the way strangers will when they encounter each other on raw, windswept coasts at the utter ends of the Earth.

He was not your average tourist. It turned out that he had been to Antarctica once before, many, many years ago—back in 1966—when he was a young mountaineer leading an expedition for the American Alpine Club to make the first ascent of Vincent Massif, at over 16,000 feet, the highest mountain in Antarctica. Those were innocent days when private citizens could still approach their own government's Antarctic programs, ask for, and receive assistance for a polar expedition.

They had been flown to McMurdo, courtesy of the U.S. Navy, which ran logistics for the U.S. Antarctic Program in those days, and then were ferried to the remote Ellsworth Mountains, where they promptly scaled Vincent Massif and went on to make first ascents of the continent's second, third, and fourth highest peaks as well. It was the last time the U.S. government would ever officially assist a private expedition—not because of anything Nicholas Clinch or his team did, but because of a belated reluctance to establish precedents, a fear of having to foot the cost of search and rescue efforts should things go awry, and an innate bureaucratic distrust of uncontrolled activities on a wide-open frontier.

"I've never been back to Antarctica until now," Nicholas told me. "It seems so strange to be coming here as a tourist; it isn't the kind of thing I had ever imagined myself doing, but I have to admit that I am enjoying it. And the hard fact remains that for most of us these days, tourism is the only possible way to get here."

The group from *Clipper Adventurer* spent about an hour on shore, before climbing back into their Zodiacs and heading back to the ship for lunch and an afternoon of lectures while they steamed toward their next landfall in the South Shetland Islands. I climbed one of the rocky hillocks and watched them go. The cruise liner left behind only its wake, and once it faded into the snowy mist, Paulet Island went back to the lonely feel it must have had for the castaways a century ago—right down to the two-masted yacht anchored in the mirror-black water, just like the one that appeared to them in their dreams.

As wild and aloof as Paulet Island had first appeared to me when we approached it that morning, it is still an island very much on the itineraries of many of the tour ships that come down here—assuming the Antarctic Strait isn't too choked with ice to allow access, and that's a big if, some years. For us, though, it had been merely a passing attraction—a convenient location for Maria's massed penguin photographs—as we made our way farther east and then south into the altogether more forbidding, remote, and seldom visited waters of the Weddell Sea.

This is the notoriously ice-choked body of water where Shackleton famously came to grief in 1915, when his ship the *Endurance* was crushed by ice. It can be a tricky—if not downright dangerous—place even these days to take a ship, let alone a yacht, but Jérome had been here many times and understood the drift of the ice and the fickle moods of the breezes as well as anyone ever has, and he wanted to show us its hard diamond beauty. And once down there we'd make for Seymour Island, Antarctica's own Jurrassic Park, a remote and oddly ice-free island covered with the fossils of gigantic penguins that stood as tall as Michael Jordan, prehistoric tortoises that reached the size of Volkswagens, and an ancient species of marsupial—the first discovery of land mammals in Antarctica—that roamed these parts during the Eocene period, between 40 million and 120 million years ago.

This is the only place in all of Antarctica where rocks from this era are exposed, giving paleontologists a unique view of what life here was like just before the continent made its final break away from the rest of the world.

Earlier, I had contacted the British Antarctic Survey, back in Cambridge, and received permission to visit its field camp on the island. The British, unlike the Americans, tend not to make permanent field camps, but opt instead for highly mobile low-impact camps that allow them to gypsy around from year to year, which is wonderful both for science and the environment but makes it a bit rough on visitors who might not know where to go. Seymour Island is more than ten miles long, and mountainous, and its coasts are thick with shifting ice, and when I last checked my e-mails, back at the

Korean base on King George Island, I'd still not had word where their camp was going to be that season.

So when we came across the British Navy ship HMS *Endurance* gliding toward us, out of the Weddell Sea, almost certainly fresh from having deployed the geologists on the island, it seemed a perfect opportunity to ask where the camp was, tell them our business, and inquire about the ice conditions ahead. I had heard, of course, many times and from many people, about the frosty rebuffs meted out to what governments regard as interlopers in Antarctica, but this was the first time I experienced it firsthand. The fact that the British Antarctic Survey had given us its official blessing to visit its camp (and later welcomed us with splendid hospitality at Rothera base) meant nothing to the Royal Navy; we never got that far in conversation.

Endurance was only about half a mile away when Jérome called them on the radio. There was no response.

He cleared his throat and tried again. "*Endurance*, this is yacht *Golden Fleece*, over."

Silence.

"Yacht *Golden Fleece* calling *Endurance*, can you read me? Over."

More silence.

The powerful naval vessel, bristling with antennas and state-of-the-art communications gear that monitored every conceivable wavelength, steamed majestically through the ice only a few hundred yards away. It could have been the *Mary Celeste* for all the life we could detect aboard her.

Jérome tried yet again, with the same result, and grew irritated, finally banging down the radio mike.

"*Bastards!* For all they know, I could have somebody dying on board. This is wrong." He was particularly incensed because in the past he and the *Golden Fleece* had assisted the British Antarctic Survey and the HMS *Endurance* with wildlife surveys. Then he had been handsomely entertained in the officers' mess aboard *Endurance*, where the gentlemen dined in full dinner kit. Now those same officers and gentlemen—men whom he knew by name and who knew him as well—were very pointedly refusing to speak to him. Antarctica—particularly this part of it—was too small a world for them not to have placed him or his yacht; it was galling.

"When they had use of me—fine—but now I do not exist."

He picked up the mike again and addressed the ether with weary irony. "Ah, well, thank you very much *Endurance*, you have been a big help. If you ever have need of anything, you know whom to call. This is Jérome Poncet, aboard the yacht *Golden Fleece*, over and out."

We stood out on the deck and watched the big red-and-white vessel steam gloriously into the bluish distance; Britannia ruling the waves, and waiving the rules. The temperature dropped noticeably once we sailed into the Weddell Sea, the air chilled by the presence of so much ice. Icebergs loomed everywhere, many of them towering above our mast. A group of Adélie penguins stood on an ice floe and stared hard at us as we floated by. Shackleton had the misfortune to sail into it during a particularly bad year for ice; we had come in a relatively good season by Weddell Sea standards. Even so, Jérome kept an anxious eye out, not just on the icebergs, pack ice, and submerged growlers crowding our path, but on the murky skies as well. A sudden shift in the wind could stir countless millions of tons of ice into chaotic motion, like a cocktail shaker, bruising, imprisoning, or even crushing the *Golden Fleece*.

I watched Jérome at the tiller, enjoying the challenge, plotting his moves ahead with the skill of a chess master. What lay before us was a beautiful, shimmering, crystal maze, constantly in subtle motion. Jérome was very, very good at what he did, but there was no arrogance to it, no showiness, just a quiet pleasure in the game. It would have been foolish for almost anyone else on the planet to try steering a yacht through this, but Jérome had the skills, a respectful knowledge of ice and winds born of 30 years' experience, and an intuitive understanding of Antarctica's moods that made it a fair contest, even if it couldn't lessen the stakes.

I leaned against the rail and admired the shapes of the bergs around us, picking out the Sphinx, the Matterhorn, and the Sydney Opera House. The tabular bergs had sheer white faces, as crisp and chiseled as freshly broken blocks of peppermint candy. All of the ice seemed to emit its own glow, their dazzling whites and hints of blue a dramatic counterpoint to the damp gray mass of clouds.

It was cold. Within a couple of hours the yacht's water pipes were frozen solid, obliging us to get our water for drinking and cooking the way the early Antarctic mariners did: using a long-handled net to scoop up chunks of hard, clear ice and melting them down in a pot on the stove. (A detail the explorers never mention in their journals is that if you don't let the ice blocks drain first on the deck, to let the seawater drip away, your drinking water is going to taste truly nasty and brackish.)

We spent that night drifting among the icebergs with a couple of minke whales coming up and taking big blowing breaths around us. Jérome slept on the sofa in the wheelhouse, taking turns with Christian, Miriam, and Katie at keeping watch.

By eight o'clock the next morning we were 12 nautical miles from Seymour Island, which looked dark and mountainous against a dismal sheen of sky. Seymour Island stands out from the rest because it doesn't have a thick snow cover, thanks to its being in the weather shadow of the lofty mountains of nearby James Ross and Snow Hill Islands.

Down at sea level the pack ice was very thick, and for a time it looked as though we might not be able to reach the island, but Jérome managed to finesse the *Golden Fleece* through a couple of long, narrow leads and brought us into the open waters of a shallow bay on the eastern side of the island.

Argentina maintains a base up on the heights of Seymour Island—Marambio, which has its own airstrip for access. We could see the tiny red dots of the base buildings on the prow of the ridge that rose up from the bay. Jérome radioed the base, and the Argentines cheerfully invited us to drop in, advising that the runway was clear. Jérome took a while to explain, in a mixture of French, English, and Spanish, that we had come by yacht, not plane. They were a little incredulous at first until somebody at the base looked out with a pair of binoculars and saw the *Golden Fleece* huddled close to the island. A new voice that spoke better English came on the radio and told us to come on up, adding: "We don't get many people coming here on yachts."

Jérome cast a sailor's eye at the weather, felt the gentle wafts of air that were passing for breezes that morning, studied the lie of the icebergs around us, and decided it would be safe enough for us to spend a few hours here. He left Christian in charge, passed around radios, and we all agreed to be back on board in three hours' time.

We landed on a beach of gooey mud that sucked in our boots up to our knees, and from there began the steep and slippery hike up to the base. It didn't take long before I realized that the base was much higher up than it had appeared from the boat and that this was going to be a much longer climb than I had expected. Antarctica was playing tricks of scale again. Back at Paulet Island I had mistaken a nearby molehill for a lofty ridge top and was startled out of my skin a few minutes later when I saw Miriam and Maria striding along it like silhouetted giants. Here I had made the opposite error, believing the ridge to be small and Marambio only a short way off, when in fact it was a more than a thousand feet up and on a plateau about three miles away. And it wasn't a matter of hiking up one simple grade to get up there, but a deceptive series of knife-edged ridges and hidden ravines.

There was no path. We went by dead reckoning, soon losing sight of both the yacht and the base. The gravelly mud was packed with fossils, mostly little types of seashells. It clung in clumps to the sides and soles of my boots. The landscape itself reminded me of the Badlands of South Dakota, with its weirdly weathered shapes and banded earth, but the view from the heights was pure Antarctica: a sweeping panorama of icebergs filling a glassy sea and a shimmering pearl-gray sky.

After a while we noticed a pair of blue specks making their way down the slopes above; a couple of Argentine Air Force officers were coming down to greet us. They led us the rest of the way to the top.

Marambio is one of Argentina's major staging posts on the peninsula, with a year-round gravel runway capable of handling four-engine Hercules cargo planes, and a hangar full of Twin Otters and helicopters for reaching smaller, outlying bases and field camps. It sits on a plateau, and although the runway is graded and reasonably well drained, the ground around it is a quagmire in the summer. A network of long wooden walkways links the buildings. It felt good to step onto the planking and out of the squishy ankle-deep mud.

The base headquarters was warm and quiet, with long corridors and a spectacular view over the Weddell Sea. We asked around if anyone there knew where the British field camp was, and, after a bit of rapid toing-and-froing in Spanish, one of the Air Force officers pointed to a spot on a wall map that was a good hard hour's hike away from the base. It had already taken us an hour to climb up from the yacht, and the ice wasn't going to stay in one place forever. So we decided to give the fossil hunters a miss. The commandant invited us to stay for lunch. They were having tripe soup that day, something that pleased Jérome very much. Me, I preferred the baked apple for dessert.

I started back down to the yacht ahead of the others; Miriam and Maria went off to take a few last pictures around the base, while Jérome and Katie were reviving old times with some acquaintances of his they'd run into in the dining hall. It had turned into a pleasant afternoon weatherwise, and it was nice to be hiking on my own. The skies were still mostly overcast but lifting, and the brighter light cast the Weddell Sea's sprawl of icebergs into sharper focus. They had shifted a bit since we had climbed up a couple of hours earlier, and from up here I could better appreciate Jérome's interest in a timely departure, and his skill in navigating us through all that.

Going down was much quicker than climbing, even if my boots did tend to slide on the loose clay. For the most part I was following the tracks we had left coming up, but when I came to a steep but firmer slope, one that angled off harmlessly to the right but seemed to promise a quicker and less mucky descent, I followed that instead. That in turn led to another diversion and another, and before I knew it I was well off my original track, following a creek down a lonely ravine with steep, unscalable walls on either side.

The others had also started back to the yacht by this time. Looking back and way above me I could see four colored dots picking their way down the slope well above me, and from their position I could guess how far I had angled from the path we had taken going up. It was farther than I had thought.

There was not much danger of becoming lost: I knew this creek must eventually lead back to our beach, and from there I could just walk along it until I came to where I could signal Christian on the yacht. It was more a question of how wet and muddy it would be trying to follow it, or if I wanted to scramble up the slopes I had just slid down and start over from where I'd left the path. Well...I'd always wanted to be an Antarctic explorer.

I pressed on. And like Scott I found that others had been there first—or at least their rubbish had. The creek was strewn with discarded bottles, plastic bits, batteries, scrap metal, oil cans, rusted-out fuel drums, an old shoe, wrappers, and foil. This could have been any mucky creek in any industrial wasteland on the rough edge of any city anywhere. The only thing I didn't find was a shopping cart. It was sobering to see. And weirdly enough, I felt oddly embarrassed at encountering it, so soon after the Argentines hale and hearty hospitality; I felt intrusive, as though while visiting the washroom at a host's house I had stumbled onto some nasty family secrets.

I picked my way along the creek, until it came out onto the beach only a few hundred yards up from the boat. Jérome and Katie were just coming down; so much for my head start and shortcut. We went out to the yacht. Maria and Miriam came down about 20 minutes later, having followed my tracks and getting an eyeful of the rubbish-dump creek for themselves.

A gentle breeze was picking up, not much but enough to make the icebergs begin their slow waltz. We drew anchor and left. It was good to be adrift again.

CHAPTER SEVENTEEN

Tourist Season

WE CLEARED THE WEDDELL SEA ICE PACK AND SLEPT THAT NIGHT IN A QUIET anchorage near some cliffs along Dundee Island. Early the next morning we set out for Esperanza, the Argentinean base at Hope Bay, on the tip of the peninsula. It was a damp gray morning, with the sharp bite of frost in the air and a few snowflakes filtering out of the sky. The sea was dark and empty but the airwaves were full of life. It was the radio operator on HMS *Endurance* having an amiable gabfest with his Spanish-accented counterpart at Esperanza.

Jérome joyfully seized the mike as they concluded their conversation, and with the chirpy voice of a man who has slept well and doesn't owe too much money cut in: "Bonjour, *Endurance*! This is yacht *Golden Fleece*. It is so good to hear your radio is back working again! I have been so worried about you since we passed the other day. But I am very glad to hear that everything is all right now."

Silence.

We sailed on, rolling easily on a southwest bearing, with the ranges of the peninsula dead ahead. Hope Bay was in a stunning setting, embraced by a sweep of frozen mountains that looked as high and mighty as anything in the Himalaya but were in fact less than four thousand feet high. Hope Bay itself was strewn with icebergs calved from the glaciers that spilled down to the water. We were a couple of miles out—and expected—when Jérome radioed the base to ask for instructions on where they wanted us to anchor the yacht. A peremptory English accent cut across the transmission: "*Golden Fleece*, get off this channel at once. It is for emergency use only."

This was too much. "*Golden Fleece* here," Jérome snapped. "Who is this speaking? Please respond, over."

Silence.

Technically the officious Englishman was correct: We were broadcasting on channel 16, which is the internationally recognized emergency channel. But in Antarctica, where there is very little radio traffic and even fewer emergencies, channel 16 is often used as a sort of party line, since everybody monitors it and you can be certain of being received. In fact, only an hour earlier the radio operator on *Endurance* had himself been using this very same channel in his chatter with the Argentines at Esperanza. Their riding-crop-across-the-snout arrogance left Jérome steaming.

I wondered what the Argentines were making of these exchanges. You could almost hear the catch of breath as their reply to Jérome was interrupted. They waited a diplomatic moment to avoid any verbal crossfire and gave Jérome instructions for approaching their wharf. Whatever they were thinking, they were certainly friendly enough when we arrived.

Esperanza is Argentina's attempt to colonize Antarctic soil, a little village-like base, complete with families and children and a schoolhouse with a little bell. At one time, back in the late 1970s, the Argentines had even gone to the baroque expedient of flying in pregnant women so they could give birth to native Argentinean–Antarcticans. As a result, there are now eight people in this world, Argentines in their early 20s, who have Antarctica noted as their place of birth on their birth certificates.

Esperanza is not as large or elaborate a village as Chile's Frei base on King George Island, and despite the presence of families and the classic little schoolhouse it looks and feels more like an Antarctic base. Some of this can be credited to its more frozen Antarctic setting, with icebergs in the bay, towering splintery ice-clad mountains in the background, and a colony of more than 100,000 penguins sprawling beside it.

"This is the most southerly schoolhouse in the world," Juan Carlos, the base commander, told me when he was showing me around. Its little classroom had a bell in the corner and its walls were bright with children's artwork, which contained an interesting mixture of palm trees and penguins. The room was silent and empty. All eight of the base's children were back in Buenos Aires on summervacation.

"We have exactly the same curriculum here as we do in all the other schools in the State of Tierra del Fuego," he said proudly.

I smiled at his reference to "all the other schools in Tierra del Fuego," my mind wandering back to Chile and the "local" yellow pages I had seen in my hotel room in Punta Arenas with listings that included Chilean Antarctica. School districts, telephone directories, and proprietary hospitality: Surely no continent in history has been more urbanely staked out.

We didn't linger long at Esperanza but set off down the western flank of the peninsula, hugging the coast, putting in at will into the quiet and inviting inlets and hidden anchorages Jérome knew about and enjoying Antarctica's wide-open freedom; as the days passed I began to understand how Huckleberry Finn must have felt on his raft.

The scenery was breathtaking: towering pinnacles of rock and ice that plunged down to the sea, deep fjords, sculpted icebergs, glassy reflections, massive glaciers that spilled onto the coast, their crevasses glowing eerie green and blue in their depths. It was a storybook landscape, enchanted and profoundly still. Some of the mountains looked like clouds. Others seemed almost magically cruel, with curved incisor-like peaks. There were splintery towers of black rock and shimmering ice soaring hundreds of feet high. I'd never imagined landscapes like this could exist outside of children's fairy tales.

We glided along the western coast of the peninsula, down an inside passage of islands and narrow straits. The water around us was dark and smooth and strewn with endless floes, like the shards of a shattered mirror. It was haunting and peaceful, under a dim silvery light that made everything seem unreal and distant.

The days melded into each other, sometimes bright and sunny, sometimes misty and gray and full of gentle snows. On one morning we called in at Astrolabe Island, a volcanic nub jutting out of the sea, as lonely as a lighthouse, where seabirds wheeled and screeched in front of cliffs. Another morning, farther south, found us in a silent bay, surrounded by icebergs. They came in fascinating shapes, some tall and angular like the rock formations in Monument Valley, others worn down by the wind and weather to something smooth, curvaceous, and stylishly art deco.

Jérome didn't mind drawing up close beside them. Cupped in the hollow of one of these deco bergs was a pool of perfectly translucent water, turquoise blue, and beside it a dozing seal. This self-contained little scene made me think alternately of an exquisitely styled advertisement for Eskimo Pies and a playful Hollywood photo shoot from the 1930s.

There were a lot of penguins about, and seals, and hauntingly beautiful pure white birds called snow petrels. They are about the size of peace doves. I remembered them from my first trip down to The Ice. I thought then, and still think, they are the most beautiful birds I have ever seen, and watching them glide above the ice and mirror-smooth water seemed the perfect summing up of Antarctica's otherworldly tranquillity.

One evening, when the sun was just a creamy warm smudge in the sky, we drifted among a pod of right whales. The bay we were in was filled with their long, shuddering sighs as they surfaced for air, then arched their backs and dived lazily, coming up again hundreds of yards away. There must have been half a dozen of them, and probably more. Occasionally they surfaced beside the yacht, and when they dived in that clear water we could look down and watch their huge tail flukes grow small in the depths.

The *Golden Fleece* was a world in itself, less than 70 feet long: wheelhouse and deck, cabins galley and saloon. Sometimes we just stood outside along the railings, in clammy cold or gentle snow, and enjoyed the solitude. Other times, when the wind turned sharp, we sat in the warmth of the wheelhouse, sipping coffee, watching Jérome guide the bow around a lazy slalom course through the floes. The water was deep, the mountains plunging into the sea as sharply as they sprang from it. Often we could pass within an easy stone's throw of a cliff face, but still be in many fathoms of water. The tops of these mountains—some of them more than 9,000 feet high—loomed out of sight above us.

We lived well, dining on lamb from Jérome's farm in the Falklands, or wild reindeer that he had shot on South Georgia Island, or some Moroccan dish or other that Katie created. Miriam had a knack for baking bread. We sat around the table in the evenings, telling stories or laughing at Jérome's anecdotes about the bureaucratic comedies of sailing a Falklands-registered yacht in and out of Argentina, or the flag-waving absurdities he had seen committed down here in the name of nationalism, or the time many years ago when he was skippering a yacht in an around-the-world race and it was rammed by a killer whale, causing it to sink in five minutes. They were well away from the customary shipping routes, had no time to give a distress call, and survived only by a miracle when an errant freighter happened to spot them, but to hear Jérome tell it the whole thing seemed such a lighthearted lark that you half wished you'd been there. He had a sharp wit and an eye for detail and would have made a hilarious mime.

All of these things—Jérome's funny stories, our own recalled pasts and anecdotes, even the events of the previous week when we had been doing the social rounds of the bases on King George Island—seemed to belong to a dim and surprisingly distant long-ago, as though they were fables that had been handed down by others. It was easy to imagine as we glided alone down this wild and frozen coast that we were the last people on Earth. The disembodied voices on the airwaves came from impossibly far away, those cruise directors coordinating their next day's movements every night at half past seven, and the drama unfolding on one of the glaciers somewhere in the mountains north of us.

We had been following the radio exchanges between a team of sea kayakers that had been nosing their way along the coast, and the New Zealand yacht that was supporting them, when we heard that a couple of the paddlers had decided to portage their kayaks across a mountain pass. One of them had tumbled into a crevasse and apparently suffered serious head and chest injuries. He had lain in the bottom of the slot until a helicopter from one of the tour ships came to his rescue. They flew him to the hospital at Frei, from where he would be evacuated to South America aboard one of the Chilean Air Force cargo planes. Listening to it unfold, it had the unreal but gripping quality of a soap opera.

To any wandering American who happened to be sailing around the southwestern tip of Wiencke Island, the old British base at Port Lockroy could almost pass for a lobsterman's shack somewhere in downeast Maine. It sits on a low rocky point, a gaunt timber-framed saltbox, built back in the 1940s; chocolate brown with red trim around the windows and a few seabirds perched evocatively on the roof. Edward Hopper could have painted it—it had that simplicity and sense of alienation you find in his paintings. All it needed was a few artistically tangled nets and floats piled under the eaves, a few pine trees, and a sign out front offering fried clam dinners to be any of a dozen little places I could think of along Penobscot Bay. Except those places wouldn't have had whalebones scattered on the rocks, gentoo penguins waddling about in the yard, or a histrionic sweep of frozen mountains towering overhead, let alone the Union Jack on the flagpole; Port Lockroy had all of it.

The British built this base as a top-secret listening post during World War II, on Churchill's direct orders, because of rumors (unfounded, as it turned out) that German ships were hiding out in the old whaler's anchorages along the Antarctic Peninsula. It was referred to as Operation Tabarin, after a bawdy Parisian nightspot; an exquisite irony since the men posted here in great secrecy in 1943 enjoyed the quietest of wars.

The base was kept open for research until it was finally abandoned in 1962. It should have been torn down and removed under the Madrid Protocol, which calls on nations to clear away their defunct bases, but in a bit of mental agility unusual in bureaucracies, a few entrepreneurial minds at the British Antarctic Survey got around this irksome obligation by linking up with the U.K. Antarctic Heritage Trust to have the old base lovingly restored in 1996, setting up a museum, gift shop, and post office, and sending down two staffers to run the place during the short summer season. The tourists love it. The British Antarctic Survey saved itself the hassle and costs of dismantling and removal, and the proceeds from the gift shop help support research. As a result, what had been a sagging wartime relic has now become the single biggest drawcard on the continent, drawing more than 8,000 visitors each summer. Not bad for a lonely-looking wooden shack at an obscure old whaler's haunt, nearly 65° south.

It was quiet the morning we came into the harbor; just a few croaks and squawks from the brood of gentoos hanging out on the rocks in front of the shack. A Swiss yacht sat at anchor nearby, casting a perfect reflection in the water. Its mast gave a nice sense of scale to the glacier wall looming behind it.

The base itself is on Goudier Island, a low, rocky mote barely 300 yards long in the waters of Port Lockroy. We dropped anchor and lowered the dinghy, and Jérome and I went ashore. Rusted mooring chains and bolts dangled from the rocks, left over from the whaling days more than 70 years ago. A couple of old scows moldered nearby. The two caretakers—Jim and Kenn—lived the lives of 19th-century lighthouse keepers: no heat, no running water, no plumbing and using hurricane lanterns during the brief hours of twilight at those latitudes. They loved it and seemed bemused by the attitudes of the tourists to their "hardships."

"The Americans just can't understand how we do it," Jim said. "The British, Australians, and New Zealanders who pass through here are a bit more used to the idea of roughing it. A lot of the older ones, or people who come from the country, say they recognize the décor."

We were having tea in their kitchen. Not the museum kitchen down the hall, which was neatly arranged just as it had been in the 1940s, with the original tins of Perce Duff custard powder, Lyle's golden syrup, Chiver's marmalade, and British pickle livening the shelves, but one nearly as old-fashioned yet still in day-to-day use. It looked like any number of farmhouse kitchens in the country. The men's bunks ran along the wall. Somebody was reading *Moby Dick*. It lay facedown and open, next to the hurricane lantern on the bedside table.

"That's a nice touch."

"Yeah, I thought this summer was the perfect opportunity to read that," Jim laughed. "It'll be something to tell my grandchildren how I read *Moby Dick* by lantern light at this old whaling post."

The two men were an Antarctic odd couple. Jim was 24, young and sharp, an electrical engineer on the staff of the British Antarctic Survey who had already done a two-year hitch at Halley Station, one of the years as base leader. Kenn was much older. He first came south in 1963, fresh from a degree in classics and Latin at Durham University. How he happened to join the survey sounded like one of those quixotic anecdotes from the days of Scott and Shackleton.

"I did it virtually on a bet," he told me. "They asked me what I studied at university, and when I told them classics, the fellow thought for a few moments and said 'Very well, we'll make you the meteorologist.' And that's what they did. Today you'd need a first in physics even to get an interview."

He was a gentle, shy, and soft-spoken man who had become enchanted with Antarctica at first sight and has never been able to break its spell. Over the years he had done several tours of duty at Halley and Rothera, a couple of times as station leader, and he now spent his summers either at Port Lockroy or another museum at the old whaling station on South Georgia Island.

Bransfield House—as the wooden building is known—is a time capsule of life in Antarctica as it was in the 1940s and '50s. The darkroom is crammed with vintage enlargers, trays, and chemical bottles; a ceramic jug of old-style Navy-issue rum—"Nelson's Blood," Kenn called it, "the real stuff"—sits in its wicker basket on the kitchen counter, and the bookshelves in the common room are crammed with faded copies of *Reader's Digest* from the 1950s, Somerset Maugham's tales of colonial life in Malaya, and World War I adventure novels by John Buchan, where his heroic South African mining engineer, Richard Hannay, time and again rescues the imperiled British Empire.

The old base was very mannish and clubby. The back door of the generator bears a full-length portrait of Marilyn Monroe, a sort of aide-mémoire for the men who stayed here for two years at a stretch.

The most popular thing in the museum, though, is the modern bright-red Royal Mail letterbox that adorns the entranceway. Letters and postcards posted from here receive a coveted Port Lockroy postmark, from the British Antarctic Territory, a philatelic novelty and the ultimate look-at-me-now gloat to send to your sedentary friends back home. More than 40,000 pieces of mail pass through that one little box in the course of a summer.

"I've been trying to catch up this morning while it's quiet," Jim said, pointing to a mountain of postcards on his desk behind the counter in the gift shop. He sat down, took up his rubber stamp, and started back to work. "All of this was left by passengers on the tour ship that called in yesterday. And there's another one due in tomorrow."

While he thumped away at his pile of mail I browsed around the shop, casting my eyes over the array of pins, caps, T-shirts, postcards, first-day covers, posters, mugs, and copies of *Lonely Planet Antarctica*. There were even woolen neckties and scarves on offer, woven in "authentic" Antarctic tartan devised by a textile firm in Scotland, a pretty pattern in white, blue, black, and orange—the colors of Antarctica and its penguins.

What is really clever about Port Lockroy, though, is that it is more than just a stylish Antarctic tourist trap—it is a science project as well. By monitoring the health and breeding successes of the gentoo penguins at such a popular spot, scientists hope to be able to gauge the impact tourism is having on wildlife. So far, the news appears to be good.

"We haven't noticed any difference between these penguins, which see tourists all the time, and the breeding success in some of the other rookeries nearby that see no tourists at all," Jim said, the pile of franked mail on his left growing steadily larger. "There have been other studies along the peninsula that have come to the same conclusion.

"The way things are right now, tourism isn't a problem. People come down, make a few brief landings and go home. By and large, the tour operators behave responsibly and do a good job of regulating themselves. And the good old Drake Passage should prevent this from becoming too much of a mass-market destination: Only somebody who is seriously interested in Antarctica would put themselves through a sea voyage like that," he laughed. "But sooner or later somebody is going to try to build a hotel down here, or an airstrip, and once that happens answers are going to have to be found for a lot of thorny legal and political questions we've all been putting off."

The morning's heavy cloud cover had slipped away, and by early afternoon the sun was shining from a taut blue sky. Out on the yacht Jérome and Katie had fired up a gas barbeque and begun sizzling chops and sausages, made from the sheep on Jerome's farm back in the Falklands. Jim and Kenn knocked off early and came out. A case of beer appeared and a couple of reds were opened. The temperature was a balmy 41°F. Life just doesn't get any better.

We sat on coils of rope, with our plates balanced on our laps, and basked in the sunshine. The mountains around us were sharp and white, soaring almost a mile straight up from sea level in a single breathtaking rush. High on the slopes of one of them we could see four tiny figures from the Swiss yacht, picking their way up a glacier. Shirtsleeve weather made it a risky day for that sort of thing. Every now and then there would come a rumble like distant thunder as the late January warmth released an avalanche somewhere up in the mountains. We'd look up from our plates, eyes scanning the slopes for a telltale puff of tumbling snow, but if it was ever in eyeshot at all we were never in time. The peaks were as still as a painting.

After lunch we took the dinghy and motored over to a nearby point, low and rocky and screechy with bird life, and looked at the gigantic bleached skeleton of a fin whale. It was a legacy of the days when more than 3,000 whales were killed in these waters between 1911 and the mid-1920s, then butchered at a Norwegian factory ship anchored near where the base is now.

Jim and Kenn were very agreeable about making the excursion and getting off their own tiny island for an hour or so. They were without a boat themselves—made castaways for a summer—since a nannying bureaucracy back at headquarters in Cambridge was worried that idle time, plus a boat, could possibly equal danger. It was safer simply to maroon the crew, particularly since the sorts of people who are keen to work in Antarctica are also likely to be adventurous, outdoorsy, and troublesomely independent.

"People are eventually going to stop wanting to come down here," Jim remarked as we headed back to the base. "The rules are just becoming so restrictive."

We dropped them back on their home island, returned to the yacht, and hoisted anchor. As we sailed away, leaving them standing beside the rusted old mooring chains, I appreciated more than ever the freedom we enjoyed on the yacht.

We didn't go far that evening, just around a point on Wiencke Island, a few miles away, and anchored for the night in a spot marked on the charts as Dorien Bay. The skies stayed clear and fine. We lowered the dinghy and cruised the mirror-smooth waters until very late at night, with the sun brushing the iced mountains pink and gold.

CHAPTER EIGHTEEN

The Polar Gentleman

IT WAS A FRENCH EXPLORER NAMED JEAN-BAPTISTE CHARCOT WHO DISCOVERED Port Lockroy in 1904, naming it in honor of the French minister of marine, Edouard Lockroy, who had helped him obtain funding for the expedition. As the first person to do a comprehensive survey of the Antarctic Peninsula, Charcot had naming rights over most of its grandest mountains, most spectacular islands, and best anchorages, in much the same way that Captain Cook seemed to have named everything of importance on the eastern coast of Australia.

I hadn't known much about Charcot, other than a vague recollection of having heard the name, but between the French-sounding names on the charts that Jérome was using for navigation and a gazetteer of Antarctic places he kept in the wheelhouse, and his frequent references to Charcot (who is one of France's great polar heroes, in much the same vein as Shackleton or Scott is to the English), I began piecing together a sketchy biography as we traveled south.

"If he had been English like Scott or Shackleton, he would be famous as the greatest of true explorers," Jérome boasted one afternoon as he piloted the *Golden Fleece* through a long stretch of drifting floes. "Charcot was much greater than the rest; they talked about science but came mostly for their own personal glory. Charcot truly did come here for science—and for his own quiet personal pleasure."

I had already picked up on the fact that Charcot was one of Jérome's heroes. It wasn't hard; the name frequently cropped up in conversation. When, in the course of the barbeque at Port Lockroy, I'd owned up to knowing very little about the man—the evening we anchored in Dorien Bay—I found a short stack of books at my place at the dinner table: English translations of Charcot's journals and a brief biography.

And for the next few days as we glided south, past more of Charcot's landmarks, I sat up in the wheelhouse, reading and repairing this gap in my education.

Charcot had style. Scott referred to him as "the polar gentleman." He was born into privilege, the son of a distinguished Parisian physician, and a skilled yachtsman. Although he became a wealthy and respected doctor in his own right, by the age of 35 he had become disillusioned with his accomplishments and wealth and decided to devote his life to science and exploration.

He sank all of his considerable inheritance into a grand Antarctic expedition—commissioning an ice-strengthened research ship—the *Francais*—to be built to the finest standards, and then furnished it with state-of-the-art scientific apparatus, comfortable accommodation for his men, and, of course, a first-rate wine cellar. His ambitions exceeded even his wealth, and he was forced to seek sponsorship, something that was no hardship for a person with his connections, credentials, and talent for invoking the glory of France. He set sail from Le Havre in August 1903, and six months later sailed into Port Lockroy.

They came in a bad year for ice, unlike the fairly easy conditions we encountered, and struggled to go much farther south, fighting their way almost yard by yard through dense pack ice, with a howling blizzard raging around them. They made it only as far as Booth Island, a melancholy pile of rocks that in fair weather is about half a day's sail below Port Lockroy. There they set up camp for the winter.

We arrived around midday. By then a somber veil of cloud had crept over the sky, and by its feeble light Booth Island seemed a haunting place, dominated by a hilltop cairn built by Charcot's men, and surrounded by a graveyard for old, weathered, grounded icebergs.

Few visitors come to this secluded spot, and the hundreds of skuas nesting on these rocks clearly like it that way. They dive-bombed above our heads, or hurtled up from behind, flicking an ear with a wingtip as they whizzed by, and sometimes giving the back of your head a generous whack. They are large brown sea birds with heavy beaks—think of a seagull on steroids—aggressive and territorial. But once they understood we were not going to stray near their chicks, and once we had an idea of where to avoid, they declared a truce.

We took a circuitous path to Charcot's old camp, skirting the areas the skuas declared off-limits. There wasn't much left: the skeleton of a whaleboat, some bits of wood and scrap iron, and a stone hut that had housed a magnetic observatory.

I climbed to the cairn. The air was raw and cold, with a chill wind, but the scramble up the hill kept me warm. There were no skuas here, just silence. On a clear day the view would have been breathtaking, but that afternoon it was simply moody. Damp gray clouds wrapped themselves around the cliffs and mountaintops in the distance and drifted heavily over the sea. The water was dark; the ice was bright. The old grounded bergs around the island resembled meringues. One of them had a hollow containing a pool of perfect turquoise water; another had a pool of delicate translucent jade. They looked like jewels in exquisite white settings. I thought about Charcot and his men wintering here, baking their croissants aboard the *Francais* every Sunday, celebrating the midwinter solstice with a picnic in –4°F cold, entertaining the penguins with a gramophone concert on Christmas Day in 1904, when the century was young and bright as a penny.

The dampness lingered. We glided up to a derelict British base at Prospect Point early the next morning under a low, moist blanket of cloud. The air was frosty, our breaths adding to the grayness. The world was an almost perfect monochrome of floating ice, dark water, snow, and black rock. In places, the mountains melded so fluidly with the gray wash of sky that their dark cliffs and crags sometimes seemed to float in space.

Everything was deathly still. Here and there a hint of color—faint blue highlights in a bergy bit, a touch of purple beneath the clouds, or a pallid yellow smudge where the sun was trying to filter through—suggested an outside world somewhere with blood in its veins, but otherwise everything was as still and cold as a carving. The base was just a gaunt wooden shack, one of a string of such meager shelters built by the British down here in the late 1950s, and nothing like as large as Bransfield House at Port Lockroy.

This one had been built in 1956 and then abandoned two years later when it became apparent that this cold and miserable location was always going to be difficult to reach because of its persistent heavy pack ice. A pile of fragile old dogsleds lay beside the hut like so many skeletons. A cruel-looking incisor-shaped peak—Mount Sharp on the map—brooded over the scene. Seabirds wheeled and screeched, eerie in the stillness. A skua perched on the roof beam and watched us.

Much of the time Antarctica comes to us as an exquisite wonderland, a magical place of purity, peace, and otherworldly splendor, done up in the softest and most heavenly of colors and untouched by sin, but on bloodless mornings like these you realize how misleading that all is. Beneath all the pretty snowscapes and elfin mountains, this is a ruthless place. The hush in the air isn't blessed tranquillity; it's conspiratorial silence.

I had been sitting in the wheelhouse that morning reading the memoirs of some of the men who had worked in these lonely outposts, and as I walked outside into the chill on deck I thought of the spine-tingling story of a sledging party that had disappeared near here more than 40 years ago.

They had set off across the sea ice one fine morning, bound for one of the outlying islands about 30 miles away. Within an hour of their leaving, one of their colleagues who had remained behind became so overcome with a sickening premonition that he dropped to his knees and, although he claimed he wasn't a religious man, began to pray. An evil wind rose during the night. The next morning he looked outside, and to his horror saw only cold black water lapping at the shore. All the ice was gone, broken up and swept out to sea—along with anybody who had been traveling on it. Over the next few weeks a couple of the missing party's dogs wandered back to base, their knife-slashed traces evidence that the desperate men had cut the dogs loose as the ice broke up around them, to give them their fair chance. But there was never any sign of the men themselves. This place kept its secrets.

This was no paradise, for all the talk of its peace and beauty; that was just a happy comforting illusion. An image came to me of the remains of a snow petrel I had come upon once in the Larsemann Hills, on the other side of the continent, on my first trip to The Ice. It had been killed by a skua, and picked clean. All that was left was a bleached breastplate with the two soft white-feathered wings still attached. It looked like a murdered angel.

We slipped past the abandoned hut and dropped anchor a few miles farther south among a lonely scatter of rocks and islets marked on the chart as The Minnows. The water was shallow around the islets, which were inhabited by penguins, seals, and shags.

We launched the dinghy, and Miriam, Christian, Maria, and I set off to explore. After snaking our way through the islets, we puttered across a span of deeper water toward a sheer ice wall where the Hoek Glacier meets the sea. The face was deeply cracked and crevassed, with huge fractured slabs of ice teetering out over the water at precarious angles. Its gnarled menace drew us closer. Ominous dustings of snow spurted from faults in the ice, suggesting imminent collapse. We approached obliquely, very slowly, cutting off the engine when we were about 656 feet away and letting the dingy float.

Just as no photograph of thousands of penguins along a rocky coast can bring home the wild briny smells and the stench of guano, pretty scenes of ice reflected in glassy water and stately mountains can't prepare you for the sounds of Antarctica's silence. As your ears tune in, the first sound you notice is the musical treble of millions of small pieces of ice bobbing in the water, tinkling together like soft chimes.

As the minutes passed and the stillness deepened, we began to notice the faint cries of the sea birds and penguins on the islets in the distance behind us. Every now and then would come the faraway rumble of an unsighted avalanche.

We waited, perched on the rubber side of the dinghy and exclaiming at each tiny puff of snow that erupted from pressure cracks in the face of the glacier. They became more frequent, gathered momentum. Flecks of ice and snow tumbled into the water. Keystone chunks weighing hundreds of tons could be seen to shift, nudging their way downward.

And then, suddenly, after one such shift, a massive slab pitched forward, breaking away from the glacier and tumbling into the sea with an almighty splash. A curving ripple spread across the surface, strong enough to make us grip the sides of the dinghy as it rolled beneath us. A newly formed bergy bit floated in front of the glacier face. I was admiring it, thinking of the philosopher's tree falling unheard in a silent forest and pleased that our ears had been the ones to give meaning to this lonely crashing, when the rest of the wall spectacularly collapsed, tumbling into the water with a long-drawn-out roar like rolling thunder.

This time there was no mere ripple spreading away, but a mini-tsunami of green water. We hastily started the engine, skittered the dinghy about, and sped away, rolling heavily when the wave eventually caught up and passed beneath us. We cut the engine and looked back at the fresh-cut wall of ice and the chain of newly hatched bergs in the water beneath it. The eerie musical hush settled once again.

We lingered the rest of the day at The Minnows, encouraged by a lightening in the sky and a few streaks of blue along the horizon. By early evening the blueness had crept across the sky. The sun shone brightly. The mountains became firm and crisp. Color breathed life into the snowscape. The glaciers were creased with blues and greens, the water shone like shot silk—violet, pink, silver, and orange—and the snow on the mountains looked creamy instead of bloodless. The floating ice continued its effervescent tinkle and pop, avalanches and calving glaciers sounded like distant cannons, and scores of penguins cackled on the rocks.

A continuous barrier of high, snowy, mountainous islands shelters the inner waters along the coast of the peninsula, so that much of the time I felt like we were drifting down an elongated lake, as smooth as oil and pretty as a chocolate box, with its perfect reflections and lofty chiseled peaks. It was its own quiet, cloistered world. Sometimes we glided through fjordlike channels that were barely a quarter mile across and looked narrower still with sheer dark cliffs towering out of sight on either side. Even in the broader expanses of water there always seemed to be a comfortable line of mountains walling in the horizons.

Growing familiarity and their subtly confining presence didn't make this inside passage any less grand or mystical, but as the days passed I began to lose a little of the sense of how remote it all was. There was no edge to look out from, nothing to put this place into a broader context, at least not until we sailed out to a sprinkling of granite outcrops, called Armstrong Reef, on the outermost part of the barrier.

We arrived on a sparkling February morning, the open sea spreading out to the west and the sky lively with screeching birds. It was a pretty place, haunting in its maritime isolation, its pale granite ledges dimpled with snow and capped by the remains of an old glacier. I set off across the largest of the islets. It was maybe half a mile across, low and uneven. Mosses and wispy tufts of grass grew in pockets of soil between the rocks, and delicate lichens spotted the surfaces, thanks to the warming influence of the sea here. I had to walk carefully, often hopscotching across ledges—from bare spot to bare spot—to avoid bruising anything. Hundreds of pairs of skuas nested here, their fuzzy chicks hiding in crevices. I kept an eye out for them, and their dive-bombing parents. Between avoiding the flora and the fauna, it took me a good hour to cross that little islet.

I sat down on an inviting hollow on a ledge overlooking the dark blue expanse of the Bellingshausen Sea. It was lovely there. The sun warmed the rock, and it felt good to be alone for a while, sitting on what felt like the rim of the world. The sweep of water encouraged me to believe that I could see the curve of the Earth along the empty horizon. A lone tabular iceberg floated in the blueness. Breakers crashed heavily against a line of submerged rocks a couple of miles away, sending up jets of dazzling white spray. In the stillness I could faintly hear, and almost feel, the powerful, rhythmic surge of the surf. No place that I had ever been—at least until then—had felt so powerfully far away, not even the South Pole.

I spotted Jérome's yellow slicker as I was making my way back to the dinghy an hour or so later. He was walking carefully around a small depression about 328 feet away, preoccupied and closely studying the ground. He spotted me, hesitated, and then waved me over. "Have you seen these?"

He was standing beside a small freshwater pond, maybe 50 feet long and no more than knee deep at its deepest, and so clear and smooth that at first there didn't appear to be any water in it at all. He picked up a melon-size rock from along the bank and knelt down. I squatted down beside him and, following the line of his pointed index finger, picked out a tiny flealike speck hopping in the crater where the rock had been.

"It is a type of wingless midge. Believe it or not, this is the largest land animal in Antarctica."

We both studied it. Africa has its elephants, North America its Alaskan moose and polar bears, and Australia its big desert kangaroos, but in the lean, icy barrenness of Antarctica, the largest creature that has been able to survive on shore is an invertebrate no more than a quarter of an inch long.

He placed the stone reverently back in its place.

Something in the way he did it, and in the quiet but purposeful way with which he had come ashore and sought out this little pond, made me think of a line in *Walden*, where Thoreau describes himself as the town's self-appointed inspector of sunsets. Jérome seemed to have his own self-appointed rounds down here: this little pond, some lonely rocks around Astrolabe Island where a colony of blue-eyed shags roost, the sculptured ice in the Weddell Sea, and scores of other places that went unremarked in our journey south but were touchstones for him in his 30 years of continuous voyaging around the peninsula.

I commented that he probably knew its hidden inlets and coves better than anyone since the old-time sealers.

"Oh, I know it much better than they did," he said, and without sounding immodest either, because it was simply the truth. "They were looking only for fur—I go and see things simply because I like to look. If they didn't think there would be seals someplace, they didn't go; I go anyway, just to see what might be there."

One of his most treasured discoveries was the world's most southerly growth of flowering plants on the cliff faces of a bleak and impossibly remote archipelago marked on the charts as the Terra Firma Islands. They lay at the southern end of the peninsula, at almost 69° south, in frozen waters beyond where it was possible to sail most seasons. Jérome had managed to put in there in 1984 and discovered the plants—two species of grasses, *Deschampsia antarctica* and *Colobanthus quitensis*—flourishing in crevices in the rock, well beyond where anyone had thought they might be found. He had published a couple of scientific papers on the find. He dug them out when we were back on the *Golden Fleece* and showed me the Terra Firma Islands on the map.

"If you'd like, we can try to go down there. Of course, everything will depend on the ice."

And that looked promising; this was a very good ice year. But then that was becoming more common. Everyone agreed that the winters were becoming warmer. Back on the *Yuzhmorgeologiya* all the talk had been about the sharp rise in temperatures since the 1940s, making the Antarctic Peninsula the fastest warming part of the globe, and for reasons that remained obscure. It appeared to be primarily a local phenomenon, the scientists had told me, not linked with any general global warming trends or patterns, but beyond that it remained a mystery. What was certain was the steady and pronounced warming over the past 60 years, and although the academic literature could provide all manner of worthy data, charts, and sinuous curves on graphs to demonstrate this, nothing illustrated the point better than a summer spent sailing these waters with open eyes. It is one thing to read sterile meteorological reports, and another to read a landscape.

On King George Island I had walked over a soggy moraine near Argentina's Jubany base that until recently had been covered by glacier ice. A geologist there had showed me photographs taken 30 years ago, demonstrating how the glacier had retreated more than a quarter mile in that time. At Port Lockroy, Kenn pointed out to me where the glacier wall had reached when he had first come south in the early 1960s. And Jérome had shown me photos he had taken out at Armstrong Reef in the early 1980s when the ice cap on the rock had extended much farther and wider than it does now.

A couple of days later, as we were picking our way farther south through the broken pack ice in Crystal Sound, we encountered a gleaming white cruise liner—the *Bremen*, registered in Nassau, with 235 souls on board—nosing its way north through "The Gullet," a narrow passage between Adelaide Island and the mainland that is often choked by ice, even late in the summer. She moved majestically through the floes, sounding her horn in greeting. Sightseers lined her decks, bright in their red parkas. They waved at us, almost in unison, and called out "Good morning!" in broad American accents. A woman in a white terrycloth robe stepped out onto the private balcony of her upper-deck stateroom and filmed us with her video camera. They were on a long and expensive cruise from New Zealand to Ushuaia, Argentina, via Antarctica, and had been battling heavy weather much of the way across the Bellingshausen Sea. We learned this over the radio from the captain, an ebullient German who had been delighted—for his queasy passengers' sake, particularly—to reach the tranquillity of the peninsula and find it relatively ice free.

We spent that day anchored amongst the reflections of the 7,000-foot peaks around us, and listening to the distant boom of avalanches and calving glaciers. The next morning we passed through The Gullet ourselves, gliding between awesomely steep cliffs that closed in the passage on our way to Britain's Rothera base, at the far southern end of Adelaide Island. Unlike the cold hostility from the Royal Navy, the English voices coming to us over the base radio were full of welcome.

I liked Rothera, with its quirky British humor and enthusiasms, its eclectic blending of old-fashioned and cutting edge, and its postcard setting on a bay surrounded by snowy peaks. It was like an errant piece of England, like something out of a poem. Many of its hundred-odd residents were here on two-and-a-half-year postings, the longest anywhere on the continent, meaning they'd not see a car or a tree or a familiar face from home in all that time. But the scarlet Dash-8 aircraft that zipped in regularly with supplies from the Falkland Islands, and the classic English ales on offer in the pub, suggested a cheerful exile.

They were overhauling an old-style wooden sled in the workshop the morning I arrived. It had just been returned to base after a hard month in the field, and the carpenters were taking it apart, piece by piece, examining each spar and runner and replacing anything that looked worn, before carefully reassembling it. The joints were then tightly bound with sinewlike cord and sealed with watertight red goo. Each of the sleds had its own handwritten log, in which every journey and every bit of maintenance was meticulously recorded. This particular sled was 20 years old.

The man who had been using it was the base's senior scientist, a tall, easygoing man named Pete who described himself as "a glorified natural historian." He was overseeing a comprehensive survey to map the outer limits of life on Earth. He had put more than 250 miles on its runners while roaming the remote Behrendt Mountains, more than two hours south by air, to collect tiny flakes of lichen from rock faces and gather soil samples in which microbes might survive.

He had been gone four weeks, just him and a companion, their snowmobiles roped together for safety against hidden crevasses. Each man towed his own sled and half a ton of food, fuel, and camping gear.

"We are virtually the last country still using these roving two-man field parties," he said. "They drop us off by plane, and then we set out into the wild blue yonder, not seeing anybody else until the plane returns to pick us up weeks or months later."

During that time they are totally self-sufficient, moving lightly across the landscape, sometimes tentbound by storms for days at a time, sometimes scaling ice ledges with ropes, ice axes, and crampons to get to a promising ledge, sometimes pulling up stakes at the end of a long day and driving for hours into the bright polar night and setting up a new camp at the next site.

He showed me the fruits of his labors: a collection of little mounds of meager powdery soil in charcoal and chocolate hues, and an arrangement of lichen samples on gravel-size chunks of rock. The dirt wasn't much to look at, but the lichens were kind of attractive in a minimalist sort of way: a sort of bonsaied Antarctic rock garden. "They probably don't look very exciting to you," he laughed, "But they are exciting to me. This was the first time biologists have gone into those mountains. We really had no idea what to expect."

I was talking to a man whose boyhood love of insects ("I was the kid with the butterfly net," he laughed) led to a doctorate in the behavior and complex aerodynamics of dragonflies. As I listened to him, I thought back to the marine biologists aboard the *Yuzhmorgeologiya*, who had projected the same sort of zeal for zooplankton. But unlike the pink sludge they trawled up, which resolved into fascinating and grotesque creatures under the close scrutiny of a microscope, Pete's samples became more interesting the farther you stepped back. Their drab simplicity, and the fact that pretty much the same monotonous group of organisms—microbes, mites, nematodes, lichens, mosses, and grasses—are found throughout the length of the Antarctic Peninsula and the outlying islands, is what makes this region the world's finest natural laboratory for studying biological consequences of climate change.

"Nowhere else on Earth can you travel through such a wide range of latitudes—from 54° south down to 69° south, and perhaps even farther—and directly observe how changes in temperature, ultraviolet radiation, and water affect the same basic communities of species," he explained. "We can do real-time experiments here using real-world conditions and start to form a genuine picture of how things adapt."

His drab little samples, I began to understand, although plain in themselves, were like the individual tiles in a grand mosaic; it just required the right sort of artistry to appreciate them and put them together.

We spent a couple of days at Rothera. It had a friendly relaxed offbeat sort of feel and quickly joined Mawson and Scott in my pantheon of favorite Antarctic bases. The base commander was an accomplished mountaineer and diving expert named Paul Rose, a brisk and cheery man in his 50s who had led expeditions up Mount Everest and carried out oceanography research in the Seychelles, and had the gift of projecting his own cheer to those around him.

I felt at home there. And I began to feel even more of a local—not just at Rothera but in Antarctica in general—the afternoon of the second day, when I saw a familiar-looking DC-3 touching down on the landing strip. It was the Kiwi pilot Max, whom I hadn't seen to talk to since Darwin Glacier—it already seemed like years ago—back in the Transantarctic Mountains.

We caught up that night in the pub, over a couple of pints of Flowers Ale. He had been having himself a glorious summer, doing charter work all over Antarctica, and was finishing off the season over here on the peninsula doing demonstration runs with the DC-3 for the British. It was good to see him, and not just because he was a nice guy with an interesting job, but also because bumping into him like that helped draw Antarctica together into a neat human-size package.

Pete had heard that we were going to try to reach the Terra Firma Islands next and sought out Jérome in the pub that night to see if we would collect some samples of the southernmost grasses and flowers for his outer limits of life survey.

"We would really love to get stuff from Terra Firma," he explained. "But we simply can't get there—nobody can without a yacht, the waters are too shallow and dangerous for a ship."

Jérome said he'd be glad to gather a few samples and call in on our way back. Before we returned to the yacht that night, Pete gave me some sample bags and instructions on how to collect in the field. I was a scientist again.

CHAPTER NINETEEN

Ne Plus Ultra

WE SET OFF AT DAWN, NAVIGATING THE SELDOM-VISITED WATERS OF Marguerite Bay by an Admiralty chart that warned of misplaced capes and uncharted reefs and concluded: "[M]ariners are advised to navigate these waters with extreme caution as numerous unidentified dangers are thought likely to exist."

I relished the medieval tone of these caveats, and the sense of sailing to the outer edge of the world. A strong wind picked up—a good force-eight, by Jérome's reckoning—as we cleared the southern tip of Adelaide Island and headed into open water. The sea was dark blue and choppy, laced with whitecaps, and the *Golden Fleece* pitched heavily. I leaned against a wall in the wheelhouse, nibbling cookies to put a little ballast in my stomach. The dark cliffs of Pourquois Pas Island—named by Charcot for his quixotic-sounding ship—towered above the sea a few miles to port, and behind it the never-ending wall of snowy peaks stretched south and vanished into the silvery haze.

Hours passed. Pourquois Pas Island was eventually left astern, but the chiseled ranges along the coast appeared immutable. I admired them, respected them, and found them beautiful in a haunting sort of way, but I wasn't sure any longer that I liked them. After a few weeks of coasting, I was starting to think of them as oppressive. They were always there, in that same unbroken silent line, and no matter how accustomed to seeing them you might become over time, they never broke their icy reserve.

Their implacability was a reminder that however deep my feelings might be for Antarctica, that affection was always going to be kept at arm's length, never reciprocated. You could love Antarctica, but it would never love you back. There was no way of ever really getting close to this strange land, although perhaps trying to do so was one of the things that draws people back year after year after year.

It was hard not to look at these exquisite landscapes, sense this gap in emotion, and not feel as though the failing was all mine; that if I could only shift some of the furniture in my mental attic, all would be clear. In my frustration, I had begun to resent them a little, their mocking aloofness starting to outweigh their grandeur.

By midafternoon we had traveled far enough south so that the bay was thickly scattered with ice—bergs, bergy bits, rafts of broken pack, and treacherous growlers, those nearly submerged chunks of ice that could easily smash a hole in the bow of even a steel-hulled yacht like the *Golden Fleece*.

As the chart had warned from the outset, these were dangerous, little-known waters. We proceeded slowly. Even so, several times Jérome had to veer at the last second to avoid striking one of these icy chunks, and once—swiftly and with a burst of startled cursing in French—he had to heel the yacht nearly to a halt as the depth gauge suddenly squawked out warnings that the seafloor was rising in a sharp spike toward the surface. We watched for a few moments with an almost detached fascination as the yacht glided forward under its own momentum and the numbers on the depth monitor continued to unwind rapidly, finally stopping at a depth of 12 feet. The *Golden Fleece* drew 9 feet.

"It didn't have to be twelve," Jérome laughed uneasily, as the depth fell away again. "It could just as easily have been two. And then..."

He didn't need to continue. This would not have been a good spot for a shipwreck; nobody comes down here at all, except Jérome.

We could see the Terra Firma Islands in the distance, looking as eerie and forbidding as islands at the utter ends of the Earth ought to look. They were a chain of black volcanic nubs, cold and windswept and lonely, that jutted up from the sea in almost perpendicular cliffs. The tallest—called Alamode—was more than 1,000 feet high. A team of British Navy explorers sighted them in 1936, but few people have ever landed. It was easy to see why. The islands are surrounded by treacherous rocks and shoals—a marine graveyard where old icebergs have foundered like so many shipwrecks.

We nearly scraped bottom ourselves as we drew up to Alamode, our depth gauge at one point actually touching the 9 feet that the *Golden Fleece* draws; there couldn't have been more than a couple inches in it. We dropped anchor in 23 feet of water, in a pool surrounded by towering rock walls and grounded bergs, and after a late dinner, set off in the dinghy to try to make a landing.

I had never thought that collecting grass and lichen samples was an activity that ought to have its own Indiana Jones soundtrack, but then again, I had never pictured it taking place on frozen craggy cliffs at a place like Alamode. The landing was the perfect scene setter: a rough and wet ride through the swirling currents and heavy swells at the base of the rock, past a hollowed-out berg where icicles dripped like fangs, and through an intimidating gorge, only a few meters wide, whose cliffs soared straight up, out of sight.

The only place we could scramble ashore was a rocky ledge, about 10 feet high and slick with frozen spray. We lashed the dinghy to a boulder, scaled the ledge—me with the sample bags in my teeth and again with a heroically brassy soundtrack playing in my mind—and then began picking our way up a precarious slope of volcanic scree that almost required, but didn't quite, using hands and feet. Alamode is made of chunks of heavy black rock—andesite and gabbro, if you want to be geological about it—that shift underfoot and clink musically. Skuas screeched and circled in the cold winds above us.

There were plenty of the flowering grasses Jérome had described, in thick beds that made me think of window boxes on stony slopes. They grew best on the north-facing parts, sheltered by overhangs or ledges where the round-the-clock summer sun could warm the soil and keep it watered by trickles from melting ice. I had expected something wind-whipped and wispy, heroically clinging to life in the leanest of circumstances, but what I saw was delicate, soft, and surprisingly lush.

"Beautiful, aren't they?" Jérome knelt carefully beside a particularly large and fine plot, on an outcropping ledge perhaps 131 feet above the sea. Both species of grasses flourished here, dense and green, together with a thick sort of moss and a suite of lichens in coppery orange, yellow, white, and large, textured flakes of greenish black. The effect was striking against the dark rock. Jérome studied the delicate buds of his grasses with the tenderness of a gardener, the face of a man cultivating his own White South.

"We will not collect from this patch, I think. It is so beautiful. To take from here would be a crime, even for science. We will take our samples from another place."

We collected from a smaller, less distinguished bed in a crevice, lower down. I bagged a few lichen-spotted rocks as well, and plucked a bit of moss. The sun broke through the silvery sheen as we climbed back down to the dinghy. A soft fan of light illuminated the mountains in the distance and danced on the sea. Jérome motioned toward the wild landscape.

"I claim all of this," he laughed. "I am a citizen of the world, and these belong to the world."

It was a brilliant ice year, and we could see open water lying to the south, a rarity and opportunity not to be missed. We pressed on and followed it. By four o'clock that afternoon we were crossing the 69th parallel, picking our way slowly south through the pack ice, aiming—aspiring—this time for an obscure mote called Rhyolite Island, at the southern end of King George VI Sound—about as far south as it is physically possible to sail in these waters. A couple of miles beyond it, a dense wall of ice cliffs fills the rest of the sound, blocking any further southerly progress, even if we had an icebreaker.

The lofty mountains of Alexandra Island rose in the distance, white and black in the haze, and made all the more majestic by the thought of how few people have ever seen them. The sky above was a fine milky blue. And still the waters remained navigable. The floes before us performed a slow, welcoming dance, opening leads and drawing us in, and by early evening we were at the entrance to King George VI Sound. The water shone like antique silver that had not been polished in a long time; it cast imprecise reflections of the gnarled old bergs floating in it. The sun had faded to a peach-colored smudge, its diffuse light giving the snowscapes an ethereal feel. There didn't seem to be any sharp edges or hard surfaces anywhere. It was like being in a dream.

I watched Jérome carefully manipulating the tiller, again, as he had up in the Weddell Sea, looking like a man trying to solve a puzzle as he threaded the *Golden Fleece* through a shifting labyrinth of floes and leads, plotting our course several moves ahead, constantly scanning for alternative routes, new openings. I was reminded again of how much we were all in his hands, appreciative of the confidence he inspired and of my own ignorance.

There had been times over the past few weeks where he would sidle the *Golden Fleece* incredibly close to a cliff-size iceberg so that Maria could add interest and perspective to her photographs. I would stand by the rail all the while, wringing my hands as the yacht drifted ever closer, until I could have reached out and touched those sheer, icy walls with a fishing rod if I had one handy, but Jérome would seem to be almost offhand about it all, chatting casually and giving the tiller only an occasional gentle nudge, as deft and sure as a big-city commuter parallel parking in front of the office.

Other times, such as when we were trawling for an anchorage in that tide-tossed cove back at Alamode, he became a worried man, scurrying in and out of the wheelhouse, anxiously consulting his depth gauge, peering over the side at the dark currents swirling around the hull, wrenching the tiller, and gunning the engines. I watched this frantic activity in wonder, my landlubber's eyes unable to discern any immediate peril, beyond the obvious menacing presence of those cliffs and rocks, but they were 50 yards away or more. Jérome's bursts of concern etched the dangers of these waters into sharp relief, as well as my own ignorance.

Some of the smaller floes we gently shunted aside, as the *Golden Fleece* prowled through the glassy water at a stately six knots. Once we collided heavily with an unsighted growler—a couple of tons of hard, clear ice floating just beneath the surface like an old World War II mine. It made a sickening jolt that sent all of us scrambling out to the bow, anxiously studying the dent on the side of the bow.

The hull was sound but dented, and the *Golden Fleece* was definitely going to be visiting a shipyard later. Watching Jérome's reactions—anxious dismay followed by profound relief—brought home the fact that traveling in these waters was not to be taken lightly, however exhilarating and thought provoking the scenery; there were risks and consequences.

It was late in the evening when we slipped up to Rhyolite Island, a high, dark, volcanic thumb of rock that jutted up from the water. Nobody was sleepy. We made a landing as soon as we dropped anchor. It was a steep scramble—fingers and toes—up its crags and talus cones. There were lichens and little beds of moss, but none of the strange flowering grasses from the Terra Firma Islands. We had crossed some invisible life boundary somewhere in all the drifting ice.

This was it. The end. There was no going any farther. I climbed high and dangled my feet over the prow of a ledge. The world from here looked peaceful and soft, with the little white and blue yacht resting at anchor in a dark pool at the base of the cliffs, and the irregular line of snow-covered mountains on the other side of the sound. I looked south, my eyes following the cracks and leads in the pack ice until they dead-ended at a massive wall of permanent ice, visible and not so very far away, which I recalled from the charts as being at about 70° south. What lay beyond that was pleasingly out of reach, aloof and untouchable, and as I sat there on that ledge in the small hours of the morning looking into the violet distance, I was glad. There was something redeeming about its aloof untouchability, the way it made the world big and mysterious again, with unknown and unexplored lands, as it had been in my imagination when I was a child. I cast my mind back a few weeks to when I had visited the South Pole, and recalled the faint, almost niggling, sense of loss that I'd felt beneath the sheer exhilaration of being there. I had reached one of the end points on the globe. There was no going past it, no farther south; I'd been as far in that direction as you can go. Part of me regretted going there, for just that reason. For all our explorations and desires for exotic travel, we all, deep inside, like to keep something aside, leave something untouched for our imaginations to pick over and speculate about in idle dreaming moments, and to draw out our sense of wonder and romance. I'd lost something of it through a little too much travel, but by great good fortune, here on this tiny frozen island, I found it again. The South Pole may be geographically the farthest south anyone can go, the ne plus ultra, but for me the very ends of the Earth will always be what I saw from that ledge on Rhyolite Island: those tantalizing breaks in the pack ice leading a few miles further south, those pristine ungraspable mountains in the distance and the ice cliffs beyond which it was impossible for us to go. I sat there and let it seep in to me, for this was the last day—when we drew anchor from here we'd start north again.

It was a glorious dawn here at the ends of the Earth. The sky was silvery-blue and the warm pink glow coming from behind a range of mountains hinted at the approach of the sun. The air was sharp and frosty, the bitter cold seeping through the layers of Gore-Tex and fleece I was wearing.

I tossed a pebble down onto a snowy ledge below me and was a little surprised to see it skitter on the icy surface that had been soft and damp when I had climbed up earlier. I drew my parka closer, and folded my arms. Sunrise wasn't long in coming. You could almost feel the world turn. And then a burst of sunbeams raked across the sky, crimson and gold, and looking like great flames where they touched the high, thin mare's tail clouds that swept overhead. The ranges were a suite of soft shadowy blues, violets, and eggshell white. The open leads of water, which had been glowing like lamplit silver in the predawn glow, suddenly became a kaleidoscope—gold and scarlet and carnation pink where the light touched it at one angle, electric blue, lavender, and delicate mint green where it shimmered at another.

The colors shifted and danced, like fine old carnival glass, except these colors seemed alive. Rafts of ice flowed southward, their slow movements heightening the play of light and color. It was mine just for a moment. And then the sun rose and washed away the colors with the plain light of day.

Acknowledgments

NOBODY TRAVELS TO ANTARCTICA ALONE—FROM THE DAYS OF THE VERY earliest explorers, and on up to today, there has always been a supporting cast of people who have made such voyages possible. Back in the good old days a thankful polar explorer could express his gratitude by naming the various mountains, ranges, glaciers, and islands he discovered after friends and benefactors back home. I can't do that. Too many have gone ahead of me, and the maps are already filled. I can only list the names here, in this preface to my book, of the many people and organizations who made my travel to Antarctica possible.

And so, starting in chronological order, I'd like to thank the Australian Antarctic Division, which opened the doors and gave me my first glimpse of this frozen wonderland back in 1993, and particularly Rob Easther and Patrick Quilty, two Antarctic veterans, who did so much to share the joy and wonder they had discovered down on The Ice.

On a more recent note, I'd like to thank the National Science Foundation, the National Oceanic and Atmospheric Administration, the British Antarctic Survey, as well as the Antarctic programs of Chile, Argentina, South Korea, Russia, and New Zealand, which allowed me to visit their bases. The supporting cast for anybody's presence in Antarctica is huge and too often unacknowledged—the ranks of pilots, cooks, cleaners, construction workers, tradesmen, mechanics, administrators, and doctors who make everything possible and whose friendly assistance made my own visits so enjoyable. A few names leap to mind, people whose names will always grace my own mental map of Antarctica: Steve Dunbar, Katie Jensen, Alex Brown, Jerry Martel, Carlton

Walker, June Barnard, Thai Verzone, Greg Thomas, Jack Hawkins, John Losure, Jeff Rein, Bryan Elsworth, Josh Landis, Mark Melcon, Kristin Sabbatini, Ivind Jensen, Sally Ayotte, Peter West, Dead Petersen, Linda Capper, Paul Rose, Pete Convey, Kenn Back, James Fox, Max Wenden, Sergio Lizasoain, Maria Ines Komlos, Oleg Sakharov, Patricio Eberhard, Alphonso Parcel, and Soon-Keun Chang. This is really just a grab bag; there were so many others as well.

Special thanks go to those scientists who hosted me at their field camps—particularly Rick Aster, Phil Kyle and Jean Wardell on Mount Erebus, Rosemary Askin and John Isbell in the Transantarctic Mountains, and Wayne Trivelpiece on Livingstone Island. Thanks also to South Pole scientists Darryn Schneider, Jeff Petersen, Dana Hrubes, Chris Martin, Jessica Dempsey, and Paulene Roberts. And I am indebted to Rennie Holt, Roger Hewitt, Valerie Loeb, Rob Rowley, and Kit Clark and the rest of the scientists and crew aboard the *Yuzhmorgeologiya* for a fascinating glimpse of life in Antarctica's cold, dark waters.

It was an incredible privilege to spend five weeks aboard the yacht *Golden Fleece* in the company of Jérome Poncet, the nearest thing Antarctica has to a true local, who showed me the hidden places along the Antarctic Peninsula that I would never have dreamed existed.

I am also grateful to the crew aboard the *Lindblad Explorer*, particularly the expedition leader Matt Drennan, who taught me so much about the joys and responsibilities of tourism in Antarctica.

Many, many thanks go to National Geographic magazine and editors Bill Allen, Bob Poole, Oliver Payne, and Lynn Addison, as well as researcher Liz Connell, photographer Maria Stenzel, and Jim Bullard of National Geographic Expeditions.

I'd also like to thank my agent, Fran Moore, of Curtis Brown, for her help and encouragement.

And finally, thanks to my wife, Cheryl, for her love and patience, and for holding down the fort at home while I gallivanted about the Last Place on Earth.

About the Author

Roff Smith was born in 1958, grew up in a small town in the White Mountains of New Hampshire, and emigrated to Australia when he was 23. He worked as a journalist for the *Sydney Morning Herald* and Melbourne's *Sunday Age* for several years, and later was a senior writer for *Time*, covering Australia, New Guinea, and the South Pacific—including Antarctica, visiting the continent for the first time in 1993 to write a story on the last sled dog team still working on The Ice.

A keen cyclist, in 1996 he set off on a solo 10,000-mile bicycle journey through the Australian outback to try to get better acquainted with his adopted country. The story of his journey appeared as a three-part series in NATIONAL GEOGRAPHIC magazine and was later made into a book, *Cold Beer and Crocodiles*, published by National Geographic. Other cycling adventures have taken him to East Africa and Zanzibar, from London to Istanbul, across the USA, the length and breadth of Britain, and once, in a lighthearted moment, he bicycled "around the world" in just under 15 seconds at the barber-striped marker at the South Pole.

He is married, has four children, and lives in South Australia.